Kant's Platonic Revolution in Moral and Political Philosophy

Kant's Platonic Revolution in Moral and Political Philosophy

* * * * * * * * * * * * * * * * *

T. K. SEUNG

THE JOHNS HOPKINS UNIVERSITY PRESS
BALTIMORE AND LONDON

© 1994 The Johns Hopkins University Press
All rights reserved. Published 1994
Printed in the United States of America on acid-free paper
03 02 01 00 99 98 97 96 95 94   5 4 3 2 1

The Johns Hopkins University Press
2715 North Charles Street
Baltimore, Maryland 21218-4319
The Johns Hopkins Press Ltd., London

LIBRARY OF CONGRESS CATALOGING-IN-PUBLICATION DATA

Seung, T. K., 1930–
    Kant's Platonic revolution in moral and political philosophy / T. K. Seung.
        p.   cm.
    Includes bibliographical references and index.
    ISBN 0-8018-4850-4 (alk. paper)
    1. Kant, Immanuel, 1724–1804. 2. Ethics. 3. Political science – Philosophy. I. Title.
B2799.E8S53 1994
170′.92 – dc20   94-7529

A catalog record for this book is available from the British Library.

For my friend

Chul Bum Lee

poet and critic for the two worlds

Contents

✳ ✳

Preface

* * * * * * * * * * * * * * * * * * *

What is the relevance of Kant's philosophy for us today? This question divides into two parts, because his philosophy was motivated by two different concerns: the problem of knowledge and the problem of value. The problem of knowledge is a legacy of Humean skepticism that goes back to Cartesian doubt; it questions the capacity of human cognition, ranging from scientific propositions about the natural world to metaphysical assertions about the supernatural world. The problem of value stems from Pascalian anxiety over the place and role of human values in the age of modern science. Kant regarded these two problems as central to his entire philosophy; they were the basis for its division into theoretical and practical philosophy.

In his theoretical philosophy, Kant deals with the problem of knowledge by demarcating the world of phenomena from the world of noumena. He fully endorsed the skepticism about the world of noumena. Although it is an object of human thought and intellect, it lies totally beyond the range of human sensibility. The supersensible world can never be known by human intellect—this was Kant's categorical repudiation of supersensible cognitive claims. But he was equally categorical in upholding our ability to know the world of phenomena. He regarded Newton's mechanics as the scientific knowledge of phenomena that could withstand any skeptical assault, because it stood on a set of a priori principles. To demonstrate their a priori truths, he tried to devise transcendental arguments in the *Critique of Pure Reason*.

Although Kant's theory of a priori knowledge appeared to vindicate Newtonian science and resolve the problem of knowledge to his satisfaction, it aggravated the problem of value. The Newtonian picture of nature left no room for human values. This was the most serious problem that had emerged with modern science, and it had distressed many even before Kant. In the olden days of Aristotelian science, the scientific picture of nature was perfectly compatible with human values. Aristotle's conception of natural science was based on his theory of substantial forms and their teleology. A living organism was the model of scientific objects; norms and values were essential features of their nature. But modern science stands on the sharp separation of fact and value. It recognizes the objective existence of only inert and dead matter scattered throughout boundless space and time. Terrified at such a chilling picture of nature, Pascal said, "The eternal silence of these infinite spaces fills me with dread." Pascalian dread was a formidable challenge for modern philosophy, as formidable as Cartesian doubt.

During the past two centuries, our knowledge of the natural world has changed radically, and most of the a priori principles Kant accepted as cornerstones for his philosophy of nature have crumbled. We can no longer share his view that Euclidean geometry is the a priori science of space or that Newtonian mechanics provides the basic principles of the physical world. It is even more difficult for us to subscribe to his view that space and time are no more than the a priori forms of perception, or pure intuitions. We can no longer take seriously his goal of providing a priori foundation for natural science, because such a foundation is impossible. Moreover, natural science today does not require such a foundation for its operation. We have already discarded Kant's conception of natural science and its philosophy because it is obsolete.

To discard Kant's scientific image of nature and natural philosophy, however, does not mean to discard all scientific images. As our scientific knowledge of nature expands and develops, we only replace one scientific image with another. We are caught in an endless succession of scientific images. Modern science is not only a product of modernity but its fate. Whether we love or hate modern science, we do not know how to liberate ourselves from its ceaselessly expanding chain. With its expansion, modern science only intensifies Pascalian dread. Many scientists at the forefront of today's science feel besieged by an ever-expanding sense of futility. Steven Weinberg laments, "The more the universe seems comprehensible, the more it seems pointless." Although we may ignore or even forget Cartesian doubt, we cannot dismiss Pascalian dread. Hence, Kant's second concern, the problem of value, remains as critical for us as it was for Kant or Pascal.

Kant tried to cope with the problem of value in his practical philosophy. We generally associate his practical philosophy with his formalist ethics, which is laid out in his theory of the categorical imperative ("Act always in such a way that your maxim will become a universal law"). His formalist ethics is then linked with the conventional demarcation between his Critical and pre-Critical philosophy. He is assumed to have entertained no original ethical ideas of his own during his pre-Critical period; at best, he is known to have had some serious encounters with British moral sense theory and Rousseau's theory of virtue and social contract. Only with his revolutionary view of human cognition, formulated in the first *Critique,* is he said to have gained the power to construct his equally revolutionary normative philosophy. Thus, Kant scholars have celebrated the Copernican revolution in his ethics as jubilantly as they have the Copernican revolution in his theory of knowledge. These two revolutions are supposed to mark Kant's dramatic transformation from a minor Leibnizian into a major philosopher in his own right.

This is roughly the conventional picture of Kant's practical philosophy. In this book, I show that his struggle with the problem of value was much more complicated than this conventional picture would indicate. Although the demarcation of Critical and pre-Critical periods is important for his theory of knowledge, it is not as important for his theory of value. Whereas he firmly resolves the problem of knowledge once and for all in the *Critique of Pure Reason,* he never makes a similar resolution for the problem of value either in that work or in any other. As for his theory of knowledge, the first *Critique* repudiates the position he had taken in the *Inaugural Dissertation* by denying the possibility of knowing the world of noumena. With regard to his theory of norms and values, however, the first *Critique* does not repudiate but reaffirms the position he had taken in the *Dissertation.*

In the *Dissertation* Kant had accepted Platonic Forms as the foundation of his normative philosophy. Eleven years later, in the *Critique,* he renamed the Platonic Forms the Ideas of pure reason. Although the Ideas of pure reason inevitably lead to metaphysical illusions in theoretical philosophy, he says, they are absolutely essential for practical philosophy, because they alone can provide normative standards for ethics, law, and religion. He gives a transcendental argument for the Ideas of practical reason. Just as the pure concepts of understanding make possible the world of experience, so the Ideas of pure reason make possible the world of practice. He does not even mention the categorical imperative, the formal principle he will present for the construction of all moral laws in the *Groundwork for the Metaphysics of Morals.* The moral laws he talks about in the first *Critique* are not formal but substantive principles based on Platonic Ideas. Nor does he give any intimation that his Platonic ethics is incompatible with his Critical Philosophy. Although there is no need to appeal to Platonic Forms for our knowledge of nature, he says, we can never dispense with them in normative philosophy.

When Kant presented his formalist ethics in the *Groundwork for the Metaphysics of Morals* (1785) four years after the publication of the first *Critique* (1781), his critics were taken by surprise because it was so different from what they had expected. They demanded that he explain the glaring divergence between his new ethics and the old one, and Kant had to write the *Critique of Practical Reason* (1788), which he had never thought of writing until his critics' outcry. But the second *Critique* further complicates the problem, because its ethical theory is not quite the same as that of the *Groundwork.* Whereas he gave three formulas of the categorical imperative in the *Groundwork,* he gives only one in the second *Critique.* Whereas he advocated only the duty of obeying the categorical imperative in the *Groundwork,* he advocates an additional duty in the second *Critique,* namely, the duty of promoting the highest good.

Kant makes the problem even worse by writing the *Critique of Judgment.* This *Critique* is supposedly to bridge the enormous chasm between phenomena and noumena that had been created by the first two *Critiques.* Although this mysterious function of mediation is supposed to be discharged by the faculty of reflective judgment, no one can figure out how it is accomplished. The final link in this chain of complications is the *Metaphysics of Morals*. It is meant to apply the principles laid out in the *Groundwork*, but there appear to be no clear connections between the principles and their alleged applications. To be sure, Kant mentions the categorical imperative, the central principle of his formalist ethics, a few times in the *Metaphysics of Morals*, but this formalist principle is only a formality in his exposition. In substance, the *Metaphysics of Morals* is a parade of Platonic Ideas whose acceptance is clearly incompatible with Kant's formalist ethics.

There is one more link in this chain of complications, namely, Kant's writings in the philosophy of history: the *Idea for Universal History from a Cosmopolitan Point of View* (1784), the *Conjectural Beginning of Human History* (1786), *The End of All Things* (1794), and *Perpetual Peace* (1795). In these essays, Kant gives his account of human historical development in terms of Platonic Ideas. By the conventional understanding of his Critical standard, his philosophy of history is outright speculative and dogmatic. Hence these historical essays have never been accepted in the corpus of Kant's Critical Philosophy. But they were all written during his so-called Critical period. Most Kant scholars have thought that the integrity of his Critical Philosophy could be maintained only by dismissing those speculative writings as aberrations.

It is my thesis that all of these writings are equally important for disclosing Kant's long struggle with the problem of value. This thesis goes against the conventional view that the *Groundwork*, together with the second *Critique*, gives the uniquely Kantian normative philosophy. In this book, I demonstrate that the Copernican revolution in ethics was not the only critical point in Kant's protracted struggle with the problem of value; his acceptance of Platonic Forms in the *Inaugural Dissertation* was even more critical and more important. It was Kant's Platonic revolution. Before this critical event, he had spent many years in groping for the foundation of his normative philosophy. Afterwards, he had to spend many more years in figuring out how Platonic Forms should function as its foundation. He wrote three *Critiques,* because he changed his mind three times about the role of Platonic Forms in his practical philosophy. The perpetual revision of his ideas did not end with the last *Critique* but went on with *Religion within the Limits of Reason Alone* and the *Metaphysics of Morals.* His Platonic revolution was a perpetual revolution.

During all these changes, Kant never abandoned the Platonic conception of transcendental normative standards. Although the spirit of criticism is important for his Critical Philosophy, it serves only a procedural and instrumental function. The substantive thematic force of Kant's philosophy comes from Platonic Ideas. They provide the ultimate goal for all his maneuvers; they give the unity and integrity to all his works. The spirit of criticism is only a dutiful handmaid to his grand Platonic vision. My aim in this book is to explicate the nature of this grand vision, which is hidden behind the complex facade of Critical Philosophy.

The plan of this book is as follows. In the first two chapters, I provide the setting for Kant's encounter with Platonic Ideas. Chapter 1 covers his early years, during which he groped for the foundation of norms and values in the chilling world of dead matter disclosed by Newtonian mechanics. Chapter 2 recounts his attempt to construct a new science of metaphysics in his *Inaugural Dissertation* and the *Critique of Pure Reason.* Although the presence of Platonic Ideas is evident in these two works, I do not discuss their relevance for Kant's normative philosophy in this chapter. Since I do not begin to explore my central thesis until after the first two chapters, some readers may wish to proceed directly to chapter 3.

In chapters 3 through 6, I show that the only viable version of Kant's normative philosophy is his Platonic constructivism and that even his formalist ethics makes much better sense when it is interpreted as a vital link in his Platonic scheme of construction. In chapter 7, I try to assess the strengths and weaknesses of his Platonic constructivism by comparing it with other forms of constructivism, which are based on natural law, normative positivism, and Hegelian absolute idealism. In the final chapter, I examine the close link between constructivism and deconstructivism. This will probably surprise many readers, because at least a few of them have never thought of associating deconstruction with construction. But deconstruction presupposes construction: what is not constructed can never be subject to deconstruction. Moreover, deconstruction also presupposes reconstruction; deconstruction can never be an end in itself except for the mindless or the insane. I show that we cannot appreciate the proper role of deconstruction without understanding it as the essential intermediary between construction and reconstruction in our normative life.

Several friends have had an active hand in the shaping of this book. Stanley Rosen has gone over the entire manuscript with care and given me his astute advice for its reorganization. I am also grateful for his enthusiastic endorsement of my Platonic interpretation of Kant's entire corpus. J. M. Balkin has given me valuable advice for reshaping the final chapter. I have benefited from my discussion with Louis Mackey and Kelly Oliver on deconstruction, and with Kathleen Higgins on aesthetics. My gratitude goes to Daniel Bonevac, Rob Koons, and Fred Kronz for continuing discussions on Kant's Platonism. Above all, I am most appreciative of the inspiration and encouragement I have received from the eminent Kant scholar John R. Silber.

Abbreviations

* * * * * * * * * * * * * * * * * * *

C_2 *Kritik der praktischen Vernunft.* In *KGS,* vol. 5. Translated by Lewis White Beck as *Critique of Practical Reason.* New York, 1956.

C_3 *Kritik der Urteilskraft.* In *KGS,* vol. 5. Translated by Werner Pluhar as *Critique of Judgment.* Indianapolis, 1987.

GMM *Grundlegung zur Metaphysik der Sitten.* In *KGS,* vol. 4. Translated by H. J. Paton as *Groundwork for the Metaphysics of Morals.* New York, 1964. Translated by Lewis White Beck as *Foundations of the Metaphysics of Morals.* New York, 1990.

ID *Inaugural Dissertation.* Translated by John Handyside. In *Kant's Inaugural Dissertation and Early Writings on Space.* Chicago, 1929. Reprinted in *Kant's Latin Writings,* ed. Lewis White Beck. New York, 1986.

KGS *Kants Gesammelte Schriften.* Prussian Academy edition. 29 vols. to date. Berlin, 1902– .

LE *Lectures on Ethics.* Translated by Louis Infield. London, 1930.

MM *Die Metaphysik der Sitten.* In *KGS,* vol. 6. Part 1 translated by John Ladd as *The Metaphysical Elements of Justice.* New York, 1965. Part 2 translated by James Ellington as *The Metaphysical Principles of Virtue.* Indianapolis, 1964.

Kant's Platonic Revolution in Moral and Political Philosophy

1 Modern Science and the Problem of Value

* * * * * * * * * * * * * * * * * * *

The emergence of modern science posed a critical challenge for the world of values. It was discrediting and replacing Aristotelian science, which had confirmed the commonsense view of nature as a place full of living things. In the physics of Galileo and Newton, nature was seen as a vast field of lifeless objects governed by the mechanical laws of inertia and blind forces. In such a world, nothing can be either good or bad, right or wrong; it has no place for human values and concerns. This is a chilling and frightening picture of nature. Pascal said, "The eternal silence of infinite spaces fills me with dread." He described the infinity of nature as twofold, infinitely small and infinitely large. A human being is wedged between these two silent infinities: "Anyone who regards himself in this way will be terrified at himself, and, seeing his mass, as given him by nature, supporting him between those two abysses of the infinity and nothingness, will tremble at these marvels."[1]

To recognize this terrifying peculiarity of human existence is Pascalian dread. But it was not the universal response to the new modern science. Instead of feeling any anxiety over his own scientific picture of nature, Newton was impressed with its order and beauty, though he could not explain them. His theory of gravity could explain the orderly orbital motions of planets around the sun, but he could not explain why the solar system had been constructed so beautifully. On that question, he fell back on the doctrine of divine creation: "This most beautiful system of the sun, planets, and comets, could only proceed from the counsel and dominion of an intelligent and powerful Being."[2] This is Newton's deism, which seems to dissolve Pascalian dread.

1. Pascal, *Pensées*, trans. A. J. Krailsheimer (London, 1966), pars. 201, 19.
2. Newton, *Mathematical Principles of Natural Philosophy*, trans. Florian Cajori, 2 vols. (Berkeley, 1962), 2:544.

Leibniz shared Pascal's view that the world of dead matter has no place for human values. He said that reason and value become possible only in the world of minds. The world of bodies and the world of minds are governed by two different principles. The principles of mechanics are sufficient to explain the motion of bodies, but they cannot account for the operation of minds. The latter requires the principles of teleology and perfection. Minds and bodies belong to two different orders: the kingdom of grace and the kingdom of nature.

In Leibniz's philosophy, the principle of teleology is higher than the principle of mechanical causation. He ridicules those natural philosophers who try to explain everything by the mechanical principles. He locates the ultimate principle of teleology in the perfection of God. Because God is the most perfect being, Leibniz holds, He creates the best of all possible worlds. Furthermore, the City of God is the most perfect state:

> Here there is no crime without punishment, no good action without a proportionate reward, and finally, as much virtue and happiness as is possible. And this takes place, not by a dislocation of nature, as if what God had planned for souls could disturb the laws of bodies, but by the very order of natural things itself, by virtue of the harmony pre-established from all time between the realms of nature and of grace, between God as architect and God as monarch, in such a way that nature leads to grace, and grace perfects nature by using it.[3]

* * The World of Dead Matter

Newtonian physics and Leibnizian metaphysics were two main forces shaping Kant's ideas during his formative years. He believed that the two were compatible, and he tried to vindicate this faith in his early but ambitious essay *Universal Natural History and Theory of the Heavens, or An Essay of the Constitution and Mechanical Origin of the Entire World-Edifice, treated according to Newton's Principles*

---

3. Leibniz, *Principles of Nature and Grace,* in *Leibniz: Philosophical Papers and Letters,* trans. Leroy Loemker, 2d ed. (Dordrecht, Netherlands, 1970), 636–42, par. 15.

(1755).[4] In this essay Kant not only accepts Newton's principles but wants to go further. Newton's theory describes the order and beauty of the solar system but does not explain how it has come about. In Kant's view, there is an even greater wonder, the order and beauty of the starry heavens, which was to occupy his attention for the rest of his life. He proposed to fill this gap in Newton's theory by formulating a theory of cosmic evolution.

In the preface, Kant states his hypothesis concerning the initial state of the universe: a universal diffusion of primitive matter. This mass of diffused matter was the original solar nebula, from which the sun and the planets were formed by the process of condensation. "Creation is not the work of a moment" (*KGS* 1:314). It begins with the production of an infinity of diffused matter, which generates an order in its center, which in turn extends itself in all directions to the peripheries of the universe. This infinite process is far from finished. Nature is always busy producing new objects, new scenes, and new worlds. This is the infinite fecundity of nature, which reflects God's infinite power.

The infinite process of creation is governed by the idea of perfection:

> Nature, which bordered immediately on [the act of] creation, was as raw, [and] as unformed as possible. But even in the essential properties of the elements that constitute the chaos, one can notice the hallmark of that perfection which they have from their origin on, insofar as their essence is a consequence of the eternal idea of the divine mind. The simplest, the most universal properties which seem to have been planned without intent, the [very] matter, which seems to be purely passive and in need of forms and arrangements, has in its simplest state a tendency to develop through natural development into a perfect constitution. (*KGS* 1:263, Jaki 114)

Kant's theory of cosmic evolution validates the Leibnizian credo: God creates the best of all possible worlds. And he feels rapture with his theory of nature:

4. The essay appears in *KGS* 1:215–368. An English translation is available in Immanuel Kant, *Universal History and Theory of Heavens*, trans. Stanley Jaki (Edinburgh, 1981).

The world-edifice puts one into a quiet astonishment by its immeasurable greatness and by the infinite manifoldness and beauty that shine forth from it on all sides. If now [on the one side] the presentation of all this perfection excites the imagination, on the other side another kind of enthrallment seizes the understanding when it considers how so much splendor, so much greatness flows from a single universal rule with an eternal and right order. (*KGS* 1:306, Jaki 148)

No doubt, Kant acknowledges, the process of creation inevitably involves the process of destruction, which takes place locally and globally. Innumerable animals and plants are destroyed daily and disappear as the victims of time, but they are replaced by nature's inexhaustible power of reproduction (*KGS* 1:317). The worlds themselves not only evolve but also deteriorate and disintegrate, but they are replaced by even greater worlds. Nature proves her riches by her prodigality. Even these worlds are small and insignificant in comparison with the infinitude that creates them. According to Kant, even terrible catastrophes lose their terror if they are taken as the common ways of providence (*KGS* 1:319). Kant even anticipates the last moment of all creation, when the entire universe will sink into nothingness.

The beauty and perfection of infinite nature are impersonal; they are on a par with the beauty of Euclidean geometry and Newtonian physics. Nature has no concern for the well-being and happiness of its parts; it cares neither more nor less for lice than for human beings: "From the highest class of thinking beings to the most abject insect, no member [of that chain] is indifferent to nature; nothing can be missing [from it] without breaking up the beauty of the whole, which consists in interconnectedness" (*KGS* 1:354, Jaki 185). This is a perfect picture of Leibnizian plenitude. Kant goes on to say that it should be senseless for the laws of nature to be subservient to the particular aims of one small atom called humankind.

Kant's picture of nature may be beautiful from the perspective of God or nature but quite chilling from the human perspective. Paul Menzer took it as a sign of pessimism underlying Kant's general outlook.[5] Paul Schilpp countered this view of Kant's mood with his claim that Kant's essay expresses his optimism, derived from his faith in the best of all possible worlds. In support of this view, Schilpp quotes from Kant's 1759 essay on optimism: "I rejoice to see myself as a citizen in a world which could not possibly have been better."[6] But Schilpp overlooks the fact that this sentence is followed by an ironic remark: "Having been selected as an insignificant member, unworthy in itself, to serve in the most perfect of possible schemes, I appreciate my existence so much the more." The answer to the question whether Kant's mood was optimistic or pessimistic depends on one's perspective. Menzer assessed his mood from the human perspective; Schilpp, from the divine. Kant's own ironic remark arises from the conflation of the two.

In the opening paragraph of the essay on optimism Kant notes that Leibniz's doctrine of the best of all possible worlds is meant to answer the vexing problem of evil. According to this doctrine, miseries and disasters are not really evils but essential elements for the constitution of the most beautiful world. Kant was forced to deal with this view of evil when the whole of Europe was shaken by the calamitous Lisbon earthquake of 1755, the year he stated his Leibnizian view of nature in *Universal Natural History and Theory of the Heavens*. The following year, Kant expressed his reflections on earthquakes in three essays (*KGS* 1:417–72). While admitting that an earthquake is a scourge of humankind, he reminds us that it brings its own benefits. Whether beneficial or harmful, he stresses, earthquakes should never be taken as an expression of God's vengeance. This view is the criminal folly of those who try to understand divine intentions from the human perspective. Natural disasters strike both the just and the unjust, both Christians and heathens. They are never intended for any one part of nature; they make sense only for the totality of nature.

The chilling picture of nature as impersonal and amoral was to

5. Menzer, "Der Entwicklungsgang der Kantischen Ethik in den Jahren 1760–1785," *Kant-Studien* 2 (1898): 290–322.

6. Schilpp, *Kant's Pre-Critical Ethics* (Evanston, 1960), 19.

haunt Kant for the rest of his life. In the *Critique of Judgment* he restates the view that nature has no special regard for human beings:

> For while he [a moral person] can expect that nature will now and then cooperate contingently [accidentally] with the purpose of his ... he can never expect nature to harmonize with it by laws and permanent rules. ... Moreover, as concerns the other righteous people he meets: no matter how worthy of happiness they may be, nature, which pays no attention to that, will still subject them to all the evils of deprivation, disease, and untimely death, just like all the other animals on the earth. And they will stay subjected to these evils always, until one vast tomb engulfs them one and all (honest or not, that makes no difference here) and hurls them, who managed to believe they were the final purpose of creation, back into the abyss of the purposeless chaos of matter from which they are taken. (C$_3$ 452, Pluhar 342)

This picture of nature is as terrifying as Pascal's. As Yirmiahu Yovel claims, one may sense some difference between Pascal's and Kant's views of nature. Whereas Kant speaks of awe, admiration, and even aesthetic pleasure in the sublimity of nature, Pascal only talks of dread or fright.[7] But for Kant the sublime is sometimes accompanied by a sense of dread (*KGS* 2:209). He calls that sort of feeling the terror-ridden sublime. Like Pascal, Kant advocates a religious resolution of the problem of human values in the world of brute nature. He says that human beings are not born to erect eternal habitats in this theater of vanity, because they have a far nobler destiny (*KGS* 1:460). He says that humans are strangers in the world of nature and are meant for a higher order of reality:

> In the universal quiet of nature and in the tranquility of mind there speaks the hidden capacity for knowledge of the immortal soul in unspecifiable language and offers undeveloped concepts that can be grasped but not described. If there are among the thinking creatures of this planet lowly beings who, unmindful of the stirrings through which such a great vision can captivate them, are in the position of fastening themselves to the servitude of vanity,

7. Yovel, *Kant and the Philosophy of History* (Princeton, 1980), 130.

then how unfortunate is this globe to have been to generate such miserable creatures! On the other hand, how fortunate is that same globe, since a road is open for them under most miserable conditions to reach a happiness and nobility which are infinitely far above those advantages which nature's most exceptional dispositions can achieve on all celestial bodies. (*KGS* 1:367–68, Jaki 196)

* * Moral Inquiry

The scientific picture of impersonal nature Kant had developed may have been useful for religious exhortation, but it had no relevance for ethics. He did not even try to relate his view of nature to ethics. Instead he adopted the perfectionist ethics, which had been developed by such Leibnizians as Christian Wolff and Alexander Baumgarten. When he got involved in moral sense theory, he tried to combine it with the ethics of perfectionism. He presented the result of this effort in the *Prize Essay* of 1764 (*KGS* 2:273–301).[8] Ethics is not the central topic of the essay: it is chiefly concerned with the methodological difference between mathematics and metaphysics. Against the prevailing view that these two disciplines employ the same method, Kant maintains that their methods are diametrically opposed. The mathematical method is synthetic; the metaphysical method is analytic. The former operates *in concreto*, the latter *in abstracto*. The bulk of the essay is given over to the clarification of this methodological difference.

Only in the last few pages of the essay does Kant discuss ethics. He says that the concept of moral obligation is governed by formal and material principles. The formal principle contains two rules, the rule of commission ("Realize the greatest perfection you can") and the rule of omission ("Do not do that which can hinder the greatest possible perfection realizable through you"). Although Kant adopts these two formal rules of perfection from Wolffian ethics, he stresses

---

8. The full title is *Untersuchung über die Deutlichkeit der Grundsätze der natürlichen Theologie und der Moral*. An English translation is available in *Kant: Selected Pre-Critical Writings and Correspondence with Beck*, ed. G. E. Kerferd and D. E. Walford (Manchester, 1968), 3–35.

their emptiness. Just as nothing comes from the formal principles of knowledge without the aid of its material principles, he says, so no obligations can be determined from its formal principles without the aid of its material principles (*KGS* 2:299).

Kant locates the material principle of obligation in moral sense: what is good or perfect is sensed by moral sense or feeling. Only in our times, he says, has the important difference between the faculty of representing the true and the faculty of perceiving the good been recognized. One belongs to knowledge, the other to feeling, and under no circumstances must these two be confused (*KGS* 2:299). This observation refers to Wolffians and British moralists. Wolffians had recognized no significant difference between knowing the true and knowing the good, because they believed that the true and the good were both objective. In Kant's view, they failed to recognize the difference between two distinct faculties. He assigns the credit of discovering their distinction to British moral sense theorists ("Hutcheson and others").

Kant's acceptance of moral sense theory appears to have been wholehearted. But it has been a matter of controversy. By endorsing Hutcheson's idea of moral sense, Paul Menzer maintains, Kant became a partisan of moral sense theory.[9] Paul Schilpp counters this view with the claim that Kant never uncritically accepted the British moralists. He goes on to make a far stronger claim, namely, that Kant never accepted feeling as the criterion for the judgment of the good.[10] Moral judgments are made, not by moral sense, but by reflective reason; at best, moral sense can express moral judgments after they are made. If this was Kant's view of moral sense, it would indeed be compatible with the rationalist position. In support of his interpretation, Schilpp quotes the following sentence from Kant's text: "It is the business of reason to dissolve and make clear the complex and confused concept of the good, by showing how it emerges out of simpler feelings of the good."[11] But this sentence does not support

9. Menzer, "Der Entwicklungsgang der Kantischen Ethik in den Jahren 1760–1785," esp. 302–5.

10. Schilpp, *Kant's Pre-Critical Ethics*, 27–40.

11. Ibid., 35.

the claim that reflective reason makes moral judgments. Kant is talking about the function of reason, not in making moral judgments, but in analyzing the concept of good and showing how it emerges from simpler feelings.

Although Schilpp cannot substantiate his claim, Menzer's claim is no more convincing. Menzer did not take seriously Kant's dualism of form and matter. If Kant had accepted moral sense as the only principle for making moral judgments, Menzer's view would be correct. For Kant, however, moral sense was only the material principle to be complemented by the formal principle. This dualism may harbor a serious ambiguity if Kant's concept of the good is not identical with his concept of obligation. Both Menzer and Schilpp assume the identity of these two concepts in their dispute. Kant indeed holds that the judgment "This is good" is made by moral sense or feeling and belongs to the material principle, but he never says that the material principle alone can determine our obligations. The concept of obligation concerns, not what is good and what is bad, but what good we should seek and what evil we should avoid. It is clearly impossible to seek all conceivable goods and avoid all conceivable evils, hence the normative gap between the concept of the good and the concept of obligation.

This normative gap does not obtain in Hutcheson's theory, in which moral sense is the only principle of moral judgments. In Kant's scheme, however, moral sense perceives the good but does not determine the obligation. In that regard, his notion of moral sense is much more restricted than Hutcheson's. Kant says that our obligations can be determined only when the material principles are subsumed under the formal principle (*KGS* 2:300). The union of these two principles creates the problem of dividing their labor. In both metaphysics and ethics, Kant says, material principles are subordinate or subject to formal principles. This subordination is unambiguous for metaphysics, because its formal principle plays only the negative function of rejecting all material principles that violate logical rules. The formal principle can exercise no substantive constraint over material principles. In that regard, its role is truly formal. But the formal principle in ethics is much stronger than the logical rules of metaphysics. The former does not merely tell us to eliminate the material principles that violate formal rules of logic. It tells us to achieve the greatest perfection; it is a substantive principle. It is for making a choice between different goods when not all of them can be pursued and for making a similar choice between different evils when not all of them can be avoided.

Wolff's principle of perfection includes not only the perfection of oneself but also the happiness of others. According to Wolff, the duty of perfection requires everyone to do as much as possible for the happiness of others.[12] Even the principles of impartiality and benevolence as advocated by Hutcheson and his followers cannot be any more substantive than this one. Why, then, does Kant designate the principle of perfection as formal, and moral feeling as material principle? What exactly is the relation of form and matter in his ethical theory? This relation takes many different shapes in Kant's long career. Even in the *Prize Essay* it takes two different shapes for metaphysics and ethics. In metaphysics, it is the relation of logical and extralogical. In ethics, I propose, it is the relation of general and particular. The relation of logical and extralogical is a special case of the relation of general and particular, because logical relations are the most general of all possible relations.

What are the respective roles of formal and material principles in determining the greatest perfection to be achieved on any given occasion? Kant never faces this question squarely, so he leaves us with an unresolvable ambiguity. He concludes the *Prize Essay* with an acknowledgment of this ambiguity and uncertainty: "It has still to be discovered in the first place whether the faculty of knowledge or feeling (the inner ground of the faculty of appetite) exclusively decides the primary principles of practical philosophy" (*KGS* 2:300, Kerferd and Walford 34).

---

12. Wolff, *Reasonable Thoughts about the Actions of Men, for the Promotion of Their Happiness* 4.1.767, in *Moral Philosophy from Montaigne to Kant*, ed. J. B. Schneewind, 2 vols. (Cambridge, 1990), 1:333-50.

* * Moral Principles

Kant reexamined moral sense theory in his *Observations on the Feeling of the Beautiful and the Sublime* (*KGS* 2:205-56).[13] Although this essay was written only a year after the *Prize Essay*, it marks a drastic change in his ideas. While the *Prize Essay* was written under the influence of Hutcheson, the *Observations* recorded the dramatic impact Rousseau's ideas had on Kant. Between these two works, Kant had avidly read *Emile* and the *Social Contract,* which had arrived in Königsberg in 1762.[14] The title of the *Observations* is aesthetical rather than ethical; it is concerned with the distinction between the beautiful and the sublime, a fashionable topic in eighteenth-century aesthetics.

The essay is divided into four sections. In the first, Kant restates the prevailing distinction between the beautiful and the sublime: the beautiful is charming and pleasant, but the sublime is awesome and terrifying. Flower-strewn meadows are beautiful, while raging storms are sublime. The beautiful charms; the sublime moves. In the second section, Kant begins to apply these aesthetical categories to human beings and their character traits: "Understanding is sublime, wit is beautiful. Courage is sublime and great, artfulness is little but beautiful" (*KGS* 2:211, Goldthwait 51). Up to this point, Kant's exposition appears to be no more than a Hutchesonian exercise.

In his *Inquiry into the Original of Our Ideas of Beauty and Virtue* Hutcheson had adopted Shaftsbury's view on the integral connection between aesthetic and moral sense and had written of the beauty and harmony of moral qualities, as well as of natural objects, using the same aesthetic categories. But Kant's exposition begins to take on a different tone when he distinguishes sublime virtue from

---

13. Translated into English by John T. Goldthwait (Berkeley, 1960).

14. There are many good accounts of Rousseau's influence on Kant. See, e.g., J. Schmucker, *Die Ursprünge der Ethik Kants in seinen vorkritischen Schriften und Reflexionen* (Meisenheim, 1961); George Kelly, *Idealism, Politics, and History* (Cambridge, 1969), 89-99; William Galston, *Kant and the Problem of History* (Chicago, 1975), 103-31; Susan Shell, *The Rights of Reason: A Study of Kant's Philosophy and Politics* (Toronto, 1980), 20-32; and Richard Velkley, *Freedom and the End of Reason* (Chicago, 1989), 32-103.

amiable and beautiful moral qualities (*KGS* 2:215). He says that virtue is sublime, but other moral qualities are only beautiful. Shaftsbury and Hutcheson had never applied this distinction to moral
qualities.[15] As far as they were concerned, all good moral qualities
were equally beautiful; they never bothered to single out some
moral attributes and elevate them to the exalted level of sublimity.

What, then, is Kant's motive for this unusual move? He is developing Rousseau's idea of virtue rather than Hutcheson's. Rousseau
had stressed a clear demarcation between the level of passions and
sentiments and the level of reason and virtue. He said that virtue
becomes possible only when humankind transcends the world of
passions and ascends to the world of reason. He was also interested
in the integral relation between ethical and aesthetical categories. It
was Rousseau who called virtue the "sublime science of simple
souls."[16] Virtue is sublime, because it is power and control. It is the
power to resist immediate impulses for the sake of some higher principles. Virtue is the power of struggle and conquest over passions.
Echoing this militant view of virtue, Kant says, "Subduing one's passions through principles is sublime" (*KGS* 2:215).

Kant stresses the difference between virtue and other moral qualities. Whereas other moral qualities are only sentiments, he says, virtue is a matter of principle. Universal affection for the entire human
species is the ultimate ground and principle of virtue. By this definition, sympathy is not a true virtue: it is a passion concerned with particular persons. The acts of sympathy may at best accord with virtue,
but they are not from virtue. If you are a person of sympathy, you
may help others in need. But your good-natured sentiment may still
be blind and misdirected. You may spend your resources for an act
of sympathy and forget to pay your debt. This is to sacrifice a higher
obligation for an immediate sentiment, and that is an injustice. Kant
describes universal affection as follows:

15. Hutcheson does not use the term *sublime,* but his category of grandeur is its equivalent (see Hutcheson, *Collected Works,* ed. Bernhard Fabian, 7 vols. [Hildesheim, 1971],
1:78).

16. Rousseau, *The First and Second Discourses,* ed. and trans. Victor Gourevitch (New
York, 1986), 27.

On the other hand, when universal affection toward the human species has become a principle within you to which you always subordinate your actions, then love toward the needy one still remains; but now, from a higher stand point, it has been placed in its true relation to your total duty. Universal affection is a ground of your interest in his plight, but also of the justice by whose rule you must now forbear this action. (*KGS* 2:216, Goldthwait 58)

This is a sound restatement of Rousseau's idea of virtue and justice. Although pity or sympathy is a valuable natural sentiment, he says, it can degenerate without the virtue of universal love:

To prevent pity from degenerating into weakness, it must, there-fore, be generalized and extended to the whole of mankind. Then one yields to it only insofar as it accords with justice, because of all the virtues justice is the one that contributes most to the com-mon good of men. For the sake of reason, for the sake of love of ourselves, we must have pity for our species still more than for our neighbor, and pity for the wicked is a very great cruelty to men.[17]

Universal love is the basis of virtue and the principle of justice, and to subject all affections and impulses to this universal principle is the height of moral perfection. Of such perfection Rousseau says in *Emile*, "What sublime sentiments stifle the germ of the petty passions in his heart!"[18] Kant calls such an emotional state a noble heart, which stands much higher than goodheartedness. He says that even such socially delightful and beautiful sentiments as complai-sance can lead only to depravities unless they are controlled by higher principles. Again from *Emile:* "Out of kindhearted fellow-ship he will be a liar, an idler, a drunkard, or the like, for he does not act by the rules that are directed to good conduct in general, but rather by an inclination that in itself is beautiful but becomes trifling when it is without support and without principles" (*KGS* 2:217, Goldthwait 59–60).

Kant's final charge against passions is that they are not stable.

---

17. Rousseau, *Emile, or On Education,* trans. Allan Bloom (New York, 1979), 253.
18. Ibid., 253.

Because our sentiments are largely determined by contingent external conditions, they are always fickle. On the other hand, virtue is stable and constant (*KGS* 2:221). This is another of the recurrent themes in Rousseau's writings. He observed that human beings, buffeted by the constantly changing social fashions and pressures, can never secure and enjoy unity and stability of their emotions without developing virtue. Virtue induces strength and vigor in the soul, enabling it to overcome its alienation and to regain its original nature. Only then can the soul permanently establish its existence.

In spite of these unmistakable Rousseauesque traits, everything Kant has said up to this point is still compatible with Hutcheson's moral theory. Kant and Rousseau's idea of universal affection is basically the same as Hutcheson's idea of universal benevolence. Hutcheson also recognizes the difference between particular and universal affections. Particular affections are directed toward particular persons or particular groups of people, while universal affection is directed toward all human beings or the human species as a whole. He also knows the danger of relying on particular affections for our moral guide and the tendency our sense of benevolence has to be confined and constricted by partial sentiment and erroneous considerations.[19] Hutcheson even calls the sentiment of universal benevolence a moral principle. For him, a moral principle is the ultimate ground for moral actions and judgments. It need not be a rational principle; it may be a sentiment.

Hutcheson's notion of moral sense includes two different types of moral sentiments: the sentiment recognizing general moral principles and the sentiment perceiving particular moral properties. One is the recognition of general principles; the other is a particular sentiment. In the *Observations*, Kant restricts the notion of moral sense to the latter, as he did in the *Prize Essay*. He then dissociates moral principles from moral sentiments. He insists that moral sentiments have no moral worth in their own right and that they are not truly virtuous unless they are governed by the basic rules of virtue (*KGS* 2:215). The stability of virtue derives from the stability of moral prin-

19. Hutcheson, *Collected Works*, 1:187–89.

ciples, and those principles should be rational, because sentiments and passions are always unstable.[20]

Although moral principles are rational, they can be felt in our moral sentiments. This is the basic difference between theoretical and practical principles: while the recognition of theoretical principles has nothing to do with sentiments, the recognition of practical principles is inseparable from sentiments. In the *Observations* Kant says: "These principles [of virtue] are not speculative rules, but the consciousness of a feeling that lives in every human breast and extends itself much further than over the particular grounds of compassion and complaisance. I believe that I sum it all up when I say it is the *feeling of beauty and dignity of human nature*. The first is a ground of universal affection, the second of universal esteem" (*KGS* 2:217, Goldthwait 60).

Kant derives the distinction between affection and esteem from Hutcheson's distinction between the natural and the moral good. Hutcheson says, "We love natural good, but esteem moral good."[21] Since moral excellence is the object of our esteem, Hutcheson says, we should have greater esteem for those with a higher moral excellence. For Kant, the object of our esteem is not moral qualities but human beings and their dignity. This is the important lesson he learned from Rousseau. Hutcheson never made universal esteem a separate moral principle from universal affection. In Kant's hand, however, universal affection and universal esteem become two principles: universal affection or love *(Wohlgewogenheit)* is directed toward human happiness or well-being; universal esteem or respect *(Achtung)*, toward human dignity. The first principle is a gift from Hutcheson. The second reflects Rousseau's influence. Kant describes a person with a strong sense of human dignity in Rousseau's language: "He values himself and regards a human being as a creature who merits respect. He suffers no depraved submissiveness, and breathes freedom in a noble breast. All chains, from the gilded ones

20. Keith Ward says that Kant's principles are still feelings and that they are special only because of their unchangeability (*The Development of Kant's View of Ethics* [Oxford, 1972], 24).

21. Hutcheson, *Collected Works*, 1:108.

worn at court to the heavy irons of galley slaves, are abominable to him" (*KGS* 2:221, Goldthwait 66).

Freedom is the most essential nature of every human being—this is perhaps the most important lesson Kant learned from Rousseau. Rousseau recognized two types of dependence every human being must learn to accept: the dependence on nature and the dependence on other human beings. The first is inevitable, but the second should not be allowed to lead to the enslavement of one human being to another. Insofar as human beings are aware of their dependence on nature, they are only natural beings. They become moral beings only when they begin to recognize their mutual dependence and their freedom. To project an ideal human development from a creature of natural order to an agent of moral order is the central theme of Rousseau's *Emile*. How can human beings come together in a social order of mutual dependence without enslaving one another? This is the central question of the *Social Contract*. Both are concerned with the dignity of human beings as agents of freedom.

Let us review Kant's accomplishments in the *Observations*. He rejects passions and sentiments as the foundation of morality. Section 1 begins by calling our attention to the variability and diversity of these feelings. What can be a source of pleasure for some people can produce aversion in others. The entire essay could have been called "Observations on the Variability of Feelings," for Kant goes on to explain temperamental differences between men of different psychological types (section 2), between men and women (section 3), and between men of different nationalities (section 4). But not all feelings are alike: some are based on principles. Only those feelings are sublime; they constitute the foundation of morality.

Establishing the subjectivity of sentiments and the objectivity of principles is Kant's most important accomplishment in the *Observations*. He abandons Hutcheson's moral sense theory at its most important juncture, the objectivity of moral sentiments: our internal sense of moral feelings can perceive objective qualities just as much as our external sense of colors and sounds can. This thesis is compatible only with the commonsense realism, which does not recognize the distinction between primary and secondary qualities and regards moral properties as being on a par with physical properties. But the commonsense realism has crumbled under the impact of modern science, and David Hume had to relegate moral sentiments to the domain of subjective feelings. Kant is only recognizing the fact that Hume has undermined the whole moral sense theory by denying the objectivity of moral sentiments.[22]

* *   The World of Freedom

After the publication of the *Observations*, Kant pondered Rousseau's view of human nature and recorded his reflections in a long series of notes, which he appended to his own copy of the *Observations*.[23] He says that he learned from Rousseau to honor all human beings, although before he had valued learning and despised the ignorant (*KGS* 20:44). Before reading Rousseau, he had sought the highest perfection in reason and knowledge of the universe; after Rousseau, he finds it in the subordination of everything to free will (*KGS* 20:144). He begins to see the important difference between the world of Newton and the world of Rousseau and realizes that the world of freedom is much nobler than the world of nature. Rousseau unlocked the secret of the world of freedom just as Newton had done for the world of nature. Thus, Kant calls Rousseau the Newton of the moral world. Like Newton, Rousseau discovered order where confusion had prevailed.

In Kant's view, Rousseau disclosed freedom as the true essence of humanity. Because freedom and dignity are essential to being human, the most serious evil and injustice for any human being is to be subject to the will of another (*KGS* 20:91). For the meaning of submission is to allow oneself to be used as a tool and to become a thing in the eyes of another. To submit to the will of another is to cancel one's own essence, which is self-contradiction. Following Rousseau, Kant recognizes an important difference between natural and human

22. Hume's subjectivist view of moral sentiments is given in book 3 of his *Treatise of Human Nature*.

23. These reflections are known as *Bemerkungen zu den Beobachtungen ueber das Gefühl des Schönen und Erhabenen* (*KGS* 20:1–192).

compulsions. The necessity of natural events is to be governed by the laws of nature; the necessity of human coercion is to be determined by the willfulness of one against another, which knows no laws (*KGS* 20:93). Hence the world of human wills is radically different from the world of natural events. Thus, Kant affirms the demarcation between the world of matter and the world of spirit. The world of matter is the domain of necessity; the world of spirit is the domain of freedom.

With the demarcation of nature and freedom, Kant reshapes the vocation of philosophy. The problem of knowledge becomes secondary to the problem of value. The former concerns nature; the latter, freedom. In this reorientation the problem of value and freedom becomes the central concern in Kant's philosophy, an event that Josef Schmucker considers as momentous as the well-known Copernican revolution for Critical Philosophy.[24] From this point on, as Dieter Henrich observes, Kant assigns only a propaedeutic or instrumental function to theoretical philosophy[25] and gives primacy to practical philosophy. Truth has no value in itself; it has value only in the service of the practical (*KGS* 20:175). The practical world is the normative world.

Because freedom is human essence, Kant holds, it is even more important than happiness. Freedom is also the source of most intractable problems of humankind. It is the ground of willfulness. Human beings are willful because they have free will. Without order and control, the world of willful agents would degenerate into a world of oppression and tyranny. Hence the really tough question for human beings is: What sort of moral order should be devised for the fulfillment of human nature as freedom? Kant seems to have gathered most of the essential ingredients for his ethics. Henrich says that the first two parts of the *Groundwork for the Metaphysics of Morals* could

24. Schmucker, *Die Ursprünge der Ethik Kants,* 174.

25. Dieter Henrich, "Der Begriff der sittlichen Einsicht und Kants Lehre vom Faktum der Vernunft," in *Die Gegenwart der Griechen im neueren Denken,* ed. Henrich et al. (Tübingen, 1960), 77–115, esp. 111–13; idem, *Identität und Objectivität: Eine Untersuchung über Kants transzendentale Deduktion* (Heidelberg, 1976), 13.

have been written in 1765.[26] But this is an exaggeration. Kant indeed had come to appreciate, from Rousseau's writings, not only the prodigious significance of human freedom but also the enormous difficulties that arise from it. But he had no definite ideas for coping with those difficulties. The ethics he could have written in 1765 would not have been significantly different from Rousseau's. Kant had yet to work out his own idea of spiritual order.

* * Spiritual Order

The *Dreams of a Spirit-Seer Explained through the Dreams of Metaphysics,* of 1766 (*KGS* 2:315–73), is Kant's first attempt to develop his idea of spiritual order.[27] The treatise is a caustic critique of the then renowned visionary Emanuel Swedenborg and his alleged power of communicating with the spirits of the other world. Kant ridicules Swedenborg's pneumatic powers as delusions of deranged brains by lumping them together with philosophical speculations in the fool's paradise of metaphysics (*KGS* 2:356). But Kant's caustic ridicule is only on the surface of the *Dreams.* Deep down, he is more concerned with the reality of spiritual order. He notes that the universe is full of dead matter, whose inertia he contrasts with the living force of immaterial substances (*KGS* 2:329). These living substances are spiritual beings, who are not subject to the mechanical laws of natural order. The immaterial beings must constitute a community, just as material substances constitute natural order (*KGS* 2:329–30).

Natural order is called the "material world"; spiritual order, the "immaterial" or "intelligible world" *(mundus intelligibilis).* Kant says that the human soul simultaneously belongs to both worlds. Then he considers the forces that move spiritual substances, in an analogy to the forces that move material substances. He is trying to construct a science of pneumatics, or spiritual forces, that can stand alongside

26. Henrich, "Über Kants Entwicklungsgeschichte," *Philosophische Rundschau* 13 (1965): 252–63, esp. 260.

27. Two English translations are available, one by Emanuel F. Goerwitz (London, 1900), the other by John Manolesco (New York, 1969).

the science of mechanics. He even proposes pneumatic, or spiritual, laws, which govern the behavior of spiritual beings, in an analogy to the mechanical laws of nature. The idea of pneumatics was not totally new: Christian Crusius had called his rational psychology pneumatology.[28] But the idea of pneumatic laws was Kant's invention.

Kant recognizes two forces that move the human soul. One is self-love, which originates in the soul. The other originates outside the human heart and causes us to shift our attention from our personal motives to those of other rational beings (*KGS* 2:334). These two forces often come into conflict, which can take various forms. The most familiar is the conflict between self-interest and social utility. One's sense of vanity and one's craving for the applause and respect of others reveal the conflict between self-concern and concern for others. Even in the most unselfish and truthful person, Kant says, there is a secret tendency to compare one's judgment of the good and the true with others' judgment and to bring them into harmony. This is perhaps due to the perception that our judgments depend on the universal human understanding. There is a hidden propensity to secure the unity of reason for all thinking beings, a propensity that Kant regards as a manifestation of the universal force.

Parallel to the intellectual unity of all thinking beings, Kant tries to develop a notion of moral unity. He points out that our self-regarding considerations always feel the restraint of some alien will acting against our own inclinations (*KGS* 2:334–35). He says that this hidden alien force acting on human souls generates moral impulses, which eventuate in the strong law of duty and the weak law of benevolence. And while these two laws are occasionally overpowered by selfish inclinations, they never fail to assert their reality in human nature (*KGS* 2:335). These phenomena indicate the dependence of our innermost motivations on the rule *(Regel)* of general will, and

---

28. Crusius divides his rational psychology into two parts: the first part, called *pneumatology*, is concerned with the powers of understanding; the second part, called *thelematology*, with the powers of volition. For details, see his *Entwurf der notwendigen Vernunftwahrheiten* [Sketch of the necessary truths of reason], secs. 281, 334, 425, 427, 432, 433, 450, 451; and J. N. Findlay's exposition in his *Kant and the Transcendental Object* (Oxford, 1981), 66–67.

thence arises in the community of all thinking beings a moral unity and a system of constitution in accordance with purely spiritual laws.

The power of general will over private wills turns out to be the ultimate source for the strong law of duty and the weak law of benevolence. Kant goes on to explain the nature of our moral feelings in pneumatic terms. He says that moral feelings are the feelings of constraint on the private will exercised by the general will (*KGS* 2:335). How does the general will affect the individual will? This is a mystery about which Kant says we are utterly ignorant. He longs for a Newtonian discovery in moral science. Newton discovered gravitation to be the true effect of a universal force inherent in matter, which he called the force of attraction. "Might it not be possible, in a similar way," Kant wonders,

> to regard the appearance of the moral impulse in thinking natures as the consequence of a truly active force by means of which spiritual natures flow into one another? The moral feeling would be this felt dependence of the private will upon the Universal Will [general will], and a consequence of the natural and universal interaction by means of which the immaterial world achieves its moral unity developing into a system of spiritual perfection according to the laws of its own structure. (*KGS* 2:335, Manolesco 51)

If such a spiritual order is possible, Kant says, we can resolve the difficulties that arise from the contradictions between our moral and physical relations here on earth. Natural order appears to be totally indifferent to our moral concerns; most of our moral intentions are frustrated and defeated by the niggardliness of nature. Kant proposes to look at the same phenomenon from a different perspective. Since the morality of an action concerns the inner state of a spiritual being, it can have its efficacy in the spiritual world even when the same action fails to produce adequate result in the physical world (*KGS* 2:336). Moral intentions and actions have different efficacies in the two worlds. Their spiritual effects are governed by spiritual laws; their physical effects, by physical laws. The spiritual laws establish the concordance of private and general will in spiritual order, even when their concordance fails to obtain in natural order. The operation of spiritual order is completely independent of the events taking place in natural order.

In the *Dreams* Kant is much more concerned with the nature and mystery of spiritual order than with the dubious contentions of Swedenborg and metaphysicians. In the *Observations*, as we have seen, he was concerned with the instability of moral feelings and tried to seek their stable foundation in the principles of virtue. As he noted, however, there are but few who act from principles. The vast majority of people act from various impulses, such as self-interest and the love of honor. Since they are driven by these unstable impulses, it appears implausible for them to maintain any semblance of moral order. And yet Kant believed in such an order: "Thus the different groups unite into a picture of splendid expression, where amidst great multiplicity unity shines forth, and the whole of moral nature exhibits beauty and dignity" (*KGS* 2:227, Goldthwait 75).

In the *Dreams* Kant is trying to discover the hidden spiritual force that establishes order and unity in the world of perpetually fluctuating moral impulses and feelings. He locates his Archimedean point in Rousseau's idea of general will. As we have seen, he believed that Rousseau had provided the key to unlock the secret of the intelligible world: "Rousseau was the first to discover underneath the variety of human forms the deeply concealed human nature and the hidden law, in accordance with which the Providence is justified by his observations. Before them [Newton and Rousseau] the objections of King Alfonso and the Manicheans were still valid. After Newton and Rousseau, God is justified and Pope's thesis is henceforth true" (*KGS* 20:58–59).

Kant recorded this observation shortly before or during the composition of the *Dreams*. King Alfonso's complaint was made against the apparent disorder of the natural world, and the Manichean complaint was against that of the moral world. By using the Copernican perspective, Newton discovered a beautiful order hidden behind an apparently unwieldy disorder.[29] By using Rousseau's notion of gen-

---

29. Kant states the connection between Newton's theory of gravitation and the Copernican perspective in the *Critique of Pure Reason*, trans. Norman Kemp Smith, 2d ed.

eral will, Kant must have felt, he was finding a new order in the moral world under its semblance of conflict and disorder. In this he vouches for the truth of Alexander Pope's thesis in the *Essay on Man*. Pope's thesis is metaphysical optimism: the whole creation is a great chain of being that realizes the Leibnizian principle of plenitude. It may contain some evils, but those evils are essential components in the creation of the best of all possible worlds. This is basically Leibnizian optimism, although Pope denied Leibniz's influence on himself. Pope sums up his thesis thus:

Showed erring Pride, WHATEVER IS, IS RIGHT;
That REASON, PASSION, answer one great aim;
That true SELF-LOVE and SOCIAL are the same;
That VIRTUE only makes our Bliss below;
And all our Knowledge is, OURSELVES TO KNOW.

To endorse Pope's optimism is to affirm the Leibnizian theodicy, which Kant had espoused in his early works. But his Leibnizian perspective in the *Dreams* is quite different from the one that underlay *Universal Natural History and Theory of the Heavens*. His earlier Leibnizian perspective was cold and impersonal; it had no room for human values. But his new Leibnizian perspective is humanized; it recognizes the existence of spiritual order. Leibniz himself had recognized the kingdom of grace alongside the kingdom of nature. In the *Dreams* Kant accepts these two kingdoms as two orders of reality.

Kant dreams of constructing a science that Leibniz had not even dreamed of, that is, the science of spiritual order, parallel to the science of physical order. He approaches spiritual reality in just the way natural scientists approach physical reality. The latter begin with physical sensations as their data and then construct their theory of physical reality on the basis of those data. Kant takes moral and visionary experiences as his data and constructs his theory of spiritual reality on the basis of those data. He talks of pneumatic

(New York, 1929), p. xii, note a. Hereinafter the *Critique of Pure Reason* will be cited by the standard A and B numbers, an A number (e.g., A142) referring to a page in the first edition, a B number (e.g., B243) to a page in the second edition.

laws in the same manner as natural scientists talk of physical laws. Spiritual order is as real as physical order.[30] But how does he know the existence and nature of spiritual order? He tries to answer this question with his theory of spiritual intuition.

* * Spiritual Intuition

Kant says that every human soul has two sets of representations, one created by immaterial intuitions, the other by sense perceptions. Spiritual beings are the objects of spiritual representations; material beings are the objects of material representations. One belongs to the soul as a pure spirit, and the other belongs to it as a corporeal human being. These two sets of representations are so radically different from each other that they cannot be combined in one consciousness. One's spiritual representations cannot enter one's consciousness as a corporeal human being, and one's physical representations cannot enter one's consciousness as a spiritual being. Human consciousness is restricted to the domain of physical perceptions; that is, we can never be directly aware of spiritual representations.

By this theory of spiritual representation, Kant means to deny Swedenborg's claim for supernatural perception and communion. How, then, can Kant account for Swedenborg's alleged supernatural experience? He proposes a theory of spiritual influx. Although spiritual intuitions cannot be objects of our direct awareness, they can invade human consciousness by producing the images of spiritual reality in the likeness of material reality. These images are not, however, the real spiritual representations, but only their symbols (*KGS* 2:339). They are similar to the analogical descriptions of divine attributes by means of human attributes of anger, jealousy, charity, and vengeance. They are also like the poetic personification of virtues and vices and the pictorial representation of time as a straight line. The spiritual influx produces the physical representations of spiritual reality, which has no physical properties and relations.

30. Richard Velkley interprets the spiritual world in the *Dreams* as an ideal entity rather than a real one (*Freedom and the End of Reason*, 110). But that is a misreading of Kant's text: his pneumatic laws are meant to be as real and as descriptive as Newton's laws.

Kant says that not everyone experiences spiritual influx. It happens only to those souls whose organs are of an exceptional sensitivity. These abnormal people take the analogical excitations of their imagination for real spiritual representations. Whereas real representations are public, those excitations of imagination are private. Hence they are only dreams and delusions. But the dreamers of these dreams mistakenly feel that they can actually see departed souls and pure spirits and even talk with them. The excitations that spiritual influx produces on our imagination are often mingled with other fancies of imagination, such as wild fantasies and grotesquely distorted figures. In such a wild state of excitation, it becomes impossible to discriminate the true from the false, the real from the imaginary. It is a mental disease or an altered balance of nerves (*KGS* 2:340).

Kant never says that the phenomenon of spiritual visions is a hoax or trickery. He firmly believes in the existence of spiritual representations and their occasional influx into human consciousness. He only denounces the simple-minded mistake of accepting the wild effects of spiritual influx for spiritual intuitions. He insists that human beings can never be directly aware of spiritual intuitions. Only because they mistake wild phantoms for real intuitions do visionaries such as Swedenborg believe that they have knowledge of supernatural reality. In this regard, metaphysicians are like visionaries. To be sure, the objects of metaphysical illusions are not phantoms and spirits but the ideas of supernatural reality. But those ideas are as delusive as the phantoms of visionaries. Metaphysicians are dreamers of reason; visionaries are dreamers of senses.

This scathing critique of metaphysicians and visionaries applies equally to Kant's own theory of the spiritual world. If human beings can never be directly aware of spiritual intuitions, how does Kant know that there are spiritual intuitions? The idea of spiritual representation is no more than an analogy; it is conceived in the likeness of physical perception. To construct the science of pneumatics on such an analogy is to follow the suit of metaphysicians and visionaries. For these reasons, Kant becomes highly self-critical and admits that he has made the common mistake of all metaphysicians in talking about the communion of spirits. He even confesses his agnosticism about spiritual reality. At best, he says, our knowledge of spiritual order is negative. Our positive knowledge is limited to the physical reality and its laws.

Kant concludes his treatise on the spiritual world by laying down stringent restrictions on the power of human reason. Causal relations can never be determined by reasoning alone but only by experience. The scope of human reasoning is restricted to the logical rules of identity and contradiction, and causal questions can never be resolved by these two rules. Whatever goes beyond these two logical rules can be settled only by experience (*KGS* 2:370–71). This is none other than British empiricism, and Kant extends it to spiritual reality. Although we have some ideas about spiritual beings, we cannot meaningfully talk of spiritual laws that connect spiritual beings to physical objects, because those laws cannot be confirmed by our experience. Human reason can invent all sorts of laws, but only experience can substantiate their reality.

Kant's empiricism and agnosticism of spiritual reality belong to his Humean perspective, which is incompatible with his Leibnizian perspective. The mixture of these two perspectives explains his peculiar notion of spiritual representations. The idea of spiritual representation belongs to Leibnizian tradition, but Kant accedes to Humean tradition in conceding that spiritual representations are not included in our awareness. Because he subscribes to two incompatible perspectives, he winds up with the paradoxical thesis that we have spiritual representations without being conscious of them. This paradoxical thesis makes the *Dreams* a nest of contradictions and ambivalence, which affects even the tone and style of his exposition. He is equally sympathetic and antipathetic toward the alleged supernatural powers of visionaries.

In his letter of April 1766 to Moses Mendelssohn (*KGS* 10:69–73), Kant confesses the difficulties he had in finding the right style of exposition for the *Dreams*. He had decided that self-mockery was the best way to forestall other people's mockery of him. He now says that even the analogy of spiritual influx to the force of universal gravitation was never meant seriously:

My analogy between a spiritual substance's actual moral influx and the force of universal gravitation is not intended seriously; but is an example of how far one can go in philosophical fabrications, completely unhindered, when there are no *data*, and it illustrates how important it is, in such exercises, first to decide what is required for a solution of the problem and whether the necessary *data* for a solution may be lacking. (*KGS* 10:72, Zweig 57)[31]

In the same letter, Kant goes on to clarify his position on metaphysics. Although he detests dubious metaphysical speculations, he is convinced that the true and lasting welfare of humankind depends on metaphysics. Advocating the need for reforming metaphysics as a science, he asks Mendelssohn to take the lead for such a move: "It befits brilliant men such as you to create a new epoch in this science, to begin completely afresh, to draw up the plans for this heretofore haphazardly constructed discipline with a master's hand" (*KGS* 10:70, Zweig 55). The first task of such a new science is to establish a proper procedure for testing the dogmatic claims of metaphysics. He claims to have gained some important insight about such a procedure, but he is still working on it.

31. Zweig's translation is from Kant, *Philosophical Correspondence*, 1759–99, ed. and trans. Zweig (Chicago, 1967).

2 Kant's Platonic Awakening in the
Inaugural Dissertation

* * * * * * * * * * * * * * * * * *

The *Dreams* was a work of desperation. Trapped in the world of dead matter, Kant made a desperate attempt to find some room for human values. He seized on the idea of spiritual order, a Christian and a Leibnizian legacy. But how do we know anything about it? Its accessibility is as much a mystery as Swedenborg's communication with spiritual beings. As long as Kant subscribed to Hume's theory of perception, he had no semantic basis even to talk about spiritual order, because Humean empiricism restricts our perception to empirical reality. But he could not abandon Hume's theory of perception and adopt Swedenborg's doctrine of spiritual communion. He had to find a way to retain the Leibnizian legacy without rejecting Hume's theory of perception. It was this reconciliation of Leibniz and Hume that Kant had in mind when he advocated reforming metaphysics as a new science. And he made his first attempt at this reform in the *Inaugural Dissertation*, of 1770.

* * The New Metaphysics

Kant reaffirmed his two-world view in the *Inaugural Dissertation*.[1] The sensible world is made of physical substances, and the intelligible world contains spiritual substances. One is known by sensibility, and the other is known by intellect. Sensibility is receptivity; it is modification of the soul by an object. It represents the object as it appears to the subject. Hence the sensible world is the world of appearances. Intellect is not receptive or passive but active and spon-

1. *KGS* 2:285–419. Its official title is *De mundi sensibilis atque intelligibilis forma et principiis.*

taneous. Instead of receiving representations, it represents the objects by its own pure concepts. Hence it knows the objects as they really are rather than as they appear to our sensibility. The intelligible world is the world of reality (*ID* 2.3–6; *KGS* 2:392–94).

Kant recognizes two functions of intellect: the logical and the real (*ID* 2.5; *KGS* 2:393). The real function is to provide the concepts of objects and their relations; the logical function is to establish the logical order of higher and lower concepts and compare them in accordance with the principle of contradiction. For our knowledge of phenomena, intellect performs only the logical function, because the concepts of objects and their relations are given by sensibility. For our knowledge of noumena, intellect performs the real function; it provides a set of pure concepts for representing objects and their relations as they really are. The concepts of this sort are the concepts of possibility, existence, necessity, substance, and cause, with their opposites or correlates (*ID* 2.8; *KGS* 2:395).

The pure concepts of understanding have two functions: the critical and the dogmatic. The critical function is to keep the sensitive concepts from being applied to noumena. This function is only negative; it does not advance our knowledge. The dogmatic function is positive; it provides the general principles of pure understanding for ontology and rational psychology. By those principles, we form the concept of some exemplar or perfection, *perfectio noumenon*. It is the common measure of all other things as far as they are real, and is conceivable only by pure intellect. In the theoretical domain, the exemplar is the supreme being, God; in the practical domain, it is the ideal of moral perfection (*ID* 2.9; *KGS* 2:396). Since the concept of moral perfection is accessible only to pure intellect, Kant says, the first principles of moral philosophy belong to pure understanding. Thus, he condemns Epicurus and Shaftsbury for reducing moral criteria to the feelings of pleasure and pain. He is repudiating moral sense theory, and he appears to be returning to the ethics of perfectionism, which he had long forgotten.

Even so, some scholars have found it difficult to believe that Kant is returning, in the *Dissertation*, to the ethics of perfectionism after his prolonged involvement with Hutcheson and Rousseau. So they have argued that in the *Dissertation* the idea of moral perfection has only a formal function.[2] That is, Kant still retains the distinction between formal and material moral principles that he had adopted in the *Prize Essay*, whereas no such distinction had been known in the Wolffian ethics of perfectionism. These conjectures are groundless. Kant is not returning to Wolffian perfectionism but is adopting Platonic ethics. He identifies the Ideas of perfection as Platonic Forms (*ID* 2.9; *KGS* 2:396).[3] Under the influence of Rousseau, he had recognized the importance of moral principles. He had come to believe that morality requires, for its basis, principles rather than sentiments. In the *Dreams*, he had entertained the view that general will was the fountainhead of moral laws and principles. In the *Dissertation*, he is relocating this fountainhead in Platonic Forms. He says that the first principles of moral judgment are the Ideas of perfection, Platonic Ideas (*ID* 2.9; *KGS* 2:396).

The metaphysics of the *Dissertation* is Leibnizian. The demarcation of the two worlds—phenomena (sensible) and noumena (intelligible)—comes from Leibniz. The physical world has no independent existence; it is made of the phenomena of perception. Space and time are not objective entities but only the forms of perception. This is quite a change from his position in the *Dreams*, where Kant had never questioned the independent existence of natural order.[4] But his acceptance of the Leibnizian view is not total. The *Dissertation* shows the influence of the *Nouveaux Essais*, Leibniz's attempt to reconcile his rationalism with British empiricism. Kant had also been reading the Leibniz-Clarke correspondence. So he retains the essential feature of empiricism within his Leibnizian metaphysical framework and regards sensation as the only source for our knowledge of phenomena. Even the restriction of intellect to its logical function in cogni-

2. Paul Schilpp, *Kant's Pre-Critical Ethics*, 105; Keith Ward, *Development of Kant's View of Ethics*, 46–47.

3. The English word *idea* has a very broad meaning, broad enough to correspond to *representation* in Kant's lexicon. But Kant assigns a highly technical sense to *Idee*, which has the same meaning as the Platonic Idea. I shall use *Idea*, with a capital *I*.

4. Kant uses the word *Erscheinung*, the German equivalent of *phenomenon*, in describing the occurrence of moral feelings; that is, they are only effects of general will (*KGS* 2:335). But he does not use the word to describe material objects.

tion of phenomena is perfectly in line with Humean empiricism.

Kant does not endorse the Leibnizian doctrine of intellectual intuition but restricts human intuition to the sensible world. He does not even mention the idea of spiritual representations. He is hesitant to say anything definite about how mental substances interact with one another even in the world of phenomena, and he is inclined to accept the theory of their physical interaction *(influxes physicus)* rather than the theories of preestablished harmony and occasionalism (*ID* 4.22; *KGS* 2:409). Since we have no intellectual intuition of the intelligible world, Kant says, our knowledge of noumena is not fully real but only symbolic (*ID* 2.10; *KGS* 2:396). Fully real knowledge is the knowledge of the concrete, which is possible only via intuition, but human intuition is restricted to the domain of space and time, which are the formal principles of intuition.

Kant's conception of noumenal knowledge in the *Dissertation* is not very different from his theory of spiritual knowledge in the *Dreams,* where he stressed the symbolic character of our representation of spiritual order. He highlights the difference between knowledge by intuition and knowledge by concept. Knowledge by concept is abstract, vague, and often confused and never has the fullness of knowledge by intuition. The former is much more deficient than the latter. Since our knowledge of noumena depends solely on pure concepts, Kant says, it is quite inferior to our knowledge of phenomena. This is a reversal of the Leibnizian position. Leibniz had maintained that our knowledge of noumena is far superior to our knowledge of phenomena, because our ideas of noumena are clear and distinct, while our perceptions of phenomena are vague and confused. This reversal is due to Kant's partial adherence to empiricism.

Kant's acceptance of Platonic Forms was perhaps the most momentous event for the development of his normative philosophy.[5] One year before the *Dissertation,* Kant had recorded in *Reflexion* 5037 that

---

5. Although Kant identified the Ideas of perfection with Platonic Ideas for the first time in the *Dissertation,* he was acquainted with them long before that, because the Ideas of perfection had been an essential feature of Leibniz's philosophy. In *Universal Natural History and Theory of the Heavens,* Kant mentions the Idea of perfection in the divine mind (*KGS* 1:263).

a "great light" had dawned on him (*KGS* 18:69). Max Wundt has proposed that the "great light" was Kant's recognition of Platonism.[6] He says that Kant was reading Plato extensively at that time, and he points out that allusions to Plato and Greek philosophy abound in the *Dissertation*, whereas they are mostly absent from his earlier writings. But Wundt's claim has been countered by another claim, namely, that the "great light" refers to the rediscovery of Leibniz, which Kant shared with the whole German intellectual world. According to Ernst Cassirer, when the *Nouveaux Essais* was published in 1765, after the manuscript had been buried in the library at Hanover for sixty years, German intellectuals were impressed with the breadth and originality of Leibniz's thought. "Leibniz once again stood among them as a contemporary, as though raised from the dead."[7]

But these two views are by no means incompatible.[8] Here is the whole passage in which Kant refers to the "great light": "I attempted quite earnestly to prove propositions and their opposites, not in order to establish a skeptical teaching, but, as I assumed there was an illusion of the understanding, in order to discover wherein the illusion lies. The year 69 gave me great light" (*KGS* 18:69). By "propositions and their opposites" Kant means the antinomies of pure reason.[9] A few pairs of contradictory propositions can be asserted and proved about the physical universe, for example, "the world is finite" and "the world is infinite." This is an absurdly incomprehensible mystery, as Kant was later to say in the *Critique of Pure Reason*, if the physical universe is taken as real, for nothing real can violate the law of contradiction. Antinomies can be explained only if the physical world is taken as a world of phenomena. This is a Platonic account of antinomies. In arguing for the unreality of perceptual entities, Plato appealed to the fact that the objects of sense have contradictory properties. That is, they can be at once large and small, beautiful and ugly, one and

6. Wundt, *Kant als Metaphysiker* (Stuttgart, 1924), 153–78.

7. Cassirer, *Kant's Life and Thought*, trans. James Haden (New Haven, 1981), 98.

8. This is Lewis White Beck's view in *Early German Philosophy* (Cambridge, Mass., 1969), 457.

9. This interpretation is supported by H. de Vleeschauer, *The Development of Kantian Thought*, trans. A.R.C. Duncan (London, 1962), 49.

many (*Republic* 523c–524d). If they were really real, they could not have contradictory properties. Thus, Plato concluded that the perceptual world is not truly real but only appears to be real. It is the world of appearances.

Leibniz was a staunch Platonist. He accepted the Platonic demarcation between the sensible and the intelligible worlds. He was especially impressed with the Socratic view of nature, which is presented in a long passage of the *Phaedo* (97–99). He made a summary translation of this passage and inserted it as a note in his *Discourse on Metaphysics*. Here is the gist of Socrates' story. As a young man, he became engrossed in natural philosophy; he was enthralled by the idea of explaining all things in terms of physical causes. But he soon realized that he was the stupidest creature in the world, because he found too many things that could not be explained by physical causes. Then he heard of Anaxagoras's idea that the mind was the cause or the ordering principle of everything. This idea made much better sense to Socrates. Immensely pleased with this new idea, he thought

> that if the world was the effect of an intelligence, everything would be done in the most perfect manner that was possible. That is why I believed that whoever wished to explain why things beget one another or perish or subsist, would have to look for what was suitable to the perfection of each thing. Thus a man would only have to consider in himself or in any thing else what would be the best and the most perfect.[10]

In the *Phaedo* Socrates points out the important difference between two conceptions of reasons and causes. In the world of physical objects, to give a reason or cause of something is to name its physical cause. In the world of intelligence, to give a reason or cause of something is to show how it is related to its perfection. The latter is a teleological view. Socrates applies it first to human behavior: he is sitting in jail instead of escaping from it as his friends have urged him to, not because of his bones and flesh, but because he thinks what he is doing is the best. He wants to extend the idea of teleological account even to

---

10. This is Leibniz's own translation, given in *Discourse on Metaphysics*, trans. Peter Lucas and Leslie Grint (Manchester, 1953), sec. 20.

the physical world. For example, the fact that the earth is round rather than flat should be explained on the ground that it is better for being so.

On many occasions, Leibniz cites this story of Socrates to support his teleological view of the universe against the Cartesians.[11] His chief complaint against them is that their science has no room for the idea of the best or the idea of perfection, because it is dominated by the idea of mechanical causes. Leibniz wants to counter this mechanistic view of nature with a Platonic view, namely, that mind rather than matter is the ultimate principle of order. Thus, he locates his ultimate ontological principle in the monads, the mental atoms, the ultimate source of all forces and activities in the Leibnizian world. Even the mechanical laws of nature have been installed by the Supreme Monad, because they are indispensable for the creation of the best of all possible worlds.

This is not to say that Leibniz was the first to revive Platonism. The Renaissance had seen the resurgence of Platonism in the writings of Nicholas of Cusa, Marsilio Ficino, Tommaso Campanella, and Giodarno Bruno. Platonism had gained popularity especially because Aristotelian science was being discredited by the rise of modern science. Even the champions of modern science never regarded Platonism as an opponent to the revival of Democritean science. Modern science was highly mathematical, and the mathematical tradition had enjoyed a long association with Platonism and Pythagoreanism. Galileo and Kepler interpreted the order and laws of nature as Platonic Forms,[12] but they restricted Platonic Forms to the physical domain. Such a truncated Platonism was interchangeable with Democritean atomism. By complaining against modern physics, Leibniz was expressing his dissatisfaction with this debased version of Platonism and trying to restore Platonism to its original fullness.

---

11. For example, in his letter to Christian Philipp (G. 4:281–82); in *Discourse on Metaphysics*, secs. 20, 21.

12. For a good discussion of this point, see Leroy Loemker, *Struggle for Synthesis* (Cambridge, Mass., 1972), 120–21.

* * The Copernican Revolution

Shortly after the publication of his *Dissertation*, Kant became highly critical of his own position. He had maintained that the knowledge of phenomena is gained by intuitions and that the knowledge of noumena is gained by concepts. As we have already noted, he had little confidence in knowledge by concepts. He had said that such conceptual knowledge was vague and confused. He now raised a more basic question: How can we be sure that the pure concepts of understanding are related to the objects of noumena? More generally, how is a representation related to its object? Kant posed this question of representation in his letter of February 1772 to Marcus Herz (*KGS* 10:129–35). In the *Dissertation*, he said, he had overlooked this critical question. Now he noted that it was especially acute for Platonists. We do not have to worry about this problem of representation for our knowledge of this world, because our intuition of this world secures the objects for our concepts. But we do not have the same assurance for the pure concepts of understanding, because they are not derived from intuitions.

Kant briefly surveys some Platonic accounts of how we can have access to the supersensible reality: Plato's theory of recollection (the human soul had direct access to Forms before its birth in this world and now recalls the Forms it used to know in the other life), Malebranche's theory of occasionalism (the human soul sees the Forms in God's mind), and Crusius's theory of implanted rules (the soul sees the basic moral laws implanted in human minds by God). In Kant's view, every one of these accounts is a deus ex machina. Not only are they circular but they have the vice of encouraging "all sorts of wild notions and every pious and speculative brainstorm" (*KGS* 10:131, Zweig 73). Kant no longer believes that concepts alone can deliver any knowledge. This concession, which he makes for British empiricism against the Leibnizian tradition, marks the beginning of his Critical Philosophy. Although he does not accept empiricism in its entirety, he acknowledges the equal importance of sensibility and intellect. What are the proper functions of these two faculties? What are their limits? These questions begin to preoccupy his attention.

In his abovementioned letter to Herz, Kant says that he is work-ing on a book that may be called "The Limits of Sense and Reason." This projected book will have two parts: the first part will be con-cerned with general phenomenology and metaphysics; the second part, with the universal principles of feeling, taste, and sensuous desire and the basic principles of morality (*KGS* 10:129). Later in the same letter, Kant refers to the projected work as a "Critique of Pure Reason." He states his plan to work out the first part of this book, which deals with metaphysics, before taking on the second part, which deals with the principles of morality. He says that he should be in a position to publish the first part within three months (*KGS* 10:132). The three months eventually turned out to be nine years, and the *Critique of Pure Reason* was published in 1781.

The most drastic change Kant introduces in this work concerns the pure concepts of understanding: he shifts their use from the nou-menal to the phenomenal world. This shift has two consequences. First, Kant has to disavow the possibility of knowing the world of noumena. Second, he has to change his theory of how the world of phenomena is known. In the *Dissertation* Kant had limited the func-tion of reason to its logical use in the cognition of phenomena. He had assumed that the concepts of physical objects and their relations were derived from sensibility. One and all, these concepts are empir-ical, and the logical function of reason is to establish the logical rela-tion of these empirical concepts. Since our knowledge of phenomena is based on empirical intuitions and concepts, it is empirical and con-tingent. This was Hume's view of empirical knowledge, and Kant had accepted it in the *Dissertation*. He had said that our knowledge of phe-nomena always remains empirical, whatever refinement it may be given by the logical use of intellect (*ID* 2.5; *KGS* 2:393–94).

By shifting the use of pure concepts from the noumenal to the phe-nomenal world in the *Critique,* Kant is now claiming a priori knowl-edge of the phenomenal world. But this shift also presents a serious problem: How can he account for the linkage of pure concepts to the world of phenomena? This is the question of representation, which does not arise for empirical concepts. Since empirical concepts are derived from empirical intuitions, their connection to objects is secured by sensibility. But the pure concepts are neither derived from the world of phenomena nor introduced by any form of intuition of objects, so they may have no legitimate connection with the world of phenomena and may produce only spurious knowledge. This was the gist of Hume's critique against all a priori ideas, especially against the idea of causation. For this reason, the question of representation becomes no less critical for our knowledge of phenomena than for our knowledge of noumena.

Kant recognizes two ways of establishing the relation of concepts to objects. Either our concepts conform to objects, or objects conform to our concepts. The latter is the priority of concepts to objects ("the conformity of objects to concepts"), and the former is the priority of objects to concepts ("the conformity of concepts to objects"). According to Kant, the traditional metaphysics had assumed the priority of objects, that is, their existence was independent of concepts. In that case, he says, there is no way to account for a priori knowledge of objects, because independently existing objects can be known only a posteriori. In order to save a priori knowledge, he advocates the priority of concepts to objects. This is known as Kant's Copernican revolution.

Does the Copernican revolution repudiate his Platonism of the *Dissertation?* On the contrary, I propose that it reinforces and extends his Platonism. In the *Dissertation* Kant had restricted Platonism to the world of noumena; in the *Critique of Pure Reason* he is extending it to the world of phenomena. This extension is made by the Copernican revolution. The objects of the phenomenal world conform to the pure concepts of understanding, Kant maintains, because the objects are constructed in accordance with the pure concepts. This is his constructivism, whose lineage goes back to Plato. In the *Timaeus* Plato gave a mythical account of creation in which the divine craftsman, or Demiurge, introduced order into the chaotic material world by shaping the formless matter according to the eternal and ideal Forms. In the *Philebus* Socrates showed how human beings introduce order to the world of phenomena by organizing its indefinite dyads. Of these two versions of Platonic constructivism, the second is much closer to Kant's constructivism, as we shall see in greater detail in chapter 7.

If Kant's constructivism is correct, there can be no order or no laws (*law* and *order* are interchangeable for Kant) in nature prior to their introduction by pure understanding. For every law or order is a product of pure understanding. Kant says, "Thus the order and regularity in the appearances, which we entitle *nature,* we ourselves introduce. We could never find them in appearances, had not we ourselves, or the nature of our mind, originally set them there" (A125). He calls pure understanding the lawgiver of nature; it gives laws to nature (A127). "Categories are concepts which prescribe laws a priori to appearances, and therefore to nature, the sum of all appearances *(natura materialiter spectata)*" (B163). The legislative function of pure understanding comes from Kant's constructivism, and it is the same function as that of Plato's Demiurge and Leibniz's God. Kant shifts this function from God and the Demiurge to the transcendental subject.

Prior to Kantian construction, does nature have any order in its own right? For example, does nature contain causal relations before the application of the causal category? Kant has answered this question both in the affirmative and in the negative. These two answers have produced two different versions of constructivism, which may be called objectival constructivism and conceptual constructivism. In the former, the categories are used to construct their objects, which do not exist prior to their construction. In the latter, the categories are used to construct, not the objects of experience, but only the concepts or propositions necessary for the recognition of objects, which exist independently of the categories.

These two versions of constructivism reflect two different views of empirical intuitions. In conceptual constructivism, empirical intuitions have their own order, whose recognition requires the construction of a priori concepts and propositions. In objectival constructivism, empirical intuitions have no order of their own; they present only the manifold of sensibility, which have to be molded into objects of experience by the transcendental subject. We may also call objectival constructivism ontic constructivism; and conceptual constructivism, eidetic constructivism. The constructed objects belong to the ontic order, and the constructed concepts belong to the eidetic order.

These two versions of constructivism can be found in Plato's *Repub-*

lic, in which Socrates constructs an ideal republic in accordance with the Form of Justice. Socrates distinguishes two kinds of construction (*Republic* 472e–473a). The first of them is to create an ideal state in speech, as he has been doing with Glaucon and Adeimantus. The second is to create an ideal state in the real world. The former is an eidetic construction, and the latter is an ontic one. These two types of construction are two methods of articulating the same Form of Justice in the context of the phenomenal world. Because the Form exists in the eternal world totally devoid of empirical conditions, it is absolutely abstract and general. It gains concreteness by these two methods of articulation.

The two methods of construction provide two ways of construing Kant's transcendental philosophy, which may be called the ontic and the eidetic transcendental idealism. The ontic transcendental idealism is the claim that the transcendental subject provides the a priori conditions for the ontic constitution of phenomenal objects and their relations. The eidetic transcendental idealism is the claim that the transcendental subject provides the a priori conditions for the eidetic construction of a priori propositions, which are necessarily true of the phenomenal world. Eidetic constructivism can also be called propositional constructivism, because it involves the eidetic construction of a priori propositions. It can also be called epistemic constructivism, in contrast to ontic constructivism. Unlike ontic constructivism, eidetic constructivism does not construct the objects of experience and their relations; it only provides the epistemic conditions for their recognition.

In the Transcendental Deduction, Kant presents his arguments for ontic, or objectival, constructivism. The heart of his arguments is the idea of synthesis. He wants to prove the validity of the categories by his theory of threefold synthesis: the synthesis of apprehension in intuition, the synthesis of reproduction in imagination, and the synthesis of recognition in a concept (A98–110). Prior to these synthetic acts, there are neither objects nor relations of objects that can correspond to the categories. The manifold of sense is totally formless. The doctrine of synthesis fully executes Kant's Copernican revolution. Objects can conform to concepts, because the former are constructed in accordance with the latter. Ontic constructivism and the Copernican revolution are two ways of describing the same Platonic process.

* *   Two Versions of Transcendental Argument

If Kant is to adhere to the program of ontic, or objectival, constructivism, there is no need to follow up the Transcendental Deduction with the Analytic of Principles. The theory of a priori synthesis, or the Copernican revolution, is sufficient to demonstrate the validity of all categories and to silence once and for all Hume's challenge against the causal principle. In fact, I have never found a satisfactory explanation of why Kant has to continue his work in the Analytic of Principles. Let us consider the conventional account of the relation between the Transcendental Deduction and the Analytic of Principles. In the Transcendental Deduction, Kant is supposed to establish only the necessity of the categories for the possibility of experience. In the Analytic of Principles, he is supposed to explain how the categories apply to the objects of experience. But this conventional account does not take seriously what is claimed by Kant's constructivism in the Transcendental Deduction. He demonstrates the necessity of categories for the possibility of experience by showing that the objects of experience cannot be constructed without the categories. If the objects of experience are indeed constructed by the categories, it is absurd and gratuitous for Kant to worry about the problem of applying the categories to those objects.

The Transcendental Deduction is self-contained. If it is correct, it can fully demonstrate the validity of the categories. There is no way to justify Kant's labor on the Analytic of Principles. Many Kant scholars have said that the Transcendental Deduction is only a preliminary to the Analytic of Principles. In their view, the Deduction only proposes, but does not really prove, Kant's thesis that the categories are necessary for the possibility of experience. His real proofs are supposed to be given in the Analytic of Principles. If the Deduction were only a preliminary to the Analytic of Principles, I doubt that Kant would have spent so much time and labor on it or attached so much significance to it. He says that he knows of no inquiries that are more important than the Transcendental Deduction (Axvi).

In my view, the Analytic of Principles presents a line of thought that is totally different from the one Kant pursued in the Transcendental Deduction. The new line of thought belongs to eidetic, or epistemic, constructivism. In the Analytic of Principles, Kant constructs a priori principles from the categories and demonstrate their necessity for the recognition of the objects of experience and their relations whose existence is independent of the categories. Whereas in the Transcendental Deduction Kant is concerned with the problem of constructing the objects of experience, in the Analytic of Principles he is concerned with the problem of constructing and validating a priori principles.

For illustration, let us consider the role of causal principle in the Second Analogy. Kant begins his proof of the Second Analogy by distinguishing between subjective and objective successions. By walking around a house, I can have a succession of perceptions. This is an example of subjective successions, whose order is only in the perceiving subject. The order of subjective succession is reversible; for example, I can see the front of a house before or after seeing its back. An objective succession, on the other hand, is irreversible, because it takes place not merely in the perceiving subject but also in the objects of perception. An example of objectively succeeding perceptions is the successive perceptions of a boat floating down a river. Kant says that the causal principle is necessary for recognizing the objective succession of perceptions, because we can recognize the irreversibility of a succession only by using the a priori causal principle (A189–99/B234–44).

In this account of the Second Analogy, Kant assumes the equivalence of objective succession and causal relation. Moreover, he presupposes that the existence of objective, or causal, successions is prior to and independent of the causal principle. The latter is only an instrument for recognizing the former. This epistemic function of the causal principle is much weaker than its ontic function. According to ontic constructivism, the manifold of senses has no independent order of its own. It can offer no objective successions to be discriminated from subjective successions. It can be given the order of objective, or causal, succession only by the act of synthesis; that is, it has to be constructed in accordance with the pure concept of cause and effect. In eidetic, or epistemic, constructivism the causal principle performs, not the awesome function of constructing objects and their relations, but the modest function of discriminating and recognizing them.

The category of substance also performs different functions for Kant's two different programs. In his program of ontic constructivism, the category of substance is necessary for putting together the manifold of senses and constructing an object that can function as a substance. In his program of eidetic, or epistemic, constructivism, its use is not for the construction of a substance but for its recognition. In the First Analogy, Kant presents several arguments for the necessity of the category of substance. First, the category is necessary for the objective determination (recognition) of succession and coexistence (A182/B225). Second, the permanent substance is necessary for the recognition of duration. Third, the category is necessary for perceiving the permanence of time (B225). In all these arguments, Kant never questions the existence of objects and their relations and only claims the service of the category of substance for their recognition. Like the Second Analogy, the First Analogy belongs to epistemic constructivism.

To be sure, Kant never distinguishes the two versions of his constructivism; he labels all his arguments as transcendental, whether they appear in the mode of ontic or eidetic constructivism. This is the most serious source of confusion in Kant scholarship. In the name of transcendental argument, he sometimes tries to prove the necessity of the categories for the construction of objects and their relations that do not exist apart from the act of synthesis. He also tries to prove the necessity of the categories for the construction of a priori principles for the recognition of objects and their relations that exist independently of those principles.

One is the problem of a priori concepts, and the other is the problem of a priori propositions. Concepts are sufficient for the task of molding the manifold of senses into objects of experience, but the recognition function requires propositions rather than concepts, because it concerns the question of truth. Concepts are neither true nor false; only propositions have truth values. While the role of propositions is central for eidetic constructivism, that of concepts is central for ontic constructivism. For these reasons, ontic, or objectival, constructivism is given in the Analytic of Concepts, while eidetic, or epistemic, constructivism is given in the Analytic of Principles.

This is an oversimplification of a much more complicated state of Kant's text. He never manages to keep the two programs completely apart from each other. Although the program of ontic constructivism predominantly controls Kant's arguments in the Transcendental Deduction, it does not completely exclude the influence of eidetic, or epistemic, constructivism. This point is much more noticeable in the B Deduction than in the A Deduction. Let us compare the two. Both Deductions stress the importance of synthesis, which constructs the objects of experience by combining the manifold of sense. But there is a notable difference. The theory of synthesis constitutes the whole of the A Deduction; however, it is not the whole of the B Deduction. After presenting the theory of synthesis in the first six sections of the B Deduction (B129–43), Kant says that he has only begun the Deduction (B144). This is a startling statement, because he has reached the point that corresponds to the end of the A Deduction. After this remark, he goes into the discussion of the necessity of applying the categories to empirical objects. To this end, he first stresses the independent existence of empirical objects: "Now *things in space and time* are given only in so far as they are perceptions (that is, representations accompanied by sensation)—therefore only through empirical representation" (B147). The things in space and time are not constructed by the act of synthesis but are given in perceptions.

The independent existence of empirical objects is incompatible with ontic constructivism, and the doctrine of synthesis cannot account for the relation of the categories to those objects. Thus, Kant introduces the idea of application: the categories have to be applied to the objects of experience, because their existence is independent of the categories (B146–56). To illustrate this point, he cites the example of perceiving a house that is used in the Second Analogy. He does not cite the example of a boat floating down a river, he finds a similar example in the perception of water freezing (B162). Thus he proceeds to demonstrate the necessity of the categories for the cognition of empirical objects. This function of categories belongs to epistemic, or eidetic, constructivism. The B Deduction is closely associated with the Analytic of Principles, whereas the A Deduction is almost completely dissociated from it.

The difference between the two Deductions also shows up in Kant's two quite different accounts of empirical laws. In the A Deduction, he extends the role of a priori construction even to empirical laws:

> Although we learn many laws through experience, they are only special determinations of still higher laws, and the highest of these, under which the others all stand, issue *a priori* from the understanding itself. They are not borrowed from experience; on the contrary, they have to confer upon appearances their conformity to law, and so to make experience possible. Thus the understanding is something more than a power of formulating rules through comparison of appearances; it is itself the lawgiver of nature. (A126, trans. Kemp Smith)

In the B Deduction, Kant repeats the claim that the categories prescribe laws a priori to nature but gives a different account of empirical laws: "Special laws, as concerning those appearances which are empirically determined, cannot in their specific character be *derived* from the categories, although they are one and all subject to them" (B165, trans. Kemp Smith). The view that empirical laws are "subject to" a priori laws is much weaker than the view that the former are "only special determinations" of the latter. According to the latter view, empirical laws are generated by the specification of a priori laws; they are products of the a priori synthesis. This view of empirical laws belongs to the program of ontic construction. On the other hand, the view that empirical laws are subject to a priori laws can concede the independent existence of empirical laws insofar as they do not run afoul of a priori laws. Hence it belongs to the program of eidetic, or epistemic, construction.

The mixing of these two programs also takes place in the Analytic of Principles. We have already noted that the program of eidetic construction predominantly controls Kant's arguments in the First and the Second Analogies. But this is not true of his arguments for the other a priori principles. Most of Kant's arguments for the Axioms of Intuition are the arguments of synthesis. He says that "the representations of a determinate space or time are generated" by the synthesis of the manifold (A162/B202). The concept of extensive magnitude is necessary for this generative synthesis. Kant makes the same argument of generative synthesis for the Anticipations of Perception (A166/B208). This type of argument belongs to ontic constructivism.

We can now mend our earlier, oversimplified characterization of the Analytic of Concepts and the Analytic of Principles. Ontic constructivism mainly controls the Analytic of Concepts, especially the A Deduction, but the B Deduction is a compromise. Epistemic, or eidetic, constructivism is predominant in the Analytic of Principles, especially in the Analogies of Experience. But the Axioms of Intuition and the Anticipations of Perception are still aligned with the program of ontic construction. The Postulates of Empirical Thought are compatible with either of Kant's two programs, because they do not determine the nature of objects.

Because throughout the *Critique of Pure Reason* Kant's two programs of construction are never clearly separated, his repeated thesis that the categories are the necessary conditions of experience is open to two systematically different interpretations. In ontic constructivism, the categories are necessary for constructing the objects of experience and their relations that do not exist prior to such a construction. In eidetic constructivism, the categories are necessary for constructing a priori propositions for recognizing the objects of experience and their relations whose existence is independent of the categories. The categories are only cognitive presuppositions for experience. They are required for the construction of a priori propositions but not for the construction of the objects of experience and their relations.

We can also give two different interpretations to Kant's Copernican revolution, the requirement that objects conform to concepts.

When objects are constructed in accordance with concepts, the former cannot avoid the necessity of conforming to the latter. But objects can also be said to conform to concepts if the former can be recognized only by virtue of the latter, though the existence of objects is independent of concepts. This is the epistemic conformity, and the former is the ontic conformity. The epistemic conformity is required by epistemic, or eidetic, constructivism; the ontic conformity, by ontic constructivism. The former is a much weaker requirement than the latter.

Finally, the two versions of Kantian constructivism have a vital bearing on the endless dispute concerning Kant's conception of the physical world, namely, the question whether the *Critique of Pure Reason* is committed to idealism or to realism.[13] Eidetic constructivism is committed to a realistic view of the physical world; it presupposes the independent existence of physical objects and their relations prior to the application of a priori principles. On the other hand, ontic constructivism is committed to an idealistic view of the physical world; it does not admit the existence of physical objects and their relations prior to the process of their construction. Since these two incompatible views can be equally supported by the text of the first *Critique,* the attempt to resolve the dispute between them has always been futile.

* * Eidetic Construction

I have liberally used two expressions that cannot be found in Kant's own text, namely, *ontic constructivism* and *eidetic constructivism.* Most Kant scholars would raise no serious objection to my account of ontic, or objectival, constructivism, because it is a harmless restatement of Kant's doctrine of synthesis. But some of them may question my account of eidetic constructivism, so I feel the need to provide some textual support for my account. We should begin with

13. For the recent round of this dispute, see Henry Allison, *Kant's Transcendental Idealism* (New Haven, 1984); Paul Guyer, *Kant and the Claims of Knowledge* (Cambridge, 1987); and Karl Ameriks, "Kantian Idealism Today," *History of Philosophy* 9 (1992): 329–42.

Kant's derivation of the categories from the Table of Judgment. He says that the forms of judgment give rise to the categories with the introduction of transcendental content:

> The same function that gives unity to the various representations *in a judgment* also gives unity to the mere synthesis of various representations *in an intuition;* and this unity, in its most general expression, we entitle the pure concepts of understanding. The same understanding, through the same operations by which in concepts, by means of analytical unity, it produced the logical form of a judgment, also introduces a transcendental content into its representations, by means of synthetic unity of the manifold in intuition in general. (A79/B104-5, trans. Kemp Smith)

Before the introduction of transcendental content, Kant says, the forms of judgment are totally empty. They are only the forms of analytic unity. With the introduction of transcendental content, they become the forms of synthetic unity. These synthetic forms are called the categories. This is a theory of transformation: the forms of judgment are transformed into the categories by the introduction of transcendental content. This process of transformation is the process of eidetic construction. The forms of judgment are purely logical or formal; they can be expressed by logical constants such as assertion and denial. But the categories are not formal but material concepts; they are descriptive terms. Kant is saying that the material concepts are constructed by adding the transcendental content to the formal concepts. This is the transformation of the formal into the material concepts.

The alleged transformation is implausible: formal concepts cannot be transformed into material concepts. The very idea of adding transcendental content to formal concepts makes no sense. Kant gives an air of plausibility to this implausible process by rearranging the Table of Judgment. The traditional table, which derives from Aristotle's fourfold distinction of propositional forms (*De Int.* 17a8–21a34), is as follows:

1. Affirmation versus Denial (or Negation)
2. Universal versus Particular
3. Simple versus Composite
4. Possible versus Necessary

Kant adds one more item to each of the four couplets, transforming them into triplets. Thus, his Table of Judgment is as follows (A70/B95):

1. Quantity – Universal, Particular, Singular
2. Quality – Affirmative, Negative, Infinite
3. Relation – Categorical, Hypothetical, Disjunctive
4. Modality – Problematic, Assertoric, Apodeitic

Kant explains the addition of the third member in each of the four divisions. For example, the addition of singular judgment to the quantity of judgment is required by transcendental considerations. He notes that in general or formal logic singular judgment is treated as a special form of universal judgment, but he says that the two forms should be distinguished in transcendental logic. Whereas general logic is the logic of empty forms, transcendental logic is the logic of transcendental content. Although singular and universal judgments are indistinguishable in terms of their logical forms, they differ with respect to the quantity of knowledge. Their difference is comparable to the difference between unity and infinity (A71/B96). The singular judgment "This swan is white" concerns only one swan, while the universal judgment "All swans are white" concerns an infinite number of swans. This is a clear case of quantitative difference. Concerning his addition of infinite judgment as the third form of the quality of judgment, Kant says that an infinite judgment ("The soul is nonmortal") is logically indistinguishable from an affirmative judgment ("The soul is mortal"), since both take the form of affirmation. But they should be distinguished in reference to their predicates (A72/B97): the affirmative judgment takes an affirmative predicate *(mortal);* the infinite judgment, an infinite predicate *(nonmortal).* Since predicates concern the content of knowledge, their difference should be taken into consideration in transcendental logic, even though it is ignored in general logic.

It should be clear by now that the addition of a third member to each of the four divisions in the Table of Judgment transforms the entire table. By this transformation, Kant completely shifts the ground of distinction. While Aristotle's distinction between affirmation and denial is based on the logical forms of a sentence, Kant's distinction between judgment forms is based on the nature of the descriptive terms of a sentence. Kant's affirmative judgment is called affirmative, not because it performs the logical function of affirmation, but because it takes an affirmative predicate. A singular judgment is called singular because it takes a singular term, and a universal judgment is called universal because it takes a universal term. Since Kant's classification of judgment forms is based on the nature of descriptive terms, it presupposes the classification of the latter. But the classification of descriptive terms is precisely the function of the categories, which are the general names for the classes of descriptive terms.

Kant's Table of Judgment presupposes the Table of Categories. His procedure of deriving the categories turns out to be exactly opposite to what he claims to do. He says that he is deriving the categories from the forms of judgment, but in fact he is deriving the forms of judgment from the categories.[14] No wonder Kant was happy to find a neat correlation between the two tables. How could he make such an absurd mistake about this important phase in his enterprise? He had assigned a far greater significance to the derivation of categories than most of his commentators do nowadays. He recognized Aristotle as the only one who had tried to collect all the categories but found fault with his haphazard method (A81/B107). He was determined to find a systematic method for deriving the categories. He spent many years in shuffling his table of categories in many different ways, thereby delaying publication of the first *Critique* year after year. For Kant, the Metaphysical Deduction was at least as important as the celebrated Transcendental Deduction, because it was the first major step in Kantian constructivism.

14. For a more rigorous account of this point, see T. K. Seung, "Kant's Conception of the Categories," *Review of Metaphysics* 43 (1989): 107–32; and idem, *Kant's Transcendental Logic* (New Haven, 1969), 3–53.

The derivation of the categories is the common basis for both ontic and eidetic constructivism. After their derivation, the two versions of constructivism diverge from each other. In epistemic, or eidetic, constructivism the categories are transformed into the transcendental schemata, which in turn are transformed into a priori principles, which, finally, are transformed into the transcendental principles of nature. Each of these transformations is a procedure of eidetic construction. In ontic, or objectival, constructivism the categories are used to construct the objects of experience and their relations. This procedure consists of two phases: a priori and a posteriori. In the a priori phase the construction makes use of only the a priori manifold of pure intuitions, namely, space and time. The a posteriori phase completes the ontic construction by providing the a posteriori manifold of sensation. Kant calls the a priori phase of objectival construction the a priori, or pure, synthesis, in contrast to the a posteriori, or impure, synthesis:

> This synthetic unity [of the pure apperception] presupposes or includes a synthesis, and if the former is to be *a priori* necessary, the synthesis must also be *a priori*. The transcendental unity of apperception thus relates to the pure synthesis of imagination, as an *a priori* condition of the possibility of all combination of the manifold in one knowledge. But only the *productive* synthesis of the imagination can take place *a priori*; the reproductive rests upon empirical conditions. Thus the principle of the necessary unity of pure (productive) synthesis of imagination, prior to apperception, is the ground of the possibility of all knowledge, especially experience. (A118, trans. Kemp Smith)[15]

In Kant scholarship, the Metaphysical Deduction is usually taken as an episode of·mystification or aberration. It is quickly dismissed as an insignificant and irrelevant architectonic feature of Kant's philosophy. Many scholars have said that how Kant derived the pure

15. This is not an isolated remark. A similar claim is repeated in many other passages in the *Critique*, for example: "By *synthesis*, in its most general sense, I understand the act of putting different representations together, and of grasping what is manifold in them in one [act of] knowledge. Such a synthesis is *pure*, if the manifold is not empirical but is given a priori, as is the manifold in space and time" (A77/B103, trans. Kemp Smith).

concepts of understanding is not important; what truly matters is his attempt to demonstrate their validity. This attempt is supposedly made in the Transcendental Deduction and the Second Analogy. Hence we should concentrate our attention on these instead of letting ourselves be distracted by the Metaphysical Deduction. This has been the conventional wisdom of Kant scholarship, which overlooks the importance of Platonism in Kant's philosophy. The lone exception was Hegel, who regarded the Metaphysical Deduction as the heart of Kant's philosophy. Gravely dissatisfied with Kant's categorial maneuver, he tried to provide the logical derivation of not only the categories but all other concepts and Ideas.

* * Two Conceptions of Rationality

If the Metaphysical Deduction is such an important link in Kant's philosophy, how, after so may years' labor, can he make such an insidious mistake in his derivation of the categories? I can offer only a conjecture. His mistake was partly due to his willfulness. He was willful and determined enough to do almost anything to pull off his scheme of categorial derivation. Let us consider some of his willful moves. He adds disjunctive judgment as the third member of the relation of judgment. Traditionally, disjunctive judgment has been paired with conjunctive judgment. Kant separates these two, retaining one and discarding the other, and gives no reasons. He derives the category of community from disjunctive judgment, though it is more natural to derive the same category from conjunctive judgment. He derives the category of totality from singular judgment, and the category of unity from universal judgment. It is more natural to reverse the two derivations: unity from singular judgment and totality from universal judgment. In comparing these two judgments, he notes the resemblance of their relation to the relation of unity and infinity. Although he associates the category of unity with singular judgment in this comparison, he still derives the category of unity from universal judgment. In his analysis of pure reason, Kant appears to have abandoned all sense of rationality.

These are only a few examples of Kant's willful and arbitrary derivation moves. But his willfulness cannot explain all the errors in his categorial derivation: an even more basic explanation lies in his mistaken conception of the categories. This error appears to stem from his attempt to combine two different conceptions of rationality. In the *Dissertation*, as we saw, Kant acknowledged two functions of reason: its logical use and its real use. The former is the use of logical principles for ordering empirical concepts for knowledge of phenomena; the latter is the use of pure concepts for understanding the world of noumena. The logical use has no access to reality, because it is restricted to the logical principles of identity and contradiction. But the real use has access to reality by means of the pure concepts, which are the concepts of objects and their relations as they really are.

These two functions of reason represent two contending traditions of philosophy, British empiricism and Continental rationalism. Hume had maintained that the ideas of reason are only copies of impressions and that the power of reason is limited to the relation of ideas, that is, their logical relation. This logical function of reason becomes the logical use of reason in Kant's lexicon. On the other hand, Leibniz had advocated a much stronger view of reason in his doctrine of innate ideas. If this doctrine is true, our knowledge cannot be restricted to the domain of impressions. Innate ideas can give us a rational access even to supersensible reality. The function of reason is not only logical but real. This Leibnizian view of reason becomes the real use of reason in Kant's lexicon.

These two views of reason concern the power and limit of rationality. The Humean view advocates the idea of formal rationality: reason has no power of dealing with the content of reality, because its power is restricted to the forms of reasoning. The Leibnizian view advocates the idea of substantive rationality: reason has the power to know the substantive content of reality. In the *Dissertation* Kant had retained both of these conflicting views by assigning knowledge of noumena to the real use and knowledge of phenomena to the logical use. He took the Humean position on knowledge of phenomena and the Leibnizian position on knowledge of noumena.

In the *Critique of Pure Reason* Kant can no longer maintain this neat division of labor between the two functions of reason. As we noted, he has shifted the use of pure concepts to the world of phenomena; both the logical and the real use of reason are to be engaged in our cognition of phenomena. To be sure, he has dropped "the logical use" and "the real use" from his lexicon and now calls them logical and real *functions* (A79/B105). Unlike the logical function of reason, its real function presents two difficult problems. One of them is more familiar than the other: the problem of the Transcendental Deduction. What guarantees the legitimate application of the categories to the objects of experience?

The other problem concerns the origin of the categories. Kant cannot give an empirical account of their genesis; that is, he cannot say that they are derived from impressions. Sometimes he appears to accept the rationalist account, namely, that they are innate to the mind, as innate as the pure intuitions of space and time. But there are times when he is not satisfied with the innatist view of the categories. He appears to regard the innate presence of categories in the mind as too mysterious to be accepted if they are taken as substantive concepts. On those occasions, he emphatically says that the categories are no more than the forms of judgment before their application to the objects of experience. This is his formalist view of the categories, to be distinguished from his substantivist view. According to the latter, the categories are not merely formal but material concepts. Thus, Kant wavers between two views of the categories. One is a logical conception, and the other is a substantive conception.

Kant expresses his logical conception of the categories when he says that they are the logical functions of judgment (A79/B105, 143). In his logical conception he does not treat *quantity, quality, relation,* and *modality* as names of categories. He uses these words only as the labels for the four triplets of judgment forms and pure concepts. There are no logical functions that can correspond to these four terms. In the material or substantive conception of the categories, however, these terms name categories that are more important than the twelve contained in the four triplets, because they are more general. The greater generality a concept commands, the greater significance it gains in the generic or substantive conception of categories.

Kant often uses these four as the chief categories in place of the twelve. Those four categories constitute the Table of Categories of Freedom in the second *Critique*. They provide the framework for his analysis of aesthetic judgment and experience in the third *Critique* and for his exposition of the principles of nature in the *Metaphysical Foundations of Natural Science*.

Kant's two conceptions of categories are again hopelessly mingled in the Schematism. He says that the problem of pure concepts lies in its application to objects of intuition. The latter cannot be subsumed under the former, because the two are not homogeneous (A138/B177). The problem of subsumption does not arise for the forms of judgment; subsumption, the relation of a particular and a universal, belongs to the generic conception of categories. Kant opens the Schematism with his generic conception of the categories. If the categories are the ultimate generic concepts, then several species fall under each of them. Aristotle calls these species the schemata (shapes or figures) of categories. For example, the primary and the secondary substances are the schemata for the category of substance; the discrete and the continuous quantities are the schemata for the category of quantity (*Cat.* 2a11–18, 4b20–21). The Aristotelian idea of schematization is to form a specific concept by adding some attribute to a generic concept. This is another case of eidetic constructivism.

Most of Kant's transcendental schemata are generated by the Aristotelian method. The schemata of intensive and extensive magnitudes are generated by adding the attributes of extension and intension to the general concept of magnitude or quantity. In this case, the term *quantity* functions as the name of a category. The schema of substance is formed by adding the attribute of permanence to the category of substance. In its original purity, substance is conceived without the attribute of permanence. The schema of causality is formed by adding the attribute of temporal succession to the category of causation. In its conceptual domain, the idea of causation need not be restricted to the domain of temporal succession. The attributes that are added to the pure concepts in their schematization are always spatiotemporal. Without those additions, the categories should apply to things in general, but their use is restricted to the world of phenomena by their schematization (A146–47/B186).

In the Schematism, Kant does not completely forget his logical conception of the categories; he stresses it in the concluding paragraph. If we eliminate all sensible conditions (attributes) from the pure concepts of understanding, he says, they cease to be concepts of an object. For example, the concept of substance is no more than the logical concept of a subject in a sentence if the temporal attribute of permanence is removed from it. "The categories, therefore, without schemata, are merely [logical] functions of the understanding for concepts; and represent no object" (A147/B187). In the logical conception of the categories, schematization converts a logical concept into a descriptive one. Kant calls this process of conversion *realization:* "the schemata of sensibility realize *(realisieren)* the categories" (A146/B185–86). The idea of realizing the categories is clearly different from the idea of subsumption or application.

These two views of the categories, formal and substantive, give Kant the framework for their derivation: the material or substantive categories are derived from the formal categories, which are the forms of judgment, which in turn belongs to formal reason. The novel link in this derivation scheme is the relation between the formal categories and formal reason. In the *Dissertation* Kant had restricted the formal or logical use of reason to the employment of logical principles and had recognized no connection between it and the forms of judgment. In the *Critique* he expands the role of formal reason to include the forms of judgment. With this expansion, the derivation of substantive from formal categories amounts to their derivation from formal reason.

The derivation scheme, if successful, can bridge the gap between the rationalist and the empiricist conceptions of reason. The material categories belong to the rationalist view of substantive reason; the formal categories, to the empiricist view of formal reason. Kant wants to believe that the material categories are derived from the formal categories, or that the formal categories are transformed into the material categories via the process of construction. This is the essence of his claim for the Metaphysical Deduction. It depends on his program of eidetic construction; his derivation scheme is his construction scheme.

The mysterious link in Kant's construction-derivation scheme is the idea of formal categories. It is a contradiction in terms. The categories are, by nature, generic concepts, and the forms of judgment are too formal even to be called concepts. The former are descriptive terms, and the latter are logical terms. If they are so different, what reasons does Kant have to regard them as identical? The plausible answer lies in Kant's systematic confusion about the relation between form and matter. As noted in chapter 1, he had two different conceptions of the form-matter relation in the *Prize Essay*. For metaphysics, he took it to be the relation of logical and descriptive principles; for ethics, he took it to be the relation of general and particular.

The latter conception of the form-matter relation was endorsed in Platonic tradition: it was understood as the relation between higher and lower concepts. In the *Sophist* (254d–259d) Plato tried to define the affirmation and the negation of a sentence by the categories of sameness (identity) and otherness (difference). To say that something is moving is to say that it is the same as motion. To say that it is not moving is to say that it is other than motion. The categories of sameness and otherness are generic or descriptive terms, and affirmation and negation are logical functions. Plato holds that the two logical functions only express the meaning of the two descriptive terms.

The categories are indeed the most general concepts. They can surely qualify as formal concepts if the form-matter relation is taken as a relation between general and particular. For this reason, Kant appears to assume the equivalence or identity of the categories in their most generic form with the forms of judgment. In this equivalence he probably saw the possibility of bridging the gap between the empiricist and the rationalist conceptions of rationality. With the identification of formal reason with forms of judgment, and the latter with formal categories, he only had to show how formal categories are related to material categories. Having no clear idea of their relation, he tried out two different accounts. In the Metaphysical

Deduction, he claimed a one-to-one correspondence between formal and material categories. In the Schematism, he claimed the transformation of formal into material categories.

In defense of Kant, one may be tempted to say that these two accounts are not only compatible but really complementary. If formal categories can be transformed into material categories, the former should stand in a one-to-one matching relation with the latter. In that case, the Schematism is compatible and complementary with the Metaphysical Deduction. But this defense has no basis, for two reasons. First, the Schematism generates, not twelve, but only eight material (or schematized) categories. Kant transforms the three formal (or unschematized) categories of quantity into one material (or schematized) category of extensive magnitude, and the three formal categories of quality into one material category of intensive magnitude (A142–43/B182–83). By this process, he reduces the six formal categories of quantity and quality to the two material categories of extensive and intensive magnitudes. These two material categories cannot retain a simple, one-to-one matching relation with formal categories. Moreover, the idea of transforming formal into material categories is just implausible. There is no way to convert logical terms into descriptive terms. The latter belong to semantics, and the former to syntax. The Kantian categorial transformation amounts to the conversion of syntactic signs into semantic ones. If successful, it will eliminate the demarcation between syntax and semantics.

Much confusion and trickery went into Kant's theory of the categories. All of his dubious and devious maneuvers were motivated by his ultimate concern to reconcile the two incompatible conceptions of rationality he had inherited from Continental rationalism and British empiricism. He thought he had found the key to his problem in the Platonic notion of eidetic construction, and he made a sustained, determined effort to use this key in resolving the central problem in his program of constructivism. It is this effort that is at the heart of his architectonic. It was because of this same effort that he took so many years to complete the *Critique of Pure Reason*. And it was again this same effort that made the *Critique* the most involuted metaphysical treatise in the whole world. But we cannot simply ignore the Kantian labyrinth of Platonic entanglement, for to find our way through this labyrinth is essential for understanding not only his involuted theory of knowledge but also his equally complicated theory of morality.

3 Normative Platonism in the First *Critique* and Kant's Philosophy of History

* * * * * * * * * * * * * * * * * * * *

If Kant is a Platonist in the first *Critique*, what type of ethics does he advocate there? This is a wrongheaded question in conventional Kant scholarship. It is the standard belief that Kant is not expected to set forth an ethical theory in the first *Critique*, because this treatise is addressed to the theoretical function of pure reason. The exposition of his ethical theory is given in the *Critique of Practical Reason*, the *Groundwork for the Metaphysics of Morals*, and the *Metaphysics of Morals*. According to this conventional understanding, there is a clear-cut division of labor between the first and the second *Critiques*: one is for theory, and the other for practice. Ethics, or moral theory, belongs to practical philosophy.

This conventional understanding is not quite accurate. For some time, Kant did not even think of writing another *Critique* to succeed the *Critique of Pure Reason*, because the latter had been conceived as complete. Toward the end of the first *Critique* he says,

> The philosophy of pure reason is either a *propaedeutic* (preparation), which investigates the faculty of reason in respect of all its pure *a priori* knowledge, and is entitled *critique (Kritik)*, or secondly, it is the system of pure reason, that is, the science which exhibits in systematic connection the whole body (true as well as illusory) of philosophical knowledge arising out of pure reason, and which is entitled *metaphysics*. (A841/B869)

The *Critique* is a propaedeutic, or preparation, for *metaphysics;* it was meant to be followed, not by another *Critique,* but by two treatises in metaphysics. In the *Critique of Pure Reason* the entire faculty of pure reason, including the practical, is subject to critical examination, and Kant gives no intimation that he is planning to write another *Critique*.[1] On the contrary, he is announcing the completion of the propaedeutic science and looking forward to his work on metaphysics proper. He divides metaphysics into two parts: theoretical and practical. The theoretical part is called the metaphysics of nature, and the practical part, the metaphysics of morals.

Kant's division of philosophy into the propaedeutic for metaphysics and metaphysics proper is much older than his first *Critique*. Eight years earlier, in 1773, he had mentioned the same division of philosophy in a letter to Marcus Herz: "I shall be glad when I have finished my transcendental philosophy, which is actually a critique of pure reason, as then I can turn to metaphysics, which has only two parts, the metaphysics of nature and the metaphysics of morals, of which I shall present the latter first. I therefore look forward to the future" (*KGS* 10:145, Zweig 78).

Kant evidently regarded the propaedeutic as tedious, and metaphysics as exciting. So he was always looking forward to the latter. But he did not follow up the *Critique of Pure Reason* with the two projected treatises in metaphysics; instead he published "foundational" works for those two treatises, the *Groundwork for the Metaphysics of Morals* (1785) and the *Metaphysical Foundations of Natural Science* (1786). In the preface to the *Groundwork* he reaffirms his division of metaphysics into the metaphysics of nature and the metaphysics of morals (*GMM* 388). He says that the *Groundwork* lays the foundation for the metaphysics of morals by a critical examination of pure practical reason. This critical examination is supposed to be given in the final section of the *Groundwork* (*GMM* 445). Because of this critical approach, Kant says, the *Groundwork* should be called the *Critique of Pure Practical Reason* (*GMM* 391). But he has decided to call it the *Groundwork for the Metaphysics of Morals* in order to avoid some possible confusion, that is, confusion with the *Critique of Pure Reason*. Even the idea of giving a critique of practical reason in the *Groundwork* goes against Kant's original intention that the *Critique of Pure Reason* was to be the critique of pure reason in its

---

1. This view is endorsed by Lewis White Beck, *A Commentary on Kant's Critique of Practical Reason* (Chicago, 1960), 9.

entirety. Kant developed this new idea for a critique of practical reason because of a radical change in his ethical outlook. In the *Groundwork* he presents a moral theory markedly different from the one he had outlined in the first *Critique*. His critics had charged that the two moral theories were incompatible.[2] It was mainly to meet this charge that he eventually had to write the second *Critique*. The moral theory expounded in the *Groundwork* and the second *Critique* is what is generally known as Kant's moral theory, which is radically different from his Platonic ethics of the first *Critique*.

* * Kant's Platonic Ethics

In the Dialectic of the first *Critique* Kant presents the pure concepts of reason, which he distinguishes from the pure concepts of understanding, and calls the former the Ideas of pure reason. Kant had not made this distinction in the *Dissertation*, where he recognized only one intellectual faculty. In the *Critique of Pure Reason* he divides the intellectual faculty into understanding and reason and assign them different functions. And the two faculties are equipped with different concepts: pure understanding with the categories, and pure reason with the Ideas. The categories are immanent; the Ideas are transcendent. The categories are used for the knowledge of phenomena, while the Ideas transcend the world of phenomena. For example, the concept of the most perfect being is a transcendental Idea; nothing in the phenomenal world corresponds to it. Kant identifies the transcendental Ideas with Platonic Forms (A313/B370).

The Ideas of pure reason lead to dialectical illusions if they are taken as a source of knowledge. This is Kant's negative teaching in the Dialectic of the first *Critique*. Although they can play no positive role on the theoretical level, that is, in advancing our knowledge, he says, they are indispensable on the practical level, that is, in ethics, politics, law, and religion. But is it not incompatible with the spirit of Critical Philosophy to accept the Ideas of pure reason even for the practical level? This is the obvious question for those who

2. For a fuller account of their criticism, see ibid., 14–15.

learn for the first time that Kant has presented a moral theory based on Platonic Ideas in the first *Critique*. How can Kant retain Platonic Ideas after renouncing the possibility of knowing the world of noumena? Most Kant scholars would intuitively sense some serious incompatibility between Platonic Ideas and Critical Philosophy. This is why they have seldom taken seriously Kant's Platonic Ethics, given in the first *Critique*.[3] Thus, it is about time for us to consider their compatibility.

In the *Dissertation* Kant had recognized the importance of Platonic Ideas not only for the practical level but also for the theoretical (*ID* 2.9; *KGS* 2:396). The theoretical Ideas of perfection concern the existence of objects, such as the existence of the most perfect being, but the practical Ideas of perfection do not concern the existence of objects. The latter perform normative functions; the former, cognitive functions. The theoretical and the practical Ideas of perfection have different relations to the question concerning the relation of concepts to objects that Kant raised in the Herz letter. The question of representation affects the theoretical Ideas of perfection but not the practical Ideas, because the latter do not relate to any objects. Hence Kant's critique of theoretical or cognitive reason does not disqualify the normative function of practical reason.

On the contrary, Kant is emphatic in asserting the necessity of Platonic Ideas for practical philosophy. He demarcates the domain of practice (what ought to be done) from the domain of theory (what happens) (A318, 633, 802/B375, 661, 830). The pure concepts of understanding are for describing what is; the Ideas of pure reason are for prescribing what ought to be. What ought to be can never be derived or deduced from what is; normative standards can never be set by positive facts. Kant takes this point as central in Plato's theory of Forms as archetypes. He recognizes two conceptions of normative standard: normative positivism and normative transcendentalism. Normative positivism treats normative standards as social facts, such as positive law or conventional morality. On the other hand,

---

3. There is another reason why Kant's Platonic ethics has never become a topic in Kant scholarship. Because it is given toward the end of a thick volume, very few students ever to get to it.

normative transcendentalism claims that ultimate normative standards transcend all social facts. Kant looks upon Plato as the father of normative transcendentalism.

Kant says that Platonic Ideas fulfill a much higher need than that of knowing the world of appearances. Although they transcend the world of phenomena, they must have "their own reality"; they are by no means "mere fictions of the brain" (A314/B371). For example, the concepts of virtue cannot be derived from experience; they are derived from the Idea of virtue, which is the eternal pattern of all virtues (A315/B371–72). Although the *Republic* of Plato has become proverbial as a striking example of a supposedly visionary perfection, he says, we should follow up the thought of the great philosopher instead of dismissing it for its impracticality. The thought we should follow up is the Idea of a constitution, which allows "*the greatest possible human freedom* in accordance with laws by which *the freedom of each is made to be consistent with that of all others*" (A316/B373).

The Ideas of pure reason are the archetypes that set transcendental normative standards for our conduct. Archetypes and standards belong to the world of noumena, whereas the rules and laws of experience belong to the world of phenomena. The world of phenomena is the domain of what is done; the world of noumena is the domain of what ought to be done. Kant does not recognize the role of eternal archetypes for understanding the world of phenomena, and he dismisses as a Platonic exaggeration the claim that there are eternal archetypes even for the production of plants and animals. While the categories are sufficient for the cognition of what is, he holds, they are inadequate for knowing what ought to be. "Nothing is more reprehensible than to derive the laws prescribing what *ought to be done* from what *is done*" (A319/B375). Just as the pure concepts of understanding make possible the world of experience, so the Ideas of pure reason make possible the world of practice. This is Kant's transcendental argument for the Ideas of practical reason.

In the *Critique of Pure Reason* Kant presents two transcendental arguments, one for the necessity of the categories and one for the necessity of moral Ideas. While the first is well known among Kant students, the second is almost forgotten. Most Kant students well remember Kant's judicious warning against the speculative use of the Ideas of pure reason, but very few of them know of the prodigious significance he attaches to their practical function. Kant's two transcendental arguments establish his division of labor between understanding and reason: understanding is the faculty of cognition, and reason is the faculty of morality. Although he never gives a systematic exposition of this point, he repeatedly mentions it informally in all three *Critiques*, stating unequivocally that the moral function of pure reason is far more majestic than the cognitive function of pure understanding.

The division of labor between understanding and reason underlies Kant's distinction between theory and practice, the domain of knowledge and the domain of faith. The world of theory can be known, but the world of practice can only be believed. This distinction is meant to be a rebuke to both rationalists and empiricists. Rationalists make immodest and illegitimate claims in extending the domain of human knowledge beyond the world of sensibility, and empiricists, while they are right to limit knowledge to the domain of sense experience, are equally dogmatic in their denial of supersensible ideals. They do irreparable injury to the practical interests of reason (A471/B499). Kant regards Epicurus and Plato as representatives of these two opposite dogmatic positions. The philosophy of Epicurus encourages and furthers knowledge, but it does so at the expense of practical philosophy. While Plato supplies excellent practical principles, he needlessly permits reason to indulge in metaphysical speculation.

Although the Ideas of pure reason cannot be used to extend our knowledge of phenomena, they are indispensable for practical reason. They give moral precepts and principles, which are the necessary conditions for morality, law, and religion, just as the categories are the necessary conditions for the possibility of experience. According to Kant, practical reason provides the "principles of the *possibility of experience*," namely, moral experience (A807/B835). He is expanding the notion of experience to include moral experience, which he says belongs to history. History is the domain of practical reason, while nature is the domain of theoretical reason. The world that operates under moral precepts is also called the moral world (A808/ B836). And the moral world is also called the intelligible world, because it is constituted by the Ideas of pure reason. On the other hand, the world of nature is called the sensible world, because it is the object of sensibility. Kant says that his distinction between sensible and intelligible worlds corresponds to Leibniz's distinction between the kingdom of nature and the kingdom of grace (A812/B841).

The Platonic Ideas Kant enumerates are the Ideas of divine and human perfection: the most perfect being and human virtues (A313–19, 571–78/B370–75, 599–606). They are exactly the same Ideas of perfection he had designated as objects of the noumenal world in the *Inaugural Dissertation*. In the first *Critique* his discussion of Platonic Ideas becomes much richer than in the *Dissertation*. Kant names two Ideas of human perfection: the Idea of virtue and the Idea of a republican constitution. At this point, he plans to use Platonic Ideas for the practical sciences of morality, legislation, and religion (A318/ B375). His conception of ethics is basically the same as the one outlined in the *Dissertation*. He gives no indication that his conception of practical principles is formal; the Ideas of pure reason are material or substantive practical principles.

Kant regards the Ideas of pure reason as the source of all moral laws: morality is the order of pure reason "according to Ideas" (A548/ B576). He divides the practical law into pragmatic law and moral law (A806/B834). Pragmatic laws are laws of prudence; they are concerned with happiness. They are technical rules that make use of empirical laws governing desires and the natural and cultural means to satisfy those desires. But there is no empirical basis for moral laws: "The latter [moral law] takes no account of desires, and the natural means of satisfying them, and considers only the freedom of a rational being in general, and the necessary conditions under which alone this freedom can harmonize with a distribution of happiness that is made in accordance with principles. This latter law can be based on mere ideas of pure reason, and known *a priori*" (A806/ B834).

Kant conceives of moral law mainly in a political framework. The function of moral law is to harmonize the freedom of one individual with the freedom of others. This is the same function he assigns to a republican constitution. In such a moral order, Kant says, "all the actions of rational beings take place just as if they had proceeded from a supreme will" (A810/B838). This is Rousseau's idea of general will, which Kant had praised in the *Dreams*. Although he traces the Idea of a republican constitution to Plato, his idea of moral law is much closer to Rousseau's. But Rousseau had never given an ontological account of moral principles and general will. Kant seeks it in Platonic Heaven. He further associates moral laws with maxims, which he calls subjective principles to distinguish them from objective principles (A666/B694). The use of maxims is not limited to the practical domain; there are maxims of theoretical reason as well. In the practical domain, Kant says, maxims provide the subjective grounds of actions (A812/B840). These subjective principles can be accepted as objective principles when they are in accord with the Ideas of pure reason.

By becoming the principles of action, the Ideas of pure reason enter the domain of practice. *Practice* means the practical employment of reason, which in turn means to realize the Ideas of pure reason in the world of phenomena. Practical reason reshapes the phenomenal world in accordance with noumenal ideals. This power is the causal power of practical reason: "Reason is here, indeed, exercising causality, as actually bringing about that which its concept contains; and of such wisdom we cannot, therefore, say disparagingly *it is only an idea*. On the contrary, just because it is the idea of the necessary unity of all possible ends, it must as an original, and at least restrictive condition, serve as standard in all that bears on the practical" (A328/B385).

Pure reason with practical causal efficacy is moral freedom. In the first *Critique* Kant propounds a relatively simple concept of moral freedom. He distinguishes between a purely animal will *(arbitrium brutum)* and free will *(arbitrium liberum)*. The former is determined by sensuous impulses, but the latter is independent of those impulses. Human beings have the power to overcome sensuous impulses, and this power derives from the faculty of pure reason, which can consider what is useful or injurious without being influenced by those impulses (A802/B830). Whereas each impulse or desire makes only its own demand and disregards everything else, pure reason takes into consideration all the factors relevant for our well-being. This is why the Idea of pure reason is called "the idea of the necessary unity of all possible ends" (A328/B385).

Practical laws are dictates of pure reason. Some of them are moral laws, whereas others are only laws of prudence. The former are a priori, the latter a posteriori. In issuing either of these practical laws, reason exercises practical freedom (A803/B831). This idea of practical freedom should be distinguished from the idea of transcendental freedom, which is freedom from all causes. Transcendental freedom is absolute spontaneity; it initiates its own action without being influenced by any prior causes. But practical freedom may turn out to be unfreedom on the transcendental level: it may be conditioned by prior causes.[4] Although Kant claims a tight link between moral freedom and transcendental freedom in the second *Critique,* he does not make the same claim in the first *Critique.* There he defines moral freedom independently of transcendental freedom. The only requirement for the morally free will is that it be bound by moral laws, and those laws are derived from the Ideas of pure reason. Hence the Platonic Ideas are the foundation of moral freedom. Practical reason transcends the dictates of sensuous impulses, because it can act in accordance with those Ideas.

This is the outline of Kant's Platonic ethics as presented in the first *Critique.* It resolves the basic practical problem he had inherited from Rousseau, namely, how to secure a spiritual order for human reason and freedom that transcends the natural order of dead matter. Kant takes the Platonic Ideas of virtue and the republican constitution as two principles for the construction of such a spiritual order. This is his Platonic resolution of Rousseau's problem. He no longer conceives of spiritual order as a supernatural community of spiritual

4. For a good discussion of the relation of these two freedoms, see Henry Allison, *Kant's Theory of Freedom* (Cambridge, 1990), 54–65; Bernard Carnois, *The Coherence of Kant's Doctrine of Freedom,* trans. David Booth (Chicago, 1987), 3–32; and Allen Wood, "Kant's Compatibilism," in Wood, ed., *Self and Nature in Kant's Philosophy* (Ithaca, 1984), 73–101.

substances, as he did in the *Dreams*. He now understands it as an ideal community of human beings to be realized in human history on this earth.

How can Kant use Platonic Forms as the basis of his ethics, while advocating the Critical thesis that the world of noumena cannot be known? How can we have access to those Forms if they belong to the noumenal world? In Kant's lexicon, the word *know* is used in a highly technical sense. It is no more true that to have the Ideas of pure reason is to know the world of noumena than it is true that to have the pure concepts of understanding is to know the world of phenomena. To have the Idea of the most perfect being is not to know God: to know God is to know the existence of something that corresponds to the Idea of the most perfect being. For Kant, the word *know* carries existential import.

Kant never says that we have no access to the concept of the most perfect being; nor does he say that it is not even a concept. In fact, he admits that it is an Idea of pure reason. Without it, the whole dialectic of pure reason cannot get off the ground. But to have the Idea of the most perfect being is not to know any noumena. Likewise, although we do not know the world of noumena, we still have the Ideas of practical reason. Like the pure concepts of understanding, the Ideas of pure reason are a priori accessible to human reason, although they do not constitute any knowledge in and of themselves. Kant's disclaimer that we can never know the world of noumena is perfectly compatible with his claim for the accessibility of Platonic Ideas.

* * The Destiny of Pure Reason

Kant says that pure reason is a system of essential ends (A832/B860). Morality is one of these ends, and the totality of these ends is called the complete or highest good or the supreme good (A810/B838). Kant defines it as the exact apportionment of happiness to morality. The ultimate end of pure reason is to realize not simply the moral good but the highest good. While Kant repeatedly insists on the exact apportionment of happiness to morality, he never fully explains why it is demanded by the concept of the highest good. Leibniz had a similar idea about the City of God: "Here there is no crime without punishment, no good action without a proportionate reward, and finally, as much virtue and happiness as is possible."[5] But Kant does not say that he is only adopting the Leibnizian ideal; rather, he claims to derive it from the premise that morality is the worthiness to be happy:

> Morality, taken by itself, and with it, the mere *worthiness* to be happy, is also far from being the complete good. To make the good complete, he who behaves in such a manner as not to be unworthy of happiness must be able to hope that he will participate in happiness. Even the reason that is free from all private purposes, should it put itself in the place of a being that had to distribute all happiness to others, cannot judge otherwise. (A813/B841)

By "the reason that is free from all private purposes" Kant means impartial reason. In other writings also he tries to justify the happiness-morality apportionment by appealing to impartial reason or an impartial observer.[6] In the eighteenth century, the concept of impartial reason or an impartial observer was the standard notion for justice. It was firmly endorsed by both the moral sense theorists and the rational intuitionists. Hence many Kant scholars have interpreted his notion of an exact apportionment of happiness to morality as a precept of justice. If the morally virtuous are worthy of happiness, justice demands that they should be happy in exact proportion to their virtue. Since the Idea of justice is one of the Platonic Forms, even Kant's concept of the highest good is based on Platonic Ideas. Moreover, Plato himself repeatedly claimed that the just ought to be rewarded with happiness, if not in this world, at least in the other world.[7]

The concept of the highest good generates the dialectic of practi-

---

5. *Principles of Nature and Grace*, par. 15, trans. Loemker.

6. In the *Groundwork* Kant says, "It need hardly be mentioned that the sight of a being adorned with no feature of a pure and good will yet enjoying lasting good fortune can never give pleasure to an impartial rational observer" (*GMM* 393, trans. Beck). For other passages of similar effect, see C_2 110, and C_3 458.

7. This claim is first intimated in the *Apology* (41a) and then elaborated in the form of three myths given in the *Gorgias* (523a–526d), the *Phaedo* (80b–84b, 107d–114d), and the

cal reason in the second *Critique*. In the Canon of Pure Reason, however, Kant does not recognize any dialectical problems of practical reason; he uses the concept of the highest good mainly for answering the practical question, "If I do what I ought to do, what may I then hope?" (A805/B833). According to Kant, one has the right to hope for a happiness commensurate with my moral dessert, as dictated by the concept of the highest good. However, he notes, the highest good is seldom realized in this world. The distribution of happiness is seldom in exact proportion to morality; on the contrary, the wicked often prosper, while the just suffer. In this world, he says, the connection between morality and happiness is contingent and accidental. Hence the realization of the highest good can be secured only by a Supreme Reason, who governs the entire moral world (A810/B838). This is Kant's well-known moral argument for the existence of God. But even the existence of God does not guarantee the complete realization of the highest good in this world. So he maintains that there must be another world for its realization. But only the immortal souls can participate in the other world and fully realize the highest good. Hence the realization of the highest good requires the immortality of the soul. Thus Kant's moral argument for the existence of God is linked to his moral argument for the immortality of the soul.

The moral argument for the existence of God is Kant's invention, which has struck many people for two reasons. First, it follows his rigorous critique and rejection of all theoretical arguments for the existence of God in the Transcendental Dialectic. Second, it is so different from traditional arguments for the existence of God. The traditional arguments locate their premises in the physical world. The cosmological argument takes as its first premise the existence of the physical world; the teleological argument, the order and design of the physical world.[8] The physical world provides sound premises

---

Republic (614b–621b). There is a good discussion of these three myths in Julia Annas, "Plato's Myths of Judgement," *Phronesis* 26 (1981): 119–43.

8. For this discussion and comparison, the ontological argument is an exception, because its premise is neither the physical nor the moral world.

for theological arguments, because its existence is solid and secure, but the moral argument for the existence of God does not seem to have such a solid and secure premise. It stands on the existence of the moral world, which many may not take to be as solid as the existence of the physical world.

How can Kant justify morality as the premise for proving the existence of God? This is the most troublesome question about his moral argument. But this is not a real problem for Kant, because he accepts the reality of the moral world as firmly as he does the reality of the phenomenal world. For him, the existence of the moral world is as real as the moral law. But most of us do not share his faith in the reality of moral law, which is the main reason why his moral argument strikes us as queer or even flimsy. If the moral world is as real as the physical world, then it can function as well as the physical world as the first premise for proving the existence of God.

In fact, the moral argument has one significant advantage over the ontological and the teleological arguments. The latter can never establish the existence of a moral deity, even if their proofs are successful, because their premises are morally neutral. Even if there is a supreme cause for the production of this physical universe, it may very well be morally neutral. It may have no concern for the question of good and evil. This is the defect of the cosmological argument. The same should be true of the supreme artisan, whose existence is claimed by the teleological argument. There is no reason to expect the artisan to be moral unless the teleological argument includes the moral design of the world in its premise, which is not the case with the standard teleological argument. But the God postulated by the moral argument should be different: it could not but be morally perfect. In Kant's moral argument for the existence of God, his moral character is guaranteed by its moral premise, that is, the existence of the moral world. This is the unique feature of his argument.

Because the existence of the moral world is the basic premise for Kant's moral argument, it is essential not to overlook the demarcation between the physical and the moral worlds in understanding his claim. But this demarcation is often overlooked in many criticisms of his moral argument. For example, Bertrand Russell regards it as an unsound argument from a scientific point of view. It begins with the premise that often the good suffer, while the wicked prosper, and ends with the conclusion that the injustice of this world can be remedied by God in the other world. If there is injustice in this part of the universe, then according to the rules of probability, we should expect to find it in the other parts of the universe as well. Suppose you open a crate of oranges and find that all the oranges in the top layer are bad. You would not argue that to redress the balance, the oranges underneath must be good.[9]

This scientific critique of the moral argument assumes the continuity between this world and the other: what obtains in this world is likely to obtain in the other world. But this continuity is rejected by Kant's demarcation between the sensible and the intelligible worlds. He maintains that although the sensible world is alien or even hostile to the systematic connection between morality and happiness, the intelligible world cannot be so, because it is a morally perfect world. It is a perfect world because it fully realizes the Ideas of reason. This point is overlooked by Russell's scientific criticism, which disregards Kant's demarcation between the kingdom of nature and the kingdom of morality.

The acceptance of the two kingdoms and their demarcation does not, however, remove all the objections against the moral argument. Even if we grant that the premise of the moral argument is different from that of traditional arguments, the moral argument appears to make the same illegitimate inference to the existence of God that traditional arguments make, and it appears to follow the same rules of inference that traditional arguments follow. Lewis White Beck labeled it "an argument of design, pure and simple."[10] The traditional argument of design has been based on the order and design of the physical world; Kant's moral argument is based on the order and design of the moral world. In either case, the existence of God is meant to explain the order and design we accept as the premise.

To differentiate the moral argument from traditional arguments,

9. Russell, *Why I Am Not a Christian* (London, 1957), 13.
10. Beck, *Commentary,* 276.

Kant says that the moral argument is not really a proof but only a practical postulate. A proof is required for knowledge; a postulate is an object of belief. Knowledge belongs to the theoretical world, and belief to the practical world. This Kantian distinction is quite confusing, because belief can be, for us, as theoretical as knowledge is. Let us consider Kant's threefold distinction of knowledge *(Wissen)*, belief *(Glauben)*, and opinion *(Meinen)*. He explains this distinction by using the notion of subjective and objective grounds for holding a judgment or making an assertion (A822/B850). When the ground for holding a judgment is subjectively and objectively sufficient, Kant calls it *knowledge*. When it is only subjectively sufficient, he calls the judgment *belief*. When it is neither subjectively nor objectively sufficient, he calls the judgment *opinion*.

Kant's characterization of belief in terms of the subjective sufficiency of its ground is quite unusual. According to him, there is no objective ground for holding a moral belief: it is based on purely subjective ground. Why should we hold a belief, Allen Wood rightly objects, if there is no objective ground for holding it?[11] To hold such a belief is clearly absurd. Perhaps to answer this question, Kant introduces the concept of pragmatic belief (A824/B852). A physician is uncertain about the cause of his patient's illness but feels the need to do something immediately for its relief. He can only form a contingent belief about the nature of the illness but has to act on it. This is a case of pragmatic belief; it is the belief we are prepared to act on. And Kant wants to regard moral belief as a special case of pragmatic belief.

Pragmatic belief is defined in reference to action, which is quite different from defining it in reference to the subjective ground of its truth. To be sure, if I believe in a proposition, I will be prepared to act on it. The subjective ground of truth can be translated into pragmatic considerations. But the pragmatic definition of belief cannot discriminate practical from theoretical beliefs. As Kant notes, any theoretical judgment can become an object of pragmatic belief (A825/B853). In fact, his example of a physician's conjecture about

---

11. Wood, *Kant's Moral Religion* (Ithaca, 1970), 17.

the cause of an illness is a theoretical belief; it becomes a pragmatic belief when he acts on it. Moreover, as Kant notes, there are two kinds of pragmatic belief, technical and moral. Technical belief is contingent, he observes, but moral belief is necessary (A824/B852). How can our belief be necessary if it is supported only by our subjective ground? There is no clear answer to this question in Kant's text.

＊ ＊ Practical Rationality

How is moral belief different from theoretical belief? This is the important question for Kant, because he holds that these two types of belief are fundamentally different. Since none of Kant's own attempts to clarify this question have been helpful, I propose another way of differentiating moral and theoretical belief. Let us consider the distinction between phenomenal and noumenal grounds for holding an assertion. Theoretical belief is concerned with the objects of the phenomenal world; those objects provide what Kant calls objective grounds for holding a belief. Moral belief is based on the moral laws, which are derived from the Ideas of pure reason. Since those Ideas belong to the world of noumena, they cannot provide objective grounds for holding a moral belief, because they are not objects of experience. But they should not be called subjective grounds, because they are not mere subjective ideas. They are the noumenal grounds of belief.

The phenomenal ground of belief is open for empirical confirmation, but the noumenal ground is not. Hence the acceptance of the latter is a matter of faith rather than knowledge. The novelty of Kant's moral argument for the existence of God lies in proposing the noumenal ground for belief. If the physical world is the only reality accessible to us, we have to accept it as the only premise for proving the existence of God. However, if the moral world is as real as the physical world, there is no reason to restrict our premise to the physical reality. For Kant, the existence of the moral world is not a hypothesis; it is as real as the moral law. But the acceptance of moral law is not knowledge, but belief or trust. It is like the acceptance of logical principles, which cannot be vindicated by empirical data. Just as we accept logical principles on trust, so we have to accept moral law, because we cannot live without it any more than we can reason without logical principles. Hence Kant holds that moral belief is necessary, though it is not objective, that is, not subject to empirical confirmation.

Moral and theoretical arguments for the existence of God differ not only in their premises but also in the rules of argument. Both cosmological and teleological arguments invoke the causal principle: the existence of God is asserted as the ultimate cause for the existence of the physical world or its order and design. Hume and Kant have shown that these causal arguments are inconclusive because the physical world may have been in existence from eternity and may have the power of producing its own order. Leibniz tries to make a case for the teleological argument by establishing the premise that the world of matter is totally inert. If it is inert, its order can be introduced only from outside, namely, by God. All of these arguments depend on empirical laws; even the inertia of matter belongs to the empirical world. Kant's one common objection to these arguments is that empirical laws cannot be extended beyond the domain of phenomena, and the existence of God transcends the world of phenomena.

The moral argument for the existence of God does not rely on any empirical laws. Its main force stems from the notion of rationality and absurdity. The highest good is demanded by the requirement of rationality; its denial is a practical absurdity, and the existence of God is required to avoid this absurdity. The whole argument is a *reductio ad absurdum*.[12] In this regard, it resembles the ontological argument, except for one important point. While the moral argument appeals to practical absurdity, the ontological argument relies on theoretical or logical absurdity. Nevertheless, the comparison is worth making.

The ontological argument begins by laying down as its premise the definition of God as the most perfect being and then shows the logical absurdity of denying the existence of God; that is, it contra-

---

12. This point is well explained by Allen Wood in ibid., 16.

dicts the premise. In his critique of this argument, Kant says that the alleged contradiction arises because the existence of God is illicitly presupposed in the premise; that is, existence is taken as one of the predicates required for the conception of the most perfect being. But Kant holds that existence is not a predicate, that its inclusion in the definition of God is logically illegitimate. Thus, the alleged contradiction or absurdity is due to the illegitimate conception of existence as a predicate (A592–602/B620–30).

The cosmological and teleological arguments are not arguments of absurdity. Consider the two hypotheses (1) that the world is created by God and (2) that the existence of the world is primordial. It is impossible to say that either of the two hypotheses is rational and the other is irrational, or that one of them is more rational than the other. The same thing goes for the two hypotheses about the order and design of the world: (3) that it has been created by God and (4) that it has been produced by the evolution of the world. These two accounts are equal as far as their rationality is concerned. In this regard, the moral argument for the existence of God is different from the cosmological and the teleological arguments.

As Lewis White Beck claims, the moral argument may resemble the teleological argument in one respect. It appears to appeal to the principle of causation: it claims the existence of God as the cause of a perfect moral order for the realization of the highest good. But this step of the argument is not essential for the integrity of the moral argument. All it is set out to prove is the existence of a perfect moral order that assures the exact apportionment of happiness to morality, and the question of how it comes about is irrelevant to the argument. There is no need for such a perfect moral order to depend on the existence of a personal deity. It may be achieved by some impersonal force, such as the *karma* of Buddhism or the *T'ien* (Heaven) of Confucianism. In whatever manner it operates, it fulfills the requirement of rationality. On the other hand, its nonexistence is an *absurdum practicum*. Hence Kant's moral argument is not for the existence of God but for the existence of a perfect moral order and the realizability of the highest good. As Yirmiahu Yovel correctly observes, the ultimate object of the moral argument is not

God but the highest good. The existence of God is only incidental to the moral argument.[13]

In the *Critique of Practical Reason* Kant presents his arguments for the existence of God and the immortality of the soul by constructing the antinomy of practical reason.[14] But the antinomy does not change the character of his arguments; he again appeals to the requirement of practical rationality. What is the basis for this requirement? Kant would say that it arises from the Ideas of pure reason. For an analogy, let us consider the requirement of rationality for set theory or mathematics. In these normative systems, we introduce certain axioms and postulates because of the requirement of rationality and rule out certain propositions because they offend against the same requirement. Likewise, the moral Ideas of pure reason, such as the Idea of justice, have their own requirement of rationality, because they are rational Ideas. For example, the punishment of an innocent person is an absurdity not on logical but on moral grounds. So is the nonfulfillment of the highest good. To be sure, this analogy holds only on the condition that the moral Ideas of pure reason exist in the same way that the ideas of set theory and mathematics do. This is the essential basis for Kant's moral argument for the existence of God.

Even if we accept the existence of moral Ideas as noumenal entities, we cannot overlook the difference between logical and practical absurdity. Logical absurdities are impossible in every possible world, but practical or moral absurdities are possible in many possible worlds. The nonexistence of a perfect moral community is a practical absurdity, which is clearly possible in this world. Why should Kant assume that such a practical absurdity is impossible in the other world? Kant seems to give two answers to this question. One answer is based on the assumption that the noumenal world is morally perfect, while the phenomenal world is imperfect. He often says that the moral imperfection of this world is due to our natural incli-

13. Yovel, *Kant and the Philosophy of History*, 116.

14. The antinomy of practical reason is so poorly stated that his commentators have difficulties in identifying its thesis and antithesis. Lewis White Beck tries to formulate the antinomy in two versions in *Commentary*, 246–48.

nations and the natural forces, which are indifferent to moral order. He also assumes that the intelligible world is devoid of these intractable natural elements. This view of the two worlds is a longstanding Platonic legacy. According to this view, a perfect moral community is possible in the intelligible world. For Plato, the other world is not only the domain of eternal Forms but also a perfect moral order in which those Forms are fully realized. And his moral theology moralizes the entire universe.

The assertion of a morally perfect universe, however, is incompatible with Kant's Critical Philosophy. He has repeatedly said that we can never know anything definite about the world of noumena. If so, we can never know whether the noumenal world is any more morally perfect than the phenomenal world. It is one thing to recognize the existence of Platonic Forms as a precondition for the possibility of a moral order but another thing to argue for the existence of a moral world in which those normative ideals are perfectly realized. One involves the existence of normative ideals; the other, the existence of a whole world. The latter clearly goes against Kant's own central argument in the Transcendental Dialectic.

If we take seriously Kant's cognitive limitation on our knowledge of the noumenal world, his moral argument becomes much weaker. At most, it lays out two moral hypotheses: (1) the existence of a perfect moral community in the other world and (2) its nonexistence. The latter hypothesis clearly offends against the requirement of moral law and thereby produces a practical absurdity, while the former hypothesis fulfills the rational requirement of moral law. Given these two possible pictures of the noumenal world, we have a choice to make. Is there any rationality requirement for making this choice?

As mentioned above, Bertrand Russell says that it is more rational to assume that the noumenal world has the same sort of practical absurdity as the phenomenal world. But this assertion also goes against the spirit of Kant's Critical Philosophy. Russell assumes the continuity and similarity of the two worlds, which is equally incompatible with Kant's claim that we have no knowledge of noumena. If we know nothing about the noumenal world, there is no rational or theoretical basis for choosing one of the two moral hypotheses. In that case, we have as much right to assume that the noumenal world is a perfect moral community as we have to assume that it is not. Cognitively, there is no reason to prefer either of the two hypotheses, but there is a practical difference: one of them turns our moral experience into a massive practical absurdity, while the other enables it to meet the requirement of rationality. Given these practical differences, Kant seems to say, it is practically rational to accept the hypothesis that the highest good can be realized in the noumenal world.

According to this interpretation, the moral argument does not really assert the existence of God or a perfect moral order. It only claims its possibility, and it links this possibility to the requirement of rationality. In the end, it comes down to the rationality of moral experience and the whole universe. But the rationality of the whole universe or even our whole morality cannot be proven; we can only hope for it. Hence it is a matter of faith. We should accept the existence of God and a perfect moral order in the other world if we believe in the rationality of our universe and our moral experience. If we do not accept the existence of God and the possibility of realizing the highest good, then we have to admit that our moral experience and the universe as a whole constitute a gigantic mass of irrationality and absurdity. This appears to be the best way to interpret the moral argument within the framework of Kant's Critical Philosophy.

* * The Nature of Human History

Kant defines the concept of the highest good in both the individual and the collective context. In the latter context, the highest good is a perfect moral community, in which rational beings secure their happiness or well-being through the exercise of their freedom (A809–10/B837–38). He recognizes many obstacles to the realization of such a community in the kingdom of nature and expects its fullest realization only in the kingdom of grace. But this is not to say that nature does not even allow its imperfect realization. Whatever happens in nature for its realization is called the history of humankind

(A807/B835). History belongs to the domain of freedom as much as it belongs to the domain of nature; it is governed by the laws of freedom as well as by the laws of nature. The history of humankind belongs to these two kingdoms, because human beings do. Kant expounds this view of history in his historical essays.

The first of Kant's historical essays is the *Idea for a Universal History from a Cosmopolitan Point of View* (1784).[15] Published three years after the *Critique of Pure Reason,* it reads like a sequel to *Universal Natural History and Theory of the Heavens.* Both are stories of evolution. In both, Kant maintains that the Ideas of perfection control the direction of evolution. In the earlier essay, Kant had said that the infinite process of cosmic evolution is governed by the Idea of perfection in the divine mind (*KGS* 1:263). In the later essay, he stresses the role of Ideas even more. Even its title begins with the word *Idea.* But there is an important change. In the earlier essay, Kant had portrayed the evolution of the physical universe as totally devoid of any concern for human beings. Now he presents a picture of nature that sustains the evolution of humankind.

Although the human world appears to be chaotic, Kant says, we can discern its slow but steady evolution (*KGS* 8:17). He wants to demonstrate that history reveals a definite "natural plan" for the evolution of humankind from the chaotic state of savagery to the international order of civilized communities. He proposes nine theses according to the following outline. It is Nature's purpose that human natural capacities be fully developed not in any individual but in the whole race. Nature intends that human beings use these capacities to work out their own way of providing for their well-being and happiness. To this end, Nature has used the device of mutual antagonism or the unsocial sociability of human beings. If humans did not possess heartless competitive vanity and the insatiable desire for possession and domination, all the excellent human capacities would remain dormant. Through competition and antagonism, human beings conquer their inclination to indolence, awaken all their powers,

15. This essay appears in *KGS* 8:15–31. An English translation by Lewis White Beck is available in Immanuel Kant, *On History,* ed. Beck (Indianapolis, 1963), 11–26.

and take momentous steps on a long journey from barbarism to culture.

The development of human capacities, however, requires a social order with the greatest possible freedom. Such a social order is a perfectly just constitution in which mutual opposition between its members becomes consistent with freedom and justice. Hence, Kant says, to design a just civic constitution is the highest problem Nature assigns to the human race. Such a civic constitution establishes a commonwealth. The passions that can be destructive in wild freedom can do the most good if they can be tamed in a civic union. But the commonwealth of individuals cannot be secured without securing peace and harmony among different commonwealths. The same antagonism that sets individuals against each other also drives different societies into hostile relations. It will take a league of nations to secure peace and harmony among sovereign states. Thus, the ultimate purpose of Nature is to lead humankind from the state of individual rivalry to the state of international harmony.

Two years later, Kant followed up the *Idea for a Universal History* with another historical essay, the *Conjectural Beginning of Human History* (1786).[16] In this essay, he is concerned with the question how human history begins. The story of this beginning is supposedly given in the first few chapters of *Genesis;* it has been understood as beginning in the hand of God. Kant turns over this beginning to the hand of human beings; his is the story of how human beings have earned their freedom from the bondage of nature. All along, Kant had been impressed with Rousseau's idea that human beings become human by subjugating their natural instinct and appetite, transcending the domain of nature and establishing the domain of culture. Kant takes this Rousseauesque perspective for his reading of *Genesis* and proposes four steps for the emergence of culture from nature.

At the time of creation, Kant says, human beings, like other animals, were ruled by instinct; human rationality was only a disposition. When it began to stir, it became curiosity about food that went

16. This essay appears in *KGS* 8:107–23. An English translation by Emil Fackenheim is available in Kant, *On History*, 53–68.

beyond the immediate reach of natural instinct (*KGS* 8:111). This was human beings' first break from the chain of nature. By this break, human beings took the first step in developing their freedom and control over nature. But this first step brought its own problems. Whereas human desires were simple and orderly while they were under the governance of nature, they become infinitely extended and multiplied in the domain of freedom. Thus the beginning of human history was the beginning of human misery.

The same transformation from nature to freedom took place for sexual desire. This was the second step. In the state of nature, human sexual desire was no different from the animal sexual desire. It was immediate and instinctual; its satisfaction was simple and orderly. But human sexual desire became complicated with the freedom of imagination: Its satisfaction was sought in what was imagined and distant rather than in what was immediate and present. It became infinite and insatiable; it even threatened the wholesale destruction of humankind. To avoid such a disaster, human beings had to make rules and customs for the governing of sexual behavior. As long as human sexual desires were under the governance of nature, there was no need for the rules of sexual behavior. Those rules are products of human freedom. This is Kant's commentary on the fig leaf story (*KGS* 8:112–13).

With the fig leaf (the development of human sexuality), Kant says, human beings began to develop their interiority. By this process, they ascended from sensual to ideal attraction, from mere animal desire to love, from the feeling of the merely pleasant to a taste of beauty. This was the first impetus for developing the sense of decency and proper manners. Now human beings became sociable for the first time since they took the first step on the way to freedom and became increasingly unruly and unsociable. The sense of decency was also the initial preparation for human beings' development as moral agents.

The third step came with the consciousness of the future (*KGS* 8:113). In the state of nature, human beings lived from immediacy to immediacy. They sought food and security as the occasion arose. With the development of rationality, human beings could anticipate future needs and dangers. This was the conscious expectation of the future, which Kant regards as the most decisive mark of human advantage. It enabled human beings to prepare themselves for distant aims and needs, but it brought with it the cares and troubles that are altogether unknown to animals. For the first time, human beings became obsessed with care. With the enhanced sense of the future, Kant says, human beings realize the inevitability of their death. The only comfort they can gain for their mortality is the prospect of living through their children.

The fourth and last step began with the recognition that human beings are the end of nature (*KGS* 8:114). They realized that they have a privileged position above all other creatures. They no longer look upon other animals as fellow creatures; instead they believe that those animals are created to serve their needs. At the same time, they recognize each other as equally important and enter into a relation of equality. They respect each human being as an end in himself or herself, not to be used as a mere means for someone else. This is the beginning of a moral community, and the last step for weaning humankind away from the womb of nature.

This is Kant's conjectural account of how human history began. There are a couple of items we should take note of. First, the nature of freedom that takes place in four steps is much more complicated than that of moral freedom. Moral freedom appears only in the last step but requires the preparation that takes place in the previous steps. The freedom that develops in the four steps is as broad as what Kant called practical freedom in the first *Critique*, or what Emil Fackenheim calls cultural freedom.[17] Second, the development of freedom is also the development of pure reason. The entire motive force of development comes from pure reason, which would not allow mankind to turn around, give up the relentless toil of progress, and return to the forgotten paradise of innocence. Kant says that restless reason irresistibly impels human beings to develop their faculties (*KGS* 8:115).

Nine years after the *Conjectural Beginning*, Kant again took up

---

17. In Fackenheim, "Kant's Concept of History," *Kant-Studien* 48 (1956–57): 388.

the theme of human evolution, in *Perpetual Peace*.[18] This essay is a continuation of the *Idea for a Universal History*. The ultimate end of human history is to achieve a peaceful order in the international community. This is not the aim of human beings, singly or collectively, but the design of Nature, the great artist (*KGS* 8:360). To this end, Nature has used the device of war. Humankind begins in the state of nature, which is the state of war, and scatters itself to the four corners of the world by a ceaseless war. Kant says that war also produces the legal order of humankind on three levels: civil law, the law of nations, and the law of world citizenship (*KGS* 8:365). He holds that the institution of legal orders is the work of Nature: she produces them whether human beings will or not.

How does Nature accomplish such a feat? Nature does this, Kant says, by placing different groups of people close to each other in antagonistic relations. Since they have to form themselves into states for their defense, war compels them to submit to public laws. War is the mother of political order. Among different political structures, he observes, the republican constitution is the only one entirely fitting to the rights of man (*KGS* 8:366). But it is the most difficult one to establish, and even harder to preserve, because of selfish human inclinations. Many have said that a republic would have to be a nation of angels, but Kant says that here again Nature comes to the aid of humankind through their selfish inclinations:

> But precisely with these inclinations nature comes to the aid of the general will established on reason, which is revered even though impotent in practice. Thus it is only a question of a good organization of the state (which does lie in man's power), whereby the powers of each selfish inclination are so arranged in opposition that one moderates or destroys the ruinous effect of the other. The consequence for reason is the same as if none of them existed, and man is forced to be a good citizen even if not a morally good person. (*KGS* 8:366, Beck 112)

18. This essay appears in *KGS* 8:341–86. An English translation by Lewis White Beck is available in Kant, *On History*, 85–135.

This reads like a political version of Adam Smith's theory of economic competition. Kant's notion of competition is not restricted to the economic sphere but it pervades the entire human existence, which has been liberated from the bondage of Nature. War is the first manifestation of the spirit for competition and antagonism on both the individual and the collective level. It is the main engine of human history. Human reason develops its ingenuity and its culture by coping with two problems: how to wage war and how to bring it to an end. Not only science and technology but even political and social institutions have been produced by the human ingenuity that has been nurtured in the art of war and competition.

The constitution of a republican order requires not virtuous people but an effective social order that balances selfish inclinations against each other for public benefits. It is a matter of social engineering. Kant says that such a social order can be designed even for a race of devils if we know the mechanism of Nature. A good constitution is not to be expected from morality, but a good moral condition of a people is to be expected only under a good constitution (*KGS* 8:366). Nature designs and produces a political order as a precondition for morality. This natural process is based on the antagonistic competition of selfish inclinations, which eventually produce the state of war among different states. Kant says that this state of war is preferable to the subjugation of all states under one superpower (*KGS* 8:367). Such a subjugation would produce a soulless despotism, which would extinguish the spirit of competition, the mainspring of human progress.

Kant believed that the state of war among states would eventually lead to a league of nations that could secure the international order and harmony for the whole world. Unlike the deadening peace under universal despotism, he says, a federation of competing nations will keep their equilibrium in the liveliest competitions (*KGS* 8:367). This is the ultimate goal of Nature, the great artist. She has not only the right design for humankind but sufficient resources to achieve it. This is the amazing claim Kant makes on behalf of Nature. *Perpetual Peace* is meant to be not so much a proposal for human endeavors as a description of natural teleology. It is a paean to the power of Nature.

It is not human beings but the mechanism of Nature that has taken humankind out of the state of nature and set it on a grand march to the global union of all civil constitutions. Kant places the standard social contract theory on its head. Against the prevailing view that human beings came out of the state of nature by establishing civil societies, he holds that the transition from the state of nature to the state of civil society has been a natural process.

* * Historical Understanding

These historical essays present many troublesome problems for Kant scholars. Let us consider two of them: (1) the apparent inconsistency among the essays and (2) their apparent inconsistency with Critical Philosophy. Let us begin with the first. The three historical essays appear to present different views about the relation between nature and history. In the *Conjectural Beginning* Kant says that history begins with freedom and that freedom emerges when reason breaks the bondage of Nature. There is no history of humankind as long as humans are governed by the instinctual force of Nature, because history is a product of pure reason. In the *Idea for a Universal History,* however, Kant says that Nature institutes social order, invents culture, and creates history. She leads humankind from the state of individual rivalry to the state of international harmony. History is a work of Nature. This view of history is sometimes known as "the cunning of nature," an analogy to Hegel's notion of the cunning of reason.[19]

These two views of Nature are indeed incompatible. Many Kant scholars have considered the *Idea for a Universal History* to be pre-Critical because it is a treatise of dogmatic teleology. On the other hand, they believe that the *Conjectural Beginning* and *Perpetual Peace* are in accord with Critical Philosophy. These two essays assign the motive force of history to reason rather than nature. There are a few oddities about this view, however. First, the *Idea for a Universal History* was published, not before, but three years after the publication

19. See Eric Weil, *Problèmes kantiens* (Paris, 1963).

of the first *Critique*. It is unlikely that Kant retained his pre-Critical ideas so long. His Critical thought does not really begin with the publication of the first *Critique*, but predates it by about a decade. Second, the *Idea for a Universal History* was published in the same year as *What Is Enlightenment?* (1784), which, like the former, tells how human reason develops and reaches maturity. But no one seems to regard the Enlightenment essay as pre-Critical. On the contrary, it has been received as a forceful expression of Critical Philosophy.

Third, the *Idea for a Universal History* is not very different from *Perpetual Peace* as far as the role of Nature is concerned. In both essays Kant personifies Nature and her enormous powers for making history. In the *Idea for a Universal History* Nature is said to have a plan for the development of humankind and to use the device of mutual antagonism for this purpose. In *Perpetual Peace* Nature is depicted as no less scheming and contriving. She uses the same mechanism of war and competition for the evolution of humankind and comes to the aid of selfish human beings in devising the republican form of government. She is called the great artist. This view of Nature is not any less dogmatic than the one presented in the earlier essay.

Many critics have been misled by Kant's personification of Nature. Let us take a close look at what she is claimed to do for humankind in the *Idea for a Universal History*. She really does nothing beyond producing human beings and leaving them to the force of mutual antagonism and competition. The chaotic state of humankind is the work, not of Nature, but of human beings, who are propelled by their own competitive instinct and aggression. In fact, their behavior had been orderly and peaceful before they were released from the bondage of Nature. Humankind evolved by constructing the world of culture to cope with the chaos of their own creation. This is basically the same idea that Kant expresses in the *Conjectural Beginning* and restates in *Perpetual Peace:* how humankind attains freedom and reason and constructs the world of culture in the world of nature.

Kant attributes this momentous process to the power of Nature in one essay and to the power of human reason in another. But there is no inconsistency in this, because the power of human reason is an extension of the power of Nature. After all, Nature is the mother of humankind and human reason. He also talks of Nature's plan, which is none other than the one humankind collectively devises under the guidance of the Ideas of reason, which are also given by Nature together with human reason. Hence their collective plan can be regarded as Nature's plan. There is no reason to take Kant's person-ification of Nature in the literal sense and attribute to him a mythi-cal conception of Nature as a scheming Lady.

The unity of the three historical essays does not eliminate the charge of dogmatism against Kant; in fact, it makes the charge even worse. Whereas many Kant scholars had thought that only one of the three essays was dogmatic, we have to say that all three of them are equally dogmatic. Kant claims to detect rational patterns in his-tory underneath its semblance of chaos. Such a cognitive claim appears to be dogmatic and irresponsible by the strict standard of his Critical Philosophy. This concerns the second of our two problems, namely, that Kant's philosophy of history is incompatible with his Critical Philosophy. Kant appears to respond to this problem in a note in another historical essay, *The End of All Things*,[20] where he appeals to the notion of the legislative reason. Here is the full text:

> We are dealing (or playing) here simply with Ideas which reason itself creates, the objects of which (if it possesses any) lie com-pletely beyond our field of vision; and although these Ideas are transcendent for our speculative cognition, they are still not on that account to be considered void in all respects. Made available to us by the legislative reason itself, these Ideas are to be regarded rather in a practical sense, not laboriously pondered with respect to their objects, whatever these are in and of themselves and according to their nature, but rather as we are required to contem-plate them on behalf of the moral principles which pertain to the ultimate purpose of all things. (In this way Ideas, which would oth-erwise be altogether empty, acquire objective practical reality.) And since we are dealing with such Ideas, we have an open field

20. This essay appears in *KGS* 8:325–39. An English translation by Robert Anchor is available in Kant, *On History*, 69–84.

before us to arrange this product of our reason. (*KGS* 8:332–33, Beck 75–76)

Here Kant is stressing the difference between the use of Ideas in the transcendent domain and their use in the immanent domain. Their use in the transcendent domain indeed goes beyond the limit of reason, but their use in the immanent domain is a different matter. In the immanent domain, Kant holds, the Ideas of pure reason are used, not for speculation on metaphysical entities, but for the practical purpose of morality. In the moral world, pure reason uses the Ideas for its legislative function in the same way that pure understanding uses the categories in prescribing laws for nature. Just as the categories gain objective reality by their legislative function, so the Ideas of pure reason gain practical reality by their legislative function. Hence history is the "product of our own reason" in the same way that nature is the product of our understanding.

* * Historical Constructivism

Humankind makes its own culture and history. This is Kant's constructivist view of the practical world. This is a much more credible view than the constructivist view of nature, according to which pure understanding constructs the objects of nature. It is the central thesis of Kant's Critical Philosophy that human reason can truly understand only what it constructs with its own concepts. If humankind constructs culture and history by the Ideas of pure reason, they should be proper objects of human understanding. Many Kant scholars misunderstand the Kantian constraint on speculative philosophy to be equivalent to the empiricist constraint. They assume that Kant's restriction of knowledge to the limit of sensibility amounts to the same requirement as that of empirical verification. By this empiricist criterion, his philosophy of history should be branded as dogmatic or speculative, but he never constricts the power of reason to this empiricist straitjacket. In fact, his aim is to save the power of pure reason from the suffocating effect of stringent empiricist restriction.

Kant presents his philosophy of history not as an empirical description but as a constructivist account.[21] His philosophy of history is to articulate the Ideas of pure reason that have shaped human culture. But those Ideas are not readily discernible; often they are hidden and remain undeveloped (A834/B862). In both the domain of practice and the domain of inquiry, they remain hidden for a long time. In the domain of practice, Kant says, human beings became fully conscious of their practical Ideas of reason only in the Enlightenment. In the domain of inquiry, we come to recognize them only in a philosophical reflection on the history of human practice. Hence the philosophy of history is to construct a schema for the self-development of pure reason (A835/B863).

Kant's constructivist view of human history closely resembles Vico's view. The latter had advocated his own epistemic theory of construction to counter the Cartesian view of cognition. According to Descartes, clear and distinct ideas are the true objects of knowledge. Against this position, Vico held that the act of making is the basis of true understanding. We can truly understand only those things we make. Hence his motto is *Verum factum convertuntur* (The true and what is made are convertible).[22] We can understand geometry because we construct geometrical figures. On this ground, he opposes his constructivist view of geometry to the analytical geometry of Descartes. Vico assumes that the Cartesian analytical method is meant to reduce geometrical propositions to clear and distinct ideas, which he believes is a mistaken conception of geometrical method.

In the *Prize Essay* Kant also advocated the constructivist view of geometry and mathematics. He labeled the mathematical method as the method of synthesis or construction and stressed its difference from the metaphysical method of analysis. In the first *Critique* he extends the same method of synthesis and the same constructivist view from mathematics to the entire science of nature. And he is fond of saying that we can truly understand only what we construct.

21. For a fuller discussion of this point, see William Booth, *Interpreting the World: Kant's Philosophy of History and Politics* (Toronto, 1986), 70.
22. Vico, *Selected Writings*, ed. and trans. Leon Pompa (Cambridge, 1982), 50–51.

Whether he was directly influenced by Vico is not known, but his constructivism is one with Vico's.

On the subject of our knowledge of history, Vico again maintained an anti-Cartesian position. Descartes had held natural science in high regard, and history in low esteem. Vico reversed this Cartesian ranking of science and history, saying that we can never truly understand nature because nature is not our making and that only God can understand it because it is his creation. On other hand, we can really understand history, because we are the author and maker of history. Our understanding of history is even more real than our geometrical understanding, because human affairs are more real than points, lines, surfaces, and figures.[23] Vico did not always stick to this constructivist view of history, but recognized the historical patterns and achievements attributable to the work of divine providence.[24] The discrepancy between this providential account and his constructivist accounts produced the same incoherence as the discrepancy between the role Kant attributed to Nature in history and the role he attributed to humankind, for Kant's account of Nature's role resembles Vico's account of the role of providence.

There is one more serious problem with Vico's view of history. His assertion that history is a human making is highly ambiguous; the agents of history may be taken either as individuals or as collective entities. Surely nations and institutions, which are regarded as objects of historical studies by Vico, are not made by individuals. If their making requires collective acts, who coordinates their collective efforts? It is perhaps to answer this question that Vico introduces the role of providence. The same problem arises for Kant, and he appears to resolve it with the providential role of Nature. As we have seen, however, Nature's only role is to do nothing in the domain of history and leave humankind to its own freedom and device. What, then, is Kant's real account of order and design in the historical development of humankind?

23. *The New Science of Giambattista Vico*, trans. Thomas Bergin and Max Fisch (Ithaca, 1968), par. 349.
24. Vico, *Selected Writings*, 104.

In my view, Kant attributes the order and design of human history to the Ideas of practical reason. The history of humankind is a story of steady progress, because the efforts and activities of individual human beings are governed by the Ideas of practical reason. These practical ideals lure and guide humankind at every stage of history, because they are the inevitable objects of human aspiration insofar as human beings are rational. In the *Observations,* as we noted in chapter 1, Kant said that unlike the objects of theoretical reason, moral ideals and principles are embedded in our feelings. Working through the subjective feelings of humanity at every stage of history, the Ideas of pure reason play their constructivist role in the making of human history, just as the categories of understanding discharge their constructivist function by organizing the manifold of sensibility. The Ideas of practical reason have their immanent force, though they transcend every particular stage of history.

The historical function of the Ideas of practical reason marks Kant's critical advance beyond Rousseau's view of history. As already noted, Kant accepted Rousseau's view that human beings become rational by breaking up their natural ties of instinct and establishing their freedom, but this idea did not provide a theoretical basis strong enough for the thesis that the history of humankind is a story of rational progress. Rousseau's view of human freedom, history, and rationality is only negative; it states only the negative freedom from nature's bondage. But this negative freedom cannot explain human rationality and progress. The fact that humankind breaks through the bonds of nature cannot explain why and how it becomes rational. According to Kant's theory of human reason, human beings become rational only when they become aware of the Ideas of pure reason and have the power to act in accordance with them. Then and only then can they terminate their bondage to nature and begin their journey of historical evolution.

The idea of historical evolution has been a great Platonic legacy. It began with the *City of God,* in which Saint Augustine compared the history of humankind to the growth of an individual human being (*De civitate dei* 10.14). This historical conception of humankind became an overriding concern with the theologians of the twelfth century, who had heavily imbibed the Christian Neoplatonism of the Pseudo-Dionysius.[25] In *De sancta trinitate et operibus eius* (On the Trinity and its works), Rupert of Deutz divided the entire human history into three periods: (1) the time of the Father (Creation), from the creation of the world to the Fall of Adam; (2) the time of the Son (Salvation), from the Fall to the Crucifixion; and (3) the time of the Holy Spirit (Sanctification), from the Resurrection to the end of the world. In *Concordia vetris et novi testamenti* (The Concordance of the Old and the New Testaments), Joachim of Floris proposed another triadic division of human history: the Age of the Father, the Age of the Son, and the Age of the Holy Spirit. This triadic demarcation is somewhat different from that of Rupert of Deutz: Whereas Rupert regarded the Fall as the demarcation point between the first and the second ages, Joachim moved this point from the Fall to the Incarnation. In spite of this difference, they shared the same idea of progress and evolution. The three ages or periods are the three periods in the history of evolution. The idea of evolution presupposes the idea of telos, the ultimate end. The ultimate end is none other than the most ideal state; hence the idea of evolution has enjoyed a special link with Platonism.

The novel feature of the triadic division of history was the introduction of the Age of the Holy Spirit as the third period. It is the period of sanctification. In Christian theology, the sanctification by the Holy Spirit constitutes the last phase in the long process of salvation. In traditional theology, sanctification was not supposed to take place until the purified soul reached the kingdom of heaven. For this reason, traditional theology had recognized only two periods in the history of humankind: the Age of the Father and the Age of the Son. By installing the Age of the Holy Spirit as the third period, Rupert of Deutz and Joachim of Floris were saying that the sanctification of the soul would be accomplished in this world. This was their radical departure from the traditional Christian teaching. According to them, Christ's mission of saving humankind was to be accomplished in this world.

25. For a fuller account, see T. K. Seung, *Cultural Thematics* (New Haven, 1976), 59–66.

The question whether the Christian mission could be accomplished in this or the other world is similar to Kant's question whether the highest good can be realized in the phenomenal or the noumenal world. This question has a long history in Platonic tradition. Plato himself wondered whether the ideal republic could be realized in this world or be found only in the other world. Kant is struggling with the same problem and considers the possibility of realizing the highest good in this world as well as in the other world. For Platonists, the question of history concerns the possibility of realizing the Ideas of pure reason in this world. For this reason, Kant's historical essays are inseparable from his philosophy if they are placed in the context of Platonic tradition. On the other hand, those same essays appear to be extraneous, irrelevant, and even antithetical to his philosophy, as many critics have charged, if their links with Platonism are not recognized.

4 The *Groundwork* and the Second *Critique:*
Kant's Formalism

* * * * * * * * * * * * * * * * * * *

The *Groundwork for the Metaphysics of Morals* contains no trace of Platonic ethics. It presents a totally different moral theory. Moral laws are not to be derived from Platonic Ideas; they are to be made by pure practical reason. This is Kant's idea of moral autonomy and his new concept of freedom. He has taken over the idea of legislative autonomy from Rousseau, who defined freedom as the obedience to the law one prescribes for oneself.[1] In the *Groundwork* Kant extends Rousseau's idea of legislative autonomy from political to moral order. Autonomy of the moral will consists in obeying the moral law of its own making. By this new standard of autonomy, to derive moral laws from Platonic Ideas is not autonomous or free. This is a drastic change in Kant's conception of freedom.

In the first *Critique,* as we saw in chapter 3, Kant had defined freedom as the power of practical reason to act in accordance with Platonic Ideas. There he associated the idea of freedom with the absence of causal necessity: If one acts from inclination, one has no freedom, because inclination is always subject to causal laws. On the other hand, if one acts in accordance with the Ideas of practical reason, one is still free, because those Ideas cannot causally determine the moral will. The freedom from causal necessity is not enough to constitute Kant's new idea of moral autonomy. By this new standard, even the acceptance of Platonic Ideas as normative principles is the heteronomy of the will. Pure reason is truly free and autonomous only when it makes moral laws without any external constraint. Thus, Kant takes the extreme position that even the ethics of Platonic Forms is incompatible with the ethics of autonomy, because they are

1. *On the Social Contract* 1.8.

external normative constraints on practical reason (*GMM* 442). His rejection of all forms of heteronomy or constraint for the sake of autonomy is known as the Copernican revolution in ethics.

* * The Copernican Revolution in Ethics

In the *Critique of Pure Reason* Kant recognizes two ways of establishing the relation of concepts to objects. Either our concepts conform to objects or objects conform to our concepts. The latter is the priority of concepts to objects ("the conformity of objects to concepts"), and the former is the priority of objects to concepts ("the conformity of concepts to objects"). According to Kant, the traditional metaphysics had assumed the priority of objects, that is, that their existence is independent of our concepts, and hence our concepts must conform to their objects as a precondition for our knowledge. In that case, our knowledge of objects is bound to be a posteriori. A priori knowledge can be accounted for only by turning this traditional view upside down. This is Kant's Copernican revolution in theoretical philosophy.

In the *Groundwork* and the second *Critique* Kant extends the Copernican revolution to practical philosophy.[2] The relation of the will and its objects is for practical philosophy what the relation of concepts and objects is for theoretical philosophy. The will is pure practical reason, the faculty of rational choice and action; it is the practical counterpart of pure theoretical reason. The object of the will is the good. There are two ways of accounting for the relation of the will to its object: either the good determines the will or the will determines the good (C_2 62). One is the priority of the will over its object, and the other is the priority of the object over the will. The good that determines the will is a material concept of the good; the good that is determined by the will is a formal concept of the

2. Kant's Copernican revolution in ethics is thoroughly discussed and explained by John R. Silber in "The Copernican Revolution in Ethics: The Good Reexamined," *Kant-Studien* 51 (1959–60): 85–101.

good. A material concept of the good refers to an object lying outside the will. But a formal concept of the good makes no such reference; it is its own goodness.

Various types of the good fall under the material concept. The objects of empirical desire obviously fit the definition of this concept, because all empirical entities lie outside pure practical reason. God also falls under the material concept of the good, because God is other than pure practical reason. Likewise, the ideals of perfection, such as Platonic Forms, fall under the same concept. All of them are substantive entities. On the other hand, the goodness of the will is not substantive but formal, because pure practical reason is purely formal. All practical principles based on a concept of the substantive good, in the empirical or the transcendent world, are called material principles. The practical principle based solely on a concept of the formal good is called a formal practical principle. All material practical principles result in the heteronomy of the will; only formal practical principle secures the autonomy of the will. According to Kant, all traditional ethics have been based on material practical principles. Hence his attempt to construct the ethics of formal practical principle is a major revolution.

Kant's idea of moral autonomy is much stronger than the standard notion of autonomy. Let us suppose that we make laws to secure the prosperity and security of a community. This legislative autonomy is heteronomous by Kant's standard, for it presupposes a material concept of the good lying outside the will, and the laws we make serve only the instrumental function of achieving the heteronomous goal. Now suppose that we make and obey moral laws for no other reason than their lawfulness. The idea of lawfulness is a formal concept, which is derived from pure reason. It is the formal concept of the good; its referent is the goodness of the pure moral will. To obey the moral law for no other reason than that it is lawful is to have respect for it, and that is precisely the autonomy of the will. There can be no respect for the law if it only serves an instrumental function. Thus, Kant defines moral duty as the necessity of an act dictated by respect for the moral law (*GMM* 400). As long as the moral law is understood in this manner, Kant holds, it does not presuppose any material concept of the good lying outside the will.

It is often said that Kant's conception of morality is rationalistic, that is, that the moral law is a dictate of pure reason. This conventional view is not useful until his conception of practical rationality is clearly spelled out. There are many other rationalistic ethics besides Kant's, for example, the ethics of Plato, Aristotle, Leibniz, Spinoza, and Hegel. But they are all different because they presuppose different conceptions of rationality. Kant's ethics is different from all of them. It is the only ethics that is based on the conception of formal rationality, which is defined by the formal concept of the good. Kant states his formal practical principle in the categorical imperative:

> Act only according to that maxim by which you can at the same time will that it should become a universal law. (*GMM* 421, trans. Beck)

This version of the categorical imperative is known as the formula of universal law. How can we tell whether a given maxim can be accepted as a universal law? This is the central question with the formula of universal law, and it cannot be fully answered without presupposing or spelling out the notion of a universal moral law. But Kant does not spell out such a notion, and therefore he leaves an intractable source of ambiguity in his doctrine of morality. His readers and commentators have the freedom to appeal to their own notions of moral law, and most of the controversies on his ethical theory stem from this interpretive freedom.

Although Kant does not define a moral law or its lawfulness in the *Groundwork,* he gives four examples for the formal test of a moral maxim as a universal law. The first example concerns the maxim of suicide: "From self-love, I make it my principle to shorten my life if its continuance threatens more evil than it promises pleasure." This principle of self-love cannot become a universal law of nature. Kant explains, "It is then seen at once that a system of nature by whose law the very same feeling whose function is to stimulate the furtherance of life should actually destroy life would contradict itself and consequently could not subsist as a system of nature" (*GMM* 422, trans. Paton). Hence the maxim of suicide cannot be adopted as a universal law.

Kant illustrates the same requirement of self-consistency with his second example, which concerns a maxim about promise making. Suppose I have an urgent need to borrow money and try to secure a loan on a false promise for its repayment. Kant describes the maxim as follows: "When I believe myself in need of money, I will borrow money and promise to repay it, although I know I shall never do so" (*GMM* 422, trans. Paton). The maxim contradicts itself. If it were to become a universal law, nobody would ever take a promise seriously, and the institution of promise making would be destroyed. In that case, the maxim of making a false promise can no longer function as a universal law.

The third example concerns whether natural talents should or should not be developed for their own sake. This question should be distinguished from the question whether natural talents should or should not be developed for their usefulness. The latter question belongs to a hypothetical imperative. Kant invites us to suppose that we are living in a place like the South Sea Islands, whose rich natural resources make it possible to lead a comfortable life without cultivating any of our talents. Under those fortunate circumstances, he admits, we can indeed live with the maxim of neglecting our talents as a universal law. Although a system of nature can exist under such a law, he says, no rational beings can will that it should become a universal law (*GMM* 423).

The fourth example concerns the question whether to help or not help others in need. Kant says that the maxim of neglecting others in need cannot be rejected on the formal consideration of self-contradiction. If this maxim is made into a universal law, all human beings have to look after their own well-being and expect no help from others. According to Kant, under such a law of self-reliance the human race could certainly exist and would fare even better than in a state where everyone talks of sympathy and good will. But, he says, it is nevertheless impossible for a rational being to will that the maxim of not helping others in need should become a universal law, for the will that wills this maxim as a universal law would be in conflict with itself. By willing such a universal law, we would deprive ourselves of all hope of aid even on those occasions when we cannot do without others' aid (*GMM* 423).

In these four examples, Kant recognizes two methods for testing moral maxims. Some maxims cannot be even thought of as universal laws without contradiction. Although some maxims do not involve such internal contradictions, they still cannot be willed as universal laws, because such a willing would contradict itself (*GMM* 424). Onora O'Neill has called these two criteria the contradiction in conception and the contradiction in the will.[3] Against this dyadic schema, Christine Korsgaard proposes three ways of interpreting the formula of universal law: (1) logical contradiction, (2) teleological contradiction, and (3) practical contradiction.[4] Roger Sullivan holds out a simpler view: there is only one formal test, and the contradiction in conception and the contradiction in the will are two features of the same test;[5] the categorical imperative is only the practical application of the logical principle of noncontradiction.[6] This unitary view is closer to H. J. Paton's idea of the contradiction in the will and Bruce Aune's idea of consistent willing.[7]

The question whether there is only one, two, or three tests for the universalization of moral maxims is the question whether Kant has only one, two, or three different conceptions of a moral law. If the test of universalization can be settled by the logical principle of contradiction alone, Kant's conception of a moral law is purely log-

3. *Acting on Principle: An Essay on Kantian Ethics* (New York, 1975), 63–93; *Constructions of Reason* (Cambridge, 1989), 96–101.

4. Korsgaard, "Kant's Formula of Universal Law," *Pacific Philosophical Quarterly* 66 (1985): 24–47.

5. Sullivan, *Immanuel Kant's Moral Theory* (Cambridge, 1989), 152.

6. Ibid., 163.

7. Paton, *The Categorical Imperative* (Chicago, 1948), 139. Aune's idea of consistent willing recognizes two types of inconsistent volition: (1) to will a maxim whose universalization is practically impossible and (2) to will a maxim the consequences of whose universalization is inconsistent with the other objects of rational desire. *Kant's Theory of Morals* (Princeton, 1979), 47–51, 57–58.

ical or formal. On the other hand, if the same test has to rely on some idea of teleological contradiction, then his conception of a moral law is teleological. Likewise, if the same test has to rely on some idea of practical contradiction, then his conception of a moral law is practical. The practical and the teleological conceptions of a moral law are obviously incompatible with his conception of formal practical reason and its autonomy, because they presuppose a material concept of the good and lead to the heteronomy of the will. Since the logical conception of a moral law alone is compatible with his conception of formal practical reason, the strictly formal test of universalization alone should be acceptable in Kant's new ethics. Let us now see how the various tests of universalization stand in terms of Kant's conception of formal rationality.

* * The Formal Test of Moral Maxims

Let us consider the strictly formal test of contradiction in conception. Are there really any maxims that cannot even be thought of as universal laws without contradiction? Some Kant scholars have thought that the maxim of making a false promise or deception involves such a self-contradiction. If the maxim of making false promises were to become a universal law, it would be impossible for anyone to act on that maxim. Everyone would know the falsity of every promise, and nobody would be fooled by a promise. Hence it is impossible to adopt this maxim as a universal law. As Bruce Aune points out, however, this example does not involve logical impossibility or contradiction.[8] If the maxim of making false promises were to become a universal law, the act of promise making would become an empty sham. Such an act is practically absurd, but it is still logically possible. This case involves what Korsgaard calls practical impossibility or practical contradiction rather than logical contradiction.[9] It presupposes practical rationality that recognizes the

8. Aune, *Kant's Theory of Morals,* 54.
9. Korsgaard, "Kant's Formula of Universal Law," 25.

importance of preserving the institution of making and keeping promises, which in turn involves a material concept of the good rather than a formal concept.

O'Neill gives a few maxims whose universalization is supposed to be logically impossible: (1) "I will receive presents, but not give them"; (2) "I will give presents, but not receive them"; and (3) "I will sell others lettuce but not buy it."[10] With the universalization of (1), no one would give presents, and it would be logically impossible for anyone to receive them. With the universalization of (2), the converse holds. With the universalization of (3), no one would buy lettuce, and it would be logically impossible for anyone to sell it. Are these maxims really immoral? Surely not. They are neither moral nor immoral; they are nonmoral or morally trivial maxims. The test of contradiction in conception cannot even discriminate these maxims from immoral ones, because it is a purely formal test. Their discrimination cannot be made without appealing to some substantive moral intuition. Nor can the formal test discriminate moral from immoral maxims. Compare the two maxims (4) "I will give help to others but never receive it" and (5) "I will receive help from others but never give it." Although both (4) and (5) fail Kant's formal test, we cannot casually dismiss either of them as nonmoral or trivial. Maxim 5 is morally unacceptable, while (4) is morally respectable. Hence we should conclude that the distinction between the morally acceptable and the morally unacceptable maxims cannot be made by a purely formal test either, because it is just as substantive as the distinction between moral and nonmoral maxims.

Let us now consider the test of contradiction in the will. As we saw, Kant says that both the maxim of neglecting one's talents and the maxim of developing them can survive the formal test of contradiction. But he says that a rational person would choose the maxim of developing one's talents because they are given for all sorts of possible ends. In support of this view, O'Neill says that to adopt the maxim of not developing one's talents creates a contradiction in the

---

10. O'Neill, *Acting on Principle*, 68.

will, or volitional incoherence.[11] Rational people should develop their talents because they want to engage in many kinds of activities and because those activities require developed talents and skills. The maxim of not developing one's talents undercuts the intention of engaging in those activities. The will that adopts this maxim is incoherent, O'Neill says, because it wills certain ends but refuses to prepare the means necessary for the fulfillment of those ends.

Anyone who neglects necessary means for his or her chosen ends is indeed irrational and incoherent. According to O'Neill's interpretation, the test of contradiction in the will is the test of instrumental rationality. It is the question whether necessary means are prepared for any given ends. By this test of instrumental rationality, however, we can find no fault with the imaginary person of the South Sea Islands in Kant's third example. He has chosen to have a carefree life and prefers this lifestyle to the one favored by the rational person of O'Neill's description. The maxim of neglecting one's talents generates no conflict in his will. In fact, it would be incoherent for him to adopt the maxim of fully developing all his talents, because he would be wasting much time and energy in preparing the means absolutely unnecessary for his chosen ends.

O'Neill assumes that the imaginary person of the South Sea Islands and a rational person of her description intend to engage in the same activities and have the same ends in life. But their ends are different, and the two different sets of ends dictate two different maxims concerning the development of talents. Neither of the maxims can be said to be more rational than the other as long as the idea of rationality is restricted to instrumental rationality. No doubt, we can extend the idea of rationality to the domain of ends and purposes and consider which of the two lifestyles is more rational. But this question cannot be handled by formal practical reason, because the rationality of ends and purposes is not a formal but a substantive issue.

O'Neill says that Kant's fourth example also involves the contra-

---

11. *Constructions of Reason*, 99.

diction in the will. Kant indeed describes it as a case of conflict. A will that adopts the maxim of not helping others in need would be in conflict with itself, because it would deny itself the help of others when it wants to have their help (*GMM* 423). But this argument is not conclusive; it can be inverted. The adoption of the other maxim would also create a contradiction in the will. The will that adopts the maxim of helping others in need assumes the duty of helping others, but this duty is in conflict with the desire not to be concerned with the well-being of others. To be sure, this conflict would not obtain for those devoid of the desire not to be burdened with the well-being of others, but most people have this desire; except for this desire, the duty of beneficence would not be a problem.

Since the maxims of both beneficence and nonbeneficence create some conflict in the will, there is no way to avoid the conflict, hence the contradiction in the will cannot be a criterion for choosing between the two maxims. The only way to make a rational choice is to adopt the maxim that will create a lesser conflict. But it is impossible to determine which of the two maxims will create a lesser conflict without reference to the desire structure of each person. Let us consider what Allen Buchanan calls the Independence Fanatic, who is so committed to the ideal of self-reliance that he has a strong desire to reject others' help at any cost.[12] His will would be in a serious conflict with itself if he were to accept the maxim of beneficence as a universal law. Hence the maxim of helping others in need cannot be accepted as a universal law. The only way to disregard the Independence Fanatic and justify the universal adoption of the maxim of beneficence is to brand him as irrational: his desire structure is abnormal and distorted. As O'Neill would say, the Independence Fanatic is not committed to "the standards of rational willing."[13] She can say this only by appealing to some normative standards, but the idea of normative standards belongs to not formal but substantive rationality.

The idea of substantive rationality is equally inevitable in the tele-

12. Buchanan, review of O'Neill's *Acting on Principle*, in *Journal of Philosophy* 75 (1978): 333.

13. *Constructions of Reason*, 99.

ological interpretation of the formula of universal law. As Korsgaard points out, this line of interpretation takes two forms: a maxim can be accepted as a universal moral law (1) if it can be endorsed as a teleological law of nature or (2) if it contributes to a systematic harmony of all human purposes.[14] For the first of these two approaches, the formula of universal law presupposes the knowledge of natural teleology. But formal practical reason cannot rely on this knowledge without losing its autonomy, because it involves a material concept of the good. Bruce Aune favors the second approach. He calls it the "typic" of the moral law: we should seek the harmony of human purposes by taking the harmony of natural purposes as its analogue.[15]

The harmony of all desires and purposes is not a natural fact but a normative ideal. And this is not a formal but a substantive ideal. The world of nature does not always assure the harmony of desires and purposes; it is full of conflicting desires and purposes. The chain of food supply is often the chain of predation in the animal kingdom. To be sure, the chain of predation is often nature's way of maintaining the ecological balance, but such a balance cannot be regarded as representing a world of harmony. It represents a world of Darwinian struggle for survival.

The world of living beings is a world of brutal competition. The purpose of one living being can be fulfilled only by frustrating the purpose of another. The conflict of desires and purposes takes place not only between two living beings but also within one living being. The desire for food and reproduction is often incompatible with the desire for peace and safety. The world of nature is indeed a Heraclitean world of perpetual conflict. Even if we adopt the harmony of all desires as a normative ideal, we do not want to seek the harmony of all purposes and desires, including irrational ones. Hence the idea of harmony presupposes the rationality of purposes and desires.[16]

14. "Kant's Formula of Universal Law," 33. Korsgaard makes this distinction in her interpretation of Paton's view.

15. Aune, *Kant's Theory of Morals*, 51–52.

16. Aune says that this involves circular reasoning. The formula of universal law is supposed to tell which of our purposes are rational and which are irrational, but its application presupposes the distinction between rational and irrational purposes (ibid., 69).

But the question of their rationality cannot be settled by a formal practical principle, because it is a substantive issue.

These are many different ways to interpret the formula of universal law, but none of them can fulfill Kant's idea of a purely formal test. The test of contradiction in the will and the teleological interpretation inevitably introduce substantive issues into its application. The purely formal test of contradiction has turned out to be indiscriminate and irrelevant; it cannot even distinguish between moral and nonmoral maxims. These considerations lead to the dilemma that either Kant's idea of formal practical reason is vacuous or it surreptitiously relies on some ideas of substantive rationality. In fact, this has been Hegel's charge against Kant.

* * The Vacuity of Formal Practical Reason

Hegel's critique of Kant's ethics is extended and involved,[17] but it stems from a relatively simple premise, namely, that Kant's conception of practical reason is purely formal, and that formal practical reason is in complete abstraction from the content of the will. This is another way of stating Kant's view that formal practical reason is totally dissociated from all material concepts of the good. Hegel says that the formal test of moral maxims is dictated by Kant's theory of formal practical reason. Since formal practical reason is empty of content, it can offer no substantive test. Hence, Hegel holds, the formal test is as vacuous as formal practical reason. The remainder of his critique illustrates and substantiates this charge.[18]

Against Kant's idea of a formal test for moral maxims, Hegel holds that any maxim can be universalized without contradiction. Hegel uses as an example the maxim of not returning deposits.

17. His critique is often repetitious and is scattered over many of his works, and is not easy to understand in all its details because it is couched in his opaque technical language. Its most systematic version is given in his *Phenomenology of Spirit*, trans. A. V. Miller (Oxford, 1977), 252–62.

18. Hegel's charge against Kant's ethics is well examined by Allen Wood in "The Emptiness of the Moral Will," *Monist* 72 (1989): 454–83, and *Hegel's Ethical Thought* (Cambridge, 1990), 140–73.

There are two ways for this maxim to be inconsistent: (1) it can be inconsistent with itself; or (2) it can be inconsistent with some existing practices or institutions. Let us call the former internal inconsistency and the latter, external inconsistency. No maxim can be internally inconsistent. Although the maxim of not returning deposits is inconsistent with the institution of making deposits, he says, it is perfectly consistent with the institution of making no deposit.[19] The external inconsistency of a maxim is always institution-relative; it ultimately turns on the question what sort of institution should be adopted or retained. It appeals to practical rationality.

Hegel's critique has provoked many negative responses from Kant scholars. For example, Allen Wood says that Hegel is wrong to link the formal test of contradiction to the idea of institutional practice. He says that the maxim of returning deposits has nothing to do with the institution of private property, because it is a question of personal trust, which can arise in any society, whether or not it has the institution of private property.[20] Before assessing the merit of this charge, let us consider Hegel's understanding of Kant's formal test. He considers it in two contexts, the logical and the practical. In the logical context the universalization of a maxim is to place the universal quantifier in front of the maxim. For example, the maxim "I will steal" becomes "Everybody will steal." Hegel maintains that no maxim can fail to pass this simple test. In the practical context, the universalization of a maxim is to have it adopted as a universal law in an institutional framework. The maxim that everybody should steal is in conflict with the institutional framework of private property. Although Kant may regard this conflict as a contradiction generated by the universalization of the maxim in question, Hegel says, this contradiction is not internal but external. It lies in its conflict with the institution of private property, and it can be eliminated by dissolving the institution of private property.

As far as logical consistency goes, Hegel holds, the institution of private property is not any more or any less rational than the insti-

19. Hegel, *Natural Law*, trans. T. M. Knox (Philadelphia, 1975), 77.
20. Wood, *Hegel's Ethical Thought*, 158.

tution of not allowing private property. No institution can ever suffer from self-contradiction. For an illustration of this point, let us consider the maxim of universal competition, "Everybody wills to be richer than somebody else." There is a practical contradiction in this maxim as a universal law: it is impossible for everybody to be richer than somebody else. And yet this maxim can be adopted as a universal law for some society and become a social institution. The maxim is operationally possible; it can be used as an operational rule for some society. The operational possibility of adopting a maxim should be distinguished from its practical possibility if the latter means the possibility of complete success. In terms of operational possibility, Hegel seems to say, no institution can suffer from practical contradiction. Even the maxim of universal stealing is operationally possible: everyone can try to steal from someone else, though not everyone may succeed. If any maxim can be institutionalized and no institution can suffer from practical contradiction, then there is no formal basis for rejecting some maxims as unfit to be universal laws.

This Hegelian reply, however, cannot meet Allen Wood's challenge that the morality of personal trust does not depend on any institutional framework. We can talk about the morality and the immorality of breaking trust in the context of personal relations, which totally transcend all social institutions. If this is so, we should also be able to talk about the same moral problem without reference to the formal test of universalization. The idea of universalization is convertible with the idea of institutionalization. When a maxim becomes a universal rule, it becomes a universal practice and a social institution. If the idea of social institution is irrelevant to the moral question of personal trust, the test of universalization should be equally irrelevant.

When we say that the breaking of a trust or murder is bad, as Allen Wood says, we do not base our judgment on its institutional impact. Nor do we base our judgment on its universalizability. Just imagine that Jack kills John. Can we say that the murder is wrong only on the ground that Jack's maxim cannot be universalized or institutionalized? On the contrary, because we know Jack's murder of John is wrong, we can say that Jack's maxim cannot be universalized or institutionalized. Our moral judgment of this act precedes the formal test of universalization. In this case, the formal test cannot establish the rightness or wrongness of the maxim. If we did not know whether Jack's murder of John were right or wrong, we would not know whether his maxim should or should not be universalized.

There are really two kinds of moral act. A certain type of act is morally bad even when it is taken by itself, and we install a universal rule against it because it is bad. Another type of act is morally neutral, for example, walking over a lawn, if it is taken by itself but produces disastrous consequences if it is done by many or most people. In that case, we have to install a rule to prevent those consequences. The inherent moral value of an act should be distinguished from its consequential value. The former is in the act even before the universalization of its maxim; the latter is not in the act, but comes into being only when it is connected to a social practice. We can assess the inherent moral value of individual acts without reference to social rules or institutions, but we cannot assess their consequential value without reference to social practices or institutions. If we are only concerned with the inherent value of a moral act, the test of universalization is as irrelevant to our assessment as its institutional repercussion. Hence Wood's criticism of Hegel is equally devastating when applied to Kant's test of universalization. Kant's formal test cannot recognize the vital distinction between the inherent and the consequential value of moral acts, because it is not a formal but a substantive distinction.

Let us consider another line of Hegel's critique of Kant's ethics. Hegel holds that the formal test is not only vacuous and indiscriminate but even eliminates a morally good maxim such as "Help the poor."[21] He says that the universalization of this maxim would eradicate poverty. Since the existence of the poor is the precondition for the operation of this maxim, it will be annihilated by its own universalization. By Kant's own standard, it would be immoral to help the poor. By the same formal standard, F. H. Bradley says, the maxims

---

21. Hegel, *Natural Law*, 80.

of helping the poor and loving one's enemies would be as objectionable as the maxim of stealing.[22] If this line of thought is extended, Robert Paul Wolff says, then the maxim of combating racial prejudice would be morally wrong.[23] It cannot be adopted as a universal law without eliminating racial prejudice, but the elimination of racial prejudice would destroy the maxim itself. Allen Buchanan notes that this objection can be far more pervasive than has been assumed: by Kant's formal standard, any moral act against an immoral institution or social practice would be morally wrong.[24]

What sort of defense can be made for Kant against this barrage of Hegelian criticism? Korsgaard says that the universalization of the maxim "Succor the poor" may eradicate poverty, but it does not defeat the purpose behind it, namely, to give the poor relief.[25] If her argument is correct, then the morality of helping the poor has nothing to do with the formal test of whether its maxim can be universalized. It depends solely on the purpose. But how do we know whether it is a morally good or morally bad purpose? There can be no formal test for discriminating good from bad purposes; we have to appeal to some substantive criteria for saying that the purpose of eradicating poverty is good. Wood offers a different defense of Kant.[26] The maxim of helping the poor is not simply to help the poor but to abolish poverty as far as possible. Hence the elimination of poverty does not eradicate or frustrate the maxim but fulfills it. This is to understand maxims as descriptions of goals and purposes rather than as rules of behavior. So we come back to the same question of discriminating good from bad purposes. In this debate, Kant's defenders do not take seriously Hegel's premise that Kant's test of universalization is really formal because it is the test of formal practical reason. Instead, one way or another, they surreptitiously appeal to some substantive criteria.

According to Hegel, because the formal test of contradiction is vac-

22. *Ethical Studies* (Oxford, 1970), 155.
23. *The Autonomy of Reason* (New York, 1973), 90.
24. Buchanan, review of *Acting on Principle*.
25. "Kant's Formula of Universal Law," 39.
26. Wood, *Hegel's Ethical Thought*, 160.

uous, Kant can produce respectable results only by introducing substantive considerations under the guise of a formal test. This is the
trick of substantive subterfuge. By this critique, Hegel exposes a
Kantian dilemma: If the formal test is taken in the logical context, it
is vacuous. It can endorse the universalization of any and all maxims
and cannot discriminate good from bad ones. On the practical level,
he admits, the formal test can appeal covertly to some substantive
considerations, such as the notion of ends, purposes, and consequences. But this is an appeal to empirical considerations, which
destroy the purity of the moral will.[27] The purely formal practical
reason must either lose its purity by smuggling in substantive considerations or retain its purity and remain vacuous.

* * Formal and Material Imperatives

The formula of universal law is the first of the three formulas for stating the categorical imperative.[28] Kant calls the second formula the
principle of humanity:

> Act in such a way that you always treat humanity, whether in your
> own person or in the person of any other, never simply as a
> means, but always at the same time as an end. (*GMM* 429, trans.
> Paton)

This version is known as the formula of humanity; it is clearly not
a formal but a substantive principle. To treat a person as an end
rather than a means presupposes the concept of an end. In practical
philosophy, the concept of an end is a material or substantive concept par excellence. Kant applies the second formula to the same
four examples to which he applied the first formula and obtains the
same results. Suicide is morally wrong because it amounts to the use
of oneself as a mere means for escaping from painful circumstances.

27. Hegel, *Faith and Knowledge* (Albany, 1977), 183–84.
28. There has been a dispute over the number of formulas for the categorical imperative. Although Kant names only three, Paton counts five in *Categorical Imperative*, 129.
Aune gives an even more elaborate classification of different formulas and their systematic relation in *Kant's Theory of Morals*, 112–20.

A deceitful promise is wrong because it uses another person as a mere means for one's advantage. Kant says that these two cases violate the simple negative injunction against using a person as a mere means.

The negative injunction is not strong enough for the third and the fourth examples, neither of which appears to involve the use of a person as a mere means. Someone who neglects his or her talents cannot be blamed for using himself or herself as a mere means. Kant locates the fault elsewhere: "Now there are in humanity capacities for greater perfection which form part of nature's purpose for humanity in our person. To neglect these can admittedly be compatible with the *maintenance* of humanity as an end in itself, but not with the *promotion* of this end" (*GMM* 430, trans. Paton). "Nature's purpose" belongs to natural teleology. Kant is assuming that human perfection is a part of natural teleology and that the development of talents is required for human perfection. He is advocating a teleological ethics of perfection. The ideas of natural purpose and perfection cannot belong to formal practical reason; they presuppose material practical reason. Hence the formula of humanity is incompatible with the formal principle of practical reason.

The fourth example presents the same problem for Kant's formalism. Happiness is the natural end of all human beings, he says, and there are positive and negative ways of contributing to the happiness of others (*GMM* 430). The negative way, which is not to harm others, is not enough, because it achieves only the negative harmony with others. The positive harmony can be achieved by positively furthering the subjective ends of others. The idea of subjective ends and their harmony is substantive; it lies beyond the scope of formal practical reason.

In his discussion of ends, Kant introduces the distinction between the dignity of human beings and the price of things (*GMM* 434). To respect a person means to recognize his or her dignity. The distinction of price and dignity belongs to a material concept of the good. Whether the formula of humanity is taken as the principle of negative or positive duty, it cannot be dissociated from a material concept of the good and a material practical principle. Insofar as the material concept and principle do not lie within purely formal practical reason, the formula of humanity goes against Kant's Copernican revolution in ethics. It reinstates the heteronomy of the will.

A material concept of the good gains even a greater significance in the third formulation of the categorical imperative, which is known as the formula of the kingdom of ends:

> Act on the maxims of a member who makes universal laws for a merely possible kingdom of ends. (*GMM* 439, trans. Paton)

The concept of the kingdom of ends is much more copious and substantive than the concept of a single person as an end. This concept does not make its first appearance in the *Groundwork:* it is the same as the Idea of the necessary unity of all possible ends, which Kant had used as the ultimate ideal of his Platonic ethics in the first *Critique* (A328/B385). With the third formula of the categorical imperative, he completely reverts to his old Platonic position.

In terms of Kant's Copernican revolution in ethics, the *Groundwork* is doubly schizophrenic. First, only the first formulation of the categorical imperative is stated in terms of formalist ethics. Kant freely employs material concepts of the good in the second and third formulations, hence they are obviously incompatible with his revolutionary notion of purely formal practical reason. Second, although the first formulation of the categorical imperative is stated in purely formal terms, Kant has to appeal, implicitly or surreptitiously, to some material concepts of the good in its application and interpretation. Hence even the formula of universal law is a formal practical principle only in appearance but a material practical principle in its operation. For these reasons, we may say that the *Groundwork* begins but does not complete the Copernican revolution in ethics.

In the *Critique of Practical Reason* Kant tries his best to improve the consistency in his formalist ethics. He gives only one formulation of the categorical imperative, the formula of universal law, and stresses its formal character (C_2 41); he does not even mention the second and third formulas. He introduces the respect for persons, which is the essence of the second formula, as a by-product of the respect for moral law (C_2 76–78). In his discussion of respect for moral law he says that respect always applies to persons only and never to things. He stresses its difference from other emotions, such as love, fear, and admiration. Whereas these emotions all reflect our reactions to empirical conditions, such as social position, talents, and achievements, our respect for persons transcends all empirical conditions. He further claims that our respect for a person is none other than our respect for the moral law (C_2 78). The respect for persons is no longer a basis for another formulation of the categorical imperative but only reflects our recognition of it as the highest law.

In the second *Critique* Kant tries to be faithful to the spirit of his Copernican revolution in ethics by rigorously sticking to the formalist account of the categorical imperative. But he does so only in the Analytic. In the Dialectic, he introduces the concept of the highest good, which has three components: (1) virtue (moral good), (2) happiness (natural good), and (3) their exact proportion. It is not a formal but a material concept. In chapter 2 of the Dialectic, Kant talks about our duty of promoting the highest good. After denying the necessary connection between morality and happiness in this world, he says, "Nevertheless, in the practical task of pure reason, i.e., in the necessary endeavor after the highest good, such a connection is postulated as necessary: we *should* seek to further the highest good" (C_2 124–25). Then he adds that it is not a privilege but a duty to promote the highest good.

The duty to promote the highest good is clearly different from the duty to obey the categorical imperative. On what ground does Kant propose this duty? Lewis White Beck has agonized over this question.[29] As Kant admits, the concept of the highest good cannot be the determining ground of the will. It is not a formal but a material concept. Hence it cannot prescribe a moral duty without impairing the autonomy of the will. In Beck's view, there is no way to account for the additional duty of promoting the highest good. Moreover, we do not have the power to perform the duty of promoting the highest good: "I can do absolutely nothing else toward apportioning happiness in accordance with desert—that is the task of a moral

---

29. *A Commentary on Kant's Critique of Practical Reason* (Chicago, 1960), 242–45.

governor of the universe, not of a laborer in the vineyard. It is not *my* task; my task is to realize the one condition of the *summum bonum* which is within my power."[30]

That one condition is to obey the categorical imperative. Beyond that we can do nothing, because we have no control over the problem of allocating happiness in accordance with moral desert. Beck concludes that the concept of the highest good is not a practical concept but only a dialectical ideal of reason. It makes no difference whatsoever for our notion of duty; its use is limited to Kant's dialectical moves for demonstrating the immortality of the soul and the existence of God. Against this negative, John Silber argues that we do have the duty of promoting the highest good.[31] He denies Beck's claim that we can do nothing toward apportioning happiness in accordance with desert: "And it is obvious, Beck's denial notwithstanding, that in rearing children, serving on juries, and grading papers one tries to do and actually can do something 'about apportioning happiness in accordance with desert.'"[32] It is interesting to note that all his examples concern questions of justice.

Silber distinguishes between the duty to promote the highest good and the duty to achieve it. The highest good can be achieved only after we realize our moral perfection and then receive happiness commensurate with our moral virtue. Both conditions are obviously impossible to obtain in this world, but Silber believes that we can do something even in this world for promoting the right proportion between happiness and virtue. Their right proportion can be obtained at any level of moral perfection, although the complete realization of the highest good becomes possible only at its highest level. For the right proportion between morality and happiness is none other than the question of desert and justice. Therefore, he assumes that the concept of the highest good can be taken as the principle of justice in this world.

The principle of justice is not a formal but a substantive one. If Silber is right, Kant gives a formal practical principle in the Analytic

30. Ibid., 244–45.
31. "The Importance of the Highest Good in Kant's Ethics," *Ethics* 73 (1963): 179–97.
32. Ibid., 183.

of the second *Critique* and a substantive principle in its Dialectic. As far as the text is concerned, Silber's reading is impeccable. Even Beck does not deny the existence of textual evidence; he only points out its glaring inconsistency with Kant's doctrine of autonomy. Anyone who can read the text without prejudice could not but concur with Silber. His reading is so impeccable and so compelling that Yirmiahu Yovel has been led to advocate a double-imperative thesis. He holds that Kant's ethical writings, with the exception of the *Groundwork*, contain two imperatives, one formal and one material.[33] The formal imperative is the categorical imperative; the material, the imperative for promoting the highest good.

The double-imperative thesis is operative not only in the second *Critique* but in the third *Critique*, *Religion within the Limits of Reason Alone*, and Kant's political and historical writings. The *Groundwork* appears to be the lone exception. Hence the central issue in the Beck-Silber dispute appears to be whether we should, on the one hand, protect Kant's doctrine of autonomy by exalting the *Groundwork* as the canonical text for his ethical theory and dismiss all his ethical writings that are inconsistent with it as unfortunate aberrations or, on the other hand, accept the double-imperative thesis as his real teaching and treat the *Groundwork* as a mysterious exception. This is a difficult choice, but there is no need to choose, because the *Groundwork* itself contains material imperatives, namely, the second and third formulas of the categorical imperative. The choice between the single- and the double-imperative thesis stands on the mistaken premise that the *Groundwork* gives only the formal imperative.

* * The Relation of Form and Matter

If the double-imperative thesis is true, we cannot avoid the question, What is the relation of formal and substantive principles in Kant's ethics? There are two ways to answer this question: (1) that the substantive principle is deducible from the formal principle; and (2) that the two principles are independent. The latter answer makes Kant's

33. *Kant and the Philosophy of History* (Princeton, 1980), 32–36.

moral theory incoherent. If the two principles are independent, they dictate two different conceptions of the moral will. The formal principle dictates the autonomous will; the substantive principle, the heteronomous will. These two conceptions of the will are incompatible. On the other hand, the first answer can secure the integrity of Kant's moral theory by deriving the substantive principle from the formal one. Jeffrie Murphy considers the possibility of deriving the moral duty to promote the highest good from the categorical imperative.[34] He begins with the following maxim: "Act so as to bring about a distribution of happiness according to the worthiness to be happy." Since the universalization of this maxim appears to involve no formal contradiction, it can be accepted as a universal law. But Murphy recognizes the difficulty of administering this universal law. It is chiefly epistemic; we seldom know enough about other people's moral worth to make a correct apportionment of happiness in proportion to virtue.[35]

There may be a much greater difficulty in the administration of this universal law than the epistemic one. Let us eliminate all epistemic difficulties by stipulating that we have accurate knowledge of each other's moral character. We will face the difficulty of measuring each other's moral worth and happiness. Let us resolve this problem by stipulating that we can invent a suitable measuring device. Then we have to face the problem of finding the right ratio between moral worth and happiness. Let us resolve this problem by stipulating that Beck's moral governor of the universe has given us the right ratio. We are now in a position to discharge the duty of promoting the highest good. If I see you enjoying a far greater or smaller share of happiness than you morally deserve, I will have the duty to increase or decrease your happiness proportionately. This universal law of happiness allocation would make all of us executives for increasing and decreasing each other's happiness in accordance with virtue.

It is one thing to say that we should abide by the principle of justice in dealing with each other but another thing to say that we have

---

34. Murphy, "The Highest Good as Content for Kant's Ethical Formalism," *Kant-Studien* 56 (1965): 102–10.

35. Ibid., 107.

the duty of apportioning each other's happiness. The latter is not a rule of duty but a rule of intrusion and interference. This intrusive law cannot be made much more tolerable by appointing public officials for its administration. Every time someone's happiness changes without a corresponding change in his or her virtue, or someone's virtue changes without a corresponding change in his or her happiness, the public institution has to step in and restore the balance between happiness and virtue. Although the maxim of moral apportionment of happiness involves no internal contradiction, why should any rational beings will it as a universal law? We cannot settle this question without invoking a substantive standard of rational willing, which is incompatible with formal practical reason. Hence there is no way to bring the duty of promoting the highest good under the formal practical principle.

In *Religion within the Limits of Reason Alone* Kant gives his own account of the relation of the moral law to the duty of promoting the highest good. He says that this duty is an extension of the duty of obeying the categorical imperative (*KGS* 6:7n). But this extension can be made only by using the concept of justice; the concept of duty under the categorical imperative cannot, all by itself, be extended to yield the concept of the highest good. The concept of justice is central to the demand of the exact apportionment of happiness to morality. The duty of promoting the highest good can be derived from the categorical imperative only if the latter is conjoined to the concept of justice. But this concept is not formal but substantive.

Let us now consider the relation of the formal and the material imperatives as they are given in the *Groundwork*. Kant says three things about the relation of the different formulas. First, they are equivalent and independent. Second, the formula of universal law states the form of the moral law; the formula of humanity gives its material. They are in the relation of form and matter, and the third formula combines form and matter into one. Third, there is a progression in the three formulas (*GMM* 436): the formula of universal law states the *unity* of the form of the will; the formula of humanity states the *plurality* of ends; and the formula of the kingdom of ends states the *totality* of the system of ends.

These three accounts are incompatible with each other. If the first two formulas are related as form and matter, how can they be equivalent and independent of each other? In the first *Critique* Kant had shown that form and matter are inseparable complements. There is a division of labor between form and matter, which cannot be interchanged. Nor can form and matter be independent of each other; on the contrary, they are mutually dependent. If the three formulas are really equivalent, how can they form a progression from unity through plurality to totality? These are the most baffling questions about Kant's formalist program in ethics.

The relation of the three formulas becomes even more mysterious when we consider Kant's formulation of the categorical imperative in the second *Critique*. There he gives only the formula of universal law and treats the respect of persons as a by-product of the respect for moral law. In that case, the first two formulas no longer stand in the relation of form and matter; their relation is more like that of cause and effect. If there is a progression, it is the progression from a cause to its effect. Even the relation of the moral law to the highest good can be characterized as the relation of cause and effect. The concept of moral virtue is said to lead necessarily to the concept of the highest good, and the duty of promoting the highest good is said to be the extension of the duty of obeying the moral law.

There is a pervasive confusion on the relation between form and matter in Kant's formalist ethics, that is, on the relation between formal and material imperatives, between formal and substantive principles. This confusion has produced the identity crisis in Kantian ethics. Of the many who have espoused Kantian ethics, most do not agree with Kant on its essential features. According to Kant, the formal practical principle was the essence of his Copernican revolution in ethics, and the formula of universal law was the ultimate basis of his moral theory (*GMM* 437). But few of his followers ever appeal to this formal principle when they advocate Kantian ethics; most appeal to the principle of humanity as the most salient Kantian ideal. But to treat a person as an end rather than a mere means is hardly unique with Kant's ethics. It is an essential feature of our commonsense morality.

John Silber has perhaps made the strongest attempt to remain faithful to the formula of universal law.[36] In his interpretation, the main function of this formula is to provide a universal standpoint that can secure the fairness of moral rules. But the astute Kantian John Rawls is convinced that Kant's formalism is too weak to provide any substantive ideals of justice. He has sought the real force of Kant's ethics in his substantive ideals of liberty and equality.[37] But these two ideals are much older than Kant. If we try to locate Kantian ideals on the substantive level, we can never be sure of finding any ideals uniquely Kantian. Robert Nozick claims his Kantian legacy as staunchly as John Rawls does.[38] We really cannot identify the essential feature of Kantian ethics if it is understood as an ethics of substantive ideals. This is the identity crisis in Kantian ethics, and it cannot be resolved without finding a way to bridge the gap between the form and substance of Kant's moral theory and secure its coherence.

For a coherent account of the relation between formal and substantive principles in Kant's ethics, we have to bring together the following ideas: (1) they are equivalent; (2) they are form and matter; and (3) they form a progression. Yovel has proposed one idea that may be useful for resolving the problem. He recognizes the duality in Kant's conception of the moral will.[39] Formal and material imperatives presuppose two types of the will: the pure will, which wills nothing but itself, and the will that wills the highest good. This proposal requires some refinement, because Yovel recognizes no distinction between formal and material imperatives within the categorical imperative. Instead he treats all the different forms of the categorical imperative as one formal imperative. No doubt, this is in tune with Kant's claim that there is only one categorical imperative. As we have seen, however, only the formula of universal law qualifies as the formal imperative, while the other formulas are material imperatives.

Yovel's duality thesis can now be stated in more general terms:

36. Silber, "Procedural Formalism in Kant's Ethics," *Review of Metaphysics* 28 (1974): 197–236.

37. Rawls, *A Theory of Justice* (Cambridge, Mass., 1971), 251.

38. Nozick, *Anarchy, State, and Utopia* (New York, 1974), 32, 228.

39. *Kant and the Philosophy of History*, 43–48.

Kant's ethics operates with both formal and substantive practical reason, which manifest themselves as the formal and the substantive will. The formal will expresses itself in the formula of universal law, while the substantive will operates with substantive principles, such as the formula of humanity or the concept of the highest good. This account is incompatible with Kant's Copernican revolution, his claim to have disengaged his ethics completely from substantive practical reason. Nor does this account appear to be compatible with the equivalence thesis. There can be no equivalence between the formal will, which wills nothing but its pure form, and the substantive will, which wills something other than its pure form. In spite of these objections, the duality thesis appears to capture the basic structure of practical reason, which clearly resembles the basic structure of theoretical reason.

In the first *Critique*, as we saw in chapter 2, Kant presented two conceptions of the categories, formal and material (or generic). We also noted that Kant's two conceptions of the categories reflect two different views of human reason, formal and substantive rationality, which he had inherited from two different sources, namely, Hume and Leibniz. He tried to reconcile these two views with his thesis that the two sets of the categories were not really two sets of pure concepts but two functions of the same pure concepts. This was a plausible view for him, because he believed that formal concepts were none other than the ultimate generic concepts. The duality of rationality is not limited to the pure understanding but extends to pure reason. In the first *Critique* Kant offers two conceptions of not only the categories but the Ideas of pure reason. When he takes the formal view of pure reason, he says that the Ideas of pure reason are produced by the application of the forms of syllogism "to the synthetic unity of intuitions under the direction of the categories" (A321/B378). The forms of syllogism belong to formal reason as much as the forms of judgment do, and they are supposed to produce the three Ideas of the self, the world, and God.

The Idea of God, however, cannot be constructed by purely formal reason, because it is the Idea of the most perfect being. The concept of perfection is not formal but substantive. To be sure, the Ideas of the self and the world do not involve the concept of perfection. Hence the transcendental psychology and cosmology are different from the transcendental theology. The latter cannot take a single step without the concept of perfection, whether it takes the form of the ontological, the cosmological, or the teleological argument for the existence of God. When Kant introduces the Ideas of pure reason to the domain of perfection, he espouses the substantive view of reason. He identifies the Ideas of pure reason with Platonic archetypes (A313/B3270). Platonic Ideas cannot be generated from the forms of syllogism.[40]

These two views of pure reason obtain not only for theoretical but also for practical reason; they underlie the distinction between formal and substantive practical reason. The formula of universal law is a formal principle that belongs to formal practical reason; the formula of humanity is a substantive principle that belongs to substantive practical reason. Kant appears to understand their relation as a form-matter relation in an analogy to the relation of formal and material categories. Just as the formal and the generic categories are only two different functions of the same pure concepts, the two formulas of the categorical imperative are two expressions of the same idea of moral law. In Kant's scheme of thought, as we noted in chapter 2, the formal concepts are identical with the generic concepts of the highest order. Since the formula of humanity is the highest general principle for moral law, Kant seems to think, it is also a formal principle and hence is equivalent to the formula of universal law.

I have tried to articulate Yovel's notion of duality in Kant's conception of the will, but it does not resolve our problem for two reasons. First, it presupposes a devious notion of the form-matter relation, which led Kant to his mistaken identification of formal and material categories in the first *Critique*. Kant dogmatically equates the most general principle with a formal principle. By this standard, all ultimate principles should be called formal, whatever substantive content they may have. Second, it is limited to the relation of the first

40. For a fuller account of Kant's two views of pure reason, see my *Kant's Transcendental Logic* (New Haven, 1969), 229–343.

and the second formulas. It says nothing about the third formula and its relation to the first and the second formulas; nor does it say anything about the concept of the highest good. To remedy these defects, let us propose a Platonic account. In chapter 2, we noted that the relation of formal and generic categories can be understood as the first step in the progression from the transcendental unity of apperception down to the a priori principles of understanding and natural science. Likewise, we should consider the relation of formal and material imperatives as a progression from the formal unity of pure moral will to the systematic unity of all moral laws.

* * Progressive Construction

As Onora O'Neill insightfully observes, the three formulas of the categorical imperative introduce different moral considerations.[41] The formula of universal law considers the notion of action on a maxim and its form; the formula of humanity, the notion of persons and ends; and the formula of the kingdom of ends, a system of laws for a community as a whole. In addition to these differential aspects, we should also note that the idea of law is the common theme for all three formulas. Since the categorical imperative is the principle of self-legislation, it presupposes the idea of law. The three formulas can be understood as three different ways for articulating the idea of law. The articulation of an idea is a process of eidetic construction.

The formula of universal law is obviously the first requirement of law. The propositions of law must be stated in the impersonal form of universal propositions. The idea of law requires the distinction between agents and recipients of an act. Although all three formulas are addressed to moral agents, the second formula singles out persons as the recipients or beneficiaries of moral acts. The precepts of law are addressed not only to each agent but to a whole community. Moreover, those precepts should form a coherent system and be designed for the community as a whole. This systematic feature of law is stated in the formula of the kingdom of ends.

41. "Universal Laws and Ends-in-Themselves," *Monist* 72 (1989): 343.

The three formulas are three moments in a progressive construction from the idea of law considered as a formal abstract concept to an increasingly comprehensive idea of law involving the agents and recipients of moral acts and eventually the whole moral community. This is the eidetic construction in self-legislation, which is analogous to the eidetic construction in the legislation of the laws of nature. As we saw in chapter 2, the pure understanding prescribes laws for nature. It begins with the pure concepts of understanding, which give only the universal form of the laws of nature. By introducing transcendental and empirical content, the pure understanding moves progressively from the pure concepts to the schematized concepts and then to a priori principles, until it produces a whole system of a priori laws for the entire nature. In the domains of both natural and moral law, Kant's idea of a priori legislation takes the process of eidetic construction from the formal to the substantive level, from general to particular.

Let us reconsider some of the requirements for the categorical imperative in this context of eidetic construction. As we said, the precepts of law should be stated in the form of universal propositions. This is required for the sake of justice, and even Kant notes this point. He says that the requirement of universalization is meant to allow no unfair exceptions for the moral laws (*GMM* 424). If you make an exception for yourself, while everyone else obeys the moral law, you are taking advantage of others. That is a case of injustice. In Henry Sidgwick's view, the formula of universal law can be justified only on the ground of equity.[42] If the categorical imperative is accepted as a requirement of equity or justice, it is no longer a formal criterion but the expression of a substantive idea.

Once we admit the formula of universal law as a requirement of justice, the moral irrelevance of Kant's formal test becomes clearer. There are many maxims that cannot be universalized without contradiction and yet are not morally objectionable; for example, "I will buy lettuce but never sell it" or "I will try to be richer than someone

42. *The Methods of Ethics*, 7th ed. (London, 1907), 209–10.

else." Since in acting on these maxims no one takes advantage of anyone else, they do not violate any precepts of justice, although they cannot be universalized. Let us now imagine that you have a monopoly of lettuce and try to buy up all available lettuce and never sell it: then you will be in a position to take advantage of all those who need to have lettuce. Under those circumstances, your lettuce maxim becomes a question of justice. The same maxim can take on different moral significances, depending on how it affects other people.

In the domain of moral law, Kant takes for granted, the agents and their recipients belong to the same class. He never questions that only rational beings belong to this class. He never recognizes the moral obligation of rational beings to nonrational beings; he has difficulty accounting for our moral obligation to animals. This restriction, which underlies the formula of humanity, is also due to his faulty conception of law. In the second *Critique,* as we saw, he designates the moral law as the primary object of our respect, and even human beings become worthy of respect by virtue of their capacity for obeying the moral law. In his view, the moral law is worthy of respect because it is law; this is the idea of law for the sake of law. This idea is inevitable if the idea of law is derived from the autonomy of pure reason. If we say that law is for the sake of human beings, we assign an instrumental function to law. To design and obey such an instrumental law is the heteronomy of practical reason. The autonomy of practical reason means that its law serves no master other than itself. In this "autonomous" conception of law, the universal form is the only essential feature of law (*GMM* 421; C_2 27). The entire function of law is exhaustively displayed in its universal form.

This eccentric idea of law is largely responsible for Kant's excessive rigorism. Let us consider Kant's infamous reply to Constant: You hide in your house a helpless girl who is being hounded by an assailant. When the assailant appears at your door and asks whether you have seen the girl, should you tell him the truth? Kant thought that you should, because not to tell the truth is against the moral law. This is the height of rigorism. Some Kant scholars have tried to defend it, while others have tried to dismiss it.[43] In my view, this sort of rigorism is an unavoidable by-product of Kant's idea that the moral law should be obeyed for its own sake and nothing else. His rigorism is disturbing only because we believe that law should be, not the master, but a servant for our needs and even the needs of animals and plants.

Many scholars have tried to understand the nature of moral law after the model of natural law, because Kant equates the formula of universal law with the formula of the law of nature. But since the law of nature can mean either the mechanical law or the teleological law, there has been a serious dispute over how to interpret the formula of the law of nature. This dispute is largely misguided, because the moral law, or the law of human beings, is basically different from the law of nature, whether the latter is taken as mechanical or teleological. The law of nature does not admit the distinction between the agent of an act and its recipient; the laws governing atoms and molecules, plants and animals, do not depend on the idea of agency. The laws of nature are descriptive, but the laws of human beings are normative, and all normative laws presuppose rational agents. Because of these differences, even Kant says in his sober moment that the law of nature is only an analogue of the moral law.

Finally, the idea of law concerns the whole community, because law is for the sake of community. This idea should be embodied in the systematic unity of law, which achieves the harmony of all ends. This is the idea of collective rationality: the law should be rational not for any particular member of the community but for the whole community.[44] What sort of collective rationality is required for the kingdom of ends? It is the rationality of ends, not a formal but a substantive rationality. It belongs to an Idea of reason, because the kingdom of ends is an Idea of pure reason. It is equivalent to the Idea of an ideal republic or constitution, which was the central Idea for Kant's ethics in the first *Critique*. This Idea can be taken as the ulti-

43. This point is well discussed by Roger Sullivan in *Immanuel Kant's Moral Theory*, 173–77.

44. This point is well noted by Allen Wood in *Hegel's Ethical Thought*, 165–66.

mate end for the progression of Kant's idea of moral law. It begins with the autonomy of legislative reason and then goes through the three formulas of the categorical imperative. The Idea of moral law and its progressive development presuppose the kingdom of ends as its ultimate goal. The various formulas of the categorical imperative can now be seen as a progressive articulation of the Idea of the kingdom of ends. This is a substantive account of the progression, because it presupposes the Idea of the kingdom of ends and its justice as its first premise.

In this constructivist account, the first formula is not any more formal than the second and the third formulas. All of them are substantive. All of them can be called formal, because they belong to the highest level of generality. In Kant's conceptual scheme, as we have noted repeatedly, formal concepts and propositions are identified as those belonging to the highest generality. But the different formulas cannot be said to be equivalent, because they introduce different considerations for articulating the Idea of moral law. Nor can they be independent of one another, because those considerations are interrelated. But there is a reason for Kant's claim for the equivalence and independence of the three formulas. By using only one of them, he thought, he could produce the same moral maxims that he could produce by using either of the other two. He could obtain such a fortunate result only because he never used any one of them independently, but in a covert conjunction with the other two. Their covert conjunction was more or less inevitable, because the three formulas are based on a set of different but inseparable considerations.

This constructivist account gives some coherence to the three formulas of the categorical imperative in the *Groundwork*. Without it, we have to say that Kant has two sets of imperatives, formal and material, which represent the duality in his conception of the will. We also have to say that the duality of the will is due to his acceptance of two incompatible conceptions of practical reason, formal and substantive rationality. Because he accepts these two incompatible conceptions, he has two derivation schemes for the categorical imperative. In the formal scheme, he derives the formal imperative from formal practical reason; in the material scheme, he derives the material imperatives from material practical reason. Since Kant assumes the independence of these two schemes, he says that the different formulas of the categorical imperative are independent. Moreover, he dogmatically asserts their equivalence for the same reason that had led him to believe the equivalence of formal and material categories in the first *Critique*. This account of Kant's position appears to be the only alternative to the constructivist account I have just given.

According to the alternative account, Kant begins the *Groundwork* with the formal scheme of derivation and then switches over to the material scheme, without giving any reasons. He never explains the relation of these two derivation schemes. Nor does he give any reason for his thesis that the three formulas are independent and equivalent. The relation of formal and material practical reason remains the greatest mystery in his moral theory. This mystery and obscurity are dissolved by the constructivist account. I have to confess that the constructivist account does not readily apply to the second *Critique*, where Kant stays faithful to the formal derivation scheme throughout. But even there we can notice something like a progressive construction. He begins with the formula of universal law and derives the respect for humanity from the respect for the moral law. Then he derives the concept of the highest good by extending the idea of moral good. This is a sort of progression from the most abstract idea of moral law to its concrete manifestation, a process of progressive articulation and concretion.

So far we have talked as though the kingdom of ends were interchangeable with the highest good. Let us see whether this is a hasty and faulty assumption. The idea of the kingdom of ends is a much richer concept than the concept of a moral community. In a stringent sense, the concept of a moral community may admit only the moral good or moral ends, but the kingdom of ends can admit many kinds of ends and values other than moral ends and values. Likewise, the concept of the highest good is a much richer concept than the concept of the moral good. The concept of the highest good can be understood in two different contexts. In the individual context, the highest good is the union of moral perfection and its commensurate happiness, and in the collective context, the highest good is the community that can realize the ends and goals of its members in a systematic harmony.

The highest good in the collective sense is equivalent to the kingdom of ends. It is neither restricted to individual morality nor confined within social institutions of justice but includes both of them and more: the harmonious development of all human talents and capacity. As we saw in chapter 3, Kant holds that the ultimate end of history is to secure right moral and social order as a prerequisite for the complete development of all human talents and capacities. The ultimate end of history is the highest good in the collective sense. And the same highest good is also the ultimate end for Kant's derivation of the three formulas of the categorical imperative. Thus the idea of progressive articulation and realization brings together Kant's moral philosophy and his philosophy of history.

This is a remarkable outcome and a great surprise. It confirms the conclusion of chapter 3 against the standard view that Kant's historical writings are extraneous to his Critical Philosophy. Some Kant scholars have even branded his historical writings as dogmatic or pre-Critical, although they were written at the height of his Critical period. Others have tried to defend him by designating his historical essays as peripheral or occasional reflections. But his philosophy of history is neither extraneous nor peripheral but essential to his moral philosophy if it is seen in the context of his Platonic constructivism. Kant says that the Ideas of pure reason constitute the ultimate end of human history. In his ethics, he says that the highest good and the kingdom of ends are the Ideas of pure reason. If ethics and history are indeed governed by the same Ideas of pure reason, they cannot be separated from each other. Their connection is inevitable and essential.[45]

45. In *Kant and the Philosophy of History* Yovel employs Kant's ethical concepts in his effort to link Kant's moral philosophy to his philosophy of history. He can make only a partially convincing case for his thesis, because he does not realize the importance of Platonism in Kant's philosophy.

5 The *Metaphysics of Morals:* Kant's Platonic Reversion

* * * * * * * * * * * * * * * * * *

In his *Metaphysics of Morals* Kant appears to forget his formalist conception of practical reason and ignore the distinction between form and content in ethics. This work comprises two parts: the *Metaphysical Principles of Justice* (*KGS* 6:203–372) and the *Metaphysical Principles of Virtue* (*KGS* 6:375–491). These two parts reflect his distinction between the duty of justice (juridical or political duties) and the duty of virtue (ethical duties). Even this distinction could not have been made within the framework of formal practical reason, because it is a substantive distinction. He assigns the duties of justice to external freedom and the duties of virtue to internal freedom. Internal freedom is the freedom of moral will; external freedom is political and social freedom. Hence his distinction between virtue and justice roughly corresponds to the traditional distinction between ethics and politics.

* * The Domain of External Freedom

The *Metaphysical Principles of Justice* presents the principle of justice. This is the principle for establishing a just social order for the exercise of external freedom. One of the lessons Kant learned from Rousseau was the importance of freedom and the difficulty of coordinating individual liberties. Without law, Kant says, our external freedom can only lead to an anarchy of terror and savagery (*LE* 17). There are many different kinds of law for establishing a social order, and most of them result in orders of injustice. A just social order can be established by regulating the external freedom of everyone by a set of rules that can be accepted as universal laws. Kant states the principle of justice as follows: "Every action is just [right] that in itself or in its maxim is such that the freedom of the will of each can coexist together with the freedom of everyone in accordance with a universal law" (*MM* 230, trans. Ladd).

The function of a universal law is to secure the equality of everyone in the exercise of freedom. The universality of law is appreciated for its substantive rather than its formal function. Equality of freedom means equality of rights; the concept of external freedom is interchangeable with the concept of rights. Kant says that the principle of innate freedom is the source of all rights (*MM* 237). The principle of innate freedom is the innate right to external freedom under universal laws. It contains the right to innate equality, independence from others, sovereignty over oneself, and liberty to do anything to others that does not by itself detract from what is theirs. The innate right eventually expands to the property right of acquisition and disposition.

All these rights belong to private law, insofar as they do not interfere with one another. Kant believes that they can be known a priori by every human being (*MM* 297). Hence they require no legislation. In this regard, public law is different from private law; the former is an expression of the collective will, which belongs to a civil society (*MM* 311). The constitution of a civil society is the collective action of a community. Kant accepts the theory of social contract (*MM* 315). He identifies the state as the general united will (*MM* 313), thereby formally installing Rousseau's theory of general will at the center of his theory of public law.

The ultimate end of a civil society is to secure equality and justice for all citizens. Kant says that the well-being of a state should not be confused with the well-being or happiness of its citizens, which can sometimes be better attained in the state of nature or under a despotic government. The well-being of a state consists only in the constitution that conforms most closely to the principles of justice (*MM* 318). The Idea of a constitution is exactly one of the Platonic Ideas Kant had accepted for his ethics in the first *Critique*. Kant has finally returned to the ethics of Platonic Ideas; his theory of justice reads like a parade of Platonic Ideas and their eidetic articulation.

In his theory of justice, Kant time and again appeals to the Ideas of pure reason. The original community of possession is an Idea; so is the concept of private possession in distinction from the empirical concept of physical possession (*MM* 250–55). The concept of civil society that limits the individual will in accordance with the general will is also an Idea of reason, because the concept of general will is an Idea (*MM* 306). The concept of a civil state is the state in the Idea *(der Staat in der Idee)* as it ought to be according to pure principles of justice; this Idea serves as an internal standard *(norma)* for every actual union of men in a commonwealth (*MM* 313). The original contract, by which individuals can get out of the state of nature, is not a historical or empirical concept but an Idea of reason (*MM* 315). So is the concept of an ideal state, which Kant identifies with a republican constitution (*MM* 341). The rational ideal of human community takes its final form in the Idea of a peaceful universal community of all nations (*MM* 352).

Kant's conception of normative political Ideas has become much richer than it was in the first *Critique*, in which he had mentioned only one normative political Idea, namely, the Idea of a republican constitution. In his theory of justice he parades a whole battery of Ideas, ranging from the Idea of the original contract to the Idea of a universal community of all nations. But he does not identify this battery of Ideas with Platonic Forms. Where and how has he gotten hold of these Ideas? Are they also located in Platonic Heaven? Can he revert to these Ideas without repudiating his doctrine of moral autonomy? These questions are our natural responses to his theory of justice.

Kant appears to recognize some order of progression or development for the Ideas of reason. We may be able to capture it by following Ernest Weinrib's genetic account for Kant's theory of law.[1] He says that Kant recognizes three stages in the development of law and that these stages are revealed in Kant's observations on Ulpian's three precepts of natural law (*MM* 236–37). These three precepts are: (1) Be an honorable man *(honeste vive)*; (2) Do no one an injustice *(neminem laede)*; and (3) Enter into a society with others in which each per-

---

1. "Law as a Kantian Idea of Reason," *Columbia Law Review* 87 (1987): 472–508.

son can get and keep what is his or her own *(suum cuique tribue)*. In Ulpian's doctrine of natural law these three precepts have no relation to any idea of development on different stages. Nor does the third precept have any connection with the idea of social contract. But Kant says that the third precept (Give to each what is his own) makes no sense as it stands, since no one can give someone something that already belongs to him. In order to make sense of it, he says, it must be read as a precept for social contract: Enter into a condition under which each person is guaranteed what is his own (*MM* 237).

Kant is conscious of giving Ulpian's three precepts a meaning quite different from their original one. He admits that he is developing a new meaning that may not have been in Ulpian's own mind. By this hermeneutic freedom, Kant converts Ulpian's three precepts of natural law into three stages of its development, from its beginning in the will of an agent to a complete system of public law. This is the central point in Weinrib's account. The first precept (Be an honorable man) is addressed to a single agent, whose existence constitutes the first stage. The second precept (Do no one an injustice) is addressed to an agent who is in interaction with another agent; it belongs to the second stage. The third precept (Give to each what is his own) is addressed to an agent who has to form a society with others; it belongs to the third stage. Let us consider these three stages in greater detail, following Weinrib's illuminating exposition.

The first stage is the recognition of a human being as a rational agent. A human being recognizes himself as a self-determining agent and also attributes to others the same capacity. The idea of self-determination is inevitably connected with the idea of possession; the power of autonomy cannot be exercised without the possibility of using objects. Hence the innate right to freedom is first manifested as the right of acquiring and using properties. But the exercise of property rights projects the agent into the public world. Hence his first duty and right is to assert himself as a juridical person. Kant calls it the matter of juridical honor: "Juridical honor consists in asserting one's own worth as a human being in relation to others, and this duty is expressed in the proposition: 'Do not make yourself into a mere means for others, but be at the same time an end for them'" (*MM* 236, trans. Ladd).

The second stage is the stage of commutative justice. Different agents come into interaction, acquire private properties, and make contracts. The interaction of free agents engages the external aspect of practical reason. That is, it is concerned not with the internal factors of intentions and motivations but with the external factors of coordination and cooperation. These external factors are still the affairs of private individuals in interaction. The second stage is the stage of private law. At this stage, the requirement of justice is satisfied as long as the freedom of each agent is compatible with the freedom of all other agents under a universal law. A world that can satisfy this requirement is not purely private or subjective. It has its own publicity and objectivity; it is a public world of private individuals.

The third stage is the stage of public law. The interaction of free agents is no longer limited to private transactions. They constitute civil society, become citizens, and promulgate public law. Public law establishes the organs of public administration and other public institutions of justice. Some of them are for the welfare of the poor; others are for the punishment of the wicked. Public law also institutes the publicly authorized coercion. All of these public institutions are for realizing the Idea of an ideal state. This Idea of justice cannot be fully realized in any single state alone, because the different states can still be in the state of nature against each other. They have to form an international order of justice. Hence Kant's theory of justice ends in his Idea of a global community of different states (*MM* 352).

The progression of these three stages is much like the progression of the three formulas of the categorical imperative in the *Groundwork*. The first stage resembles the first formula. It recognizes only the freedom of a single agent, which is purely formal or potential, just as the first formula recognizes the universality of moral laws, their purely formal aspect. The second stage recognizes the relation of a free agent to others, which is also the case with the second formula of the categorical imperative. The third stage is concerned with civil society; the third formula is for the kingdom of ends. Civil society is a kingdom of ends on the political level.

This progression can also be characterized as a movement from the internal world of individuals to the external world of civil society. It moves from the innate right to freedom to the external rights of possession and transaction. In this progression, Kant makes no pretense of using any formal scheme of derivation; from beginning to end he remains faithful to his substantive scheme. Even the concept of the innate right is not formal but substantive. It is as substantive as the concepts of private and public law, which are derived from it. Kant's derivation of legal rights and duties is a progression of substantive Ideas in pure reason. The progression of these Ideas belongs to Kant's scheme of eidetic construction. It begins with one ultimate Idea of a perfect community and articulates its character by constructing a series of Ideas as it descends to the context of empirical and historical conditions. Hence it is a story of descent from Platonic Heaven to this world; it is a story of progressive realization.

Autonomy of the moral will or practical reason should now be reconceived as the will of the agent who undertakes the program of eidetic construction. By this process, practical reason gives itself the law for governing its practical affairs. That is, it makes its own social order, and this is the essence of practical autonomy. Even the initial Idea, with which practical reason begins its eidetic construction, should not be construed as an external imposition on its autonomy, because the transcendental normative Ideas are not external to pure reason. They are its innermost possessions; they constitute its essential ends (A819/B847).

* * The Kingdom of Ends

Kant defines ethical duties as those ends that are at the same time duties. There are two duties of this kind: the perfection of oneself and the happiness of others (*MM* 385). Because these ends are at the same time duties, he says, they generate their own maxims. Hence the maxims of ethical duties are quite different from the maxims of juridical duties. The latter must meet only the formal requirement; the former must fulfill the material requirement. "The [juridical duties] can only concern the formal element of the maxims; the [ethical virtues], however, concerns their matter, namely an end which is at the same time conceived as a duty" (*MM* 394–95, trans. Ellington). Kant now recognizes two different types of maxim, formal and material. The formal maxim is concerned only with its form; the material maxim, with its matter. The matter of a maxim is the end of its action. A formal maxim is valid if and only if it can be accepted as a universal law for governing the domain of external freedom, regardless of the end of its action. A material maxim is valid if and only if it is linked to an end that is at the same time a duty. The duties of justice are determined by formal maxims; the duties of virtue, by material maxims. Because justice and virtue involve different types of maxim, the principle of virtue is different from the principle of justice. The principle of virtue is:

> Act according to a maxim whose ends are such that there can be a universal law that everyone have these ends. (*MM* 395, trans. Ellington)

In the principle of virtue, universal laws are end-dependent; in the principle of justice, universal laws are end-independent. For the clarification of this difference, let us consider the following two formulas:

1. A maxim is valid if it can be universalized.
2. A maxim can be universalized if it is valid.

The principle of justice takes formula 1, while the principle of virtue takes formula 2. Formula 1 first determines whether a maxim can or cannot be accepted as a universal law without reference to an end. It produces a legalistic conception of ethics. Formula 2 first determines whether an end should or should not be accepted universally. A universally acceptable end yields a universalizable maxim. Formula 2 yields a teleological conception of ethics; the nature of an end is the ultimate ethical consideration. In these two formulas, universalization plays different roles. In formula 1, it serves as the test for adopting a maxim as a universal law; in formula 2, it is the result of accepting an end as obligatory.

In chapter 4, we noted the distinction between the intrinsic and the consequential values of a moral act. This distinction is also relevant for explaining the difference between formulas 1 and 2. If we accept or reject a moral maxim on the basis of the consequential value of an act, we rely on formula 1. On the other hand, if we accept or reject a moral maxim on the basis of its intrinsic value, we rely on formula 2. Before the *Metaphysics of Morals*, Kant tried to resolve all ethical problems by formula 1. Hence his conception of ethics was highly legalistic and too restrictive.[2]

In his *Lectures on Ethics* Kant had already experienced the awkwardness of accommodating all ethical duties within his legalistic formula. What reasons could he give for condemning private vices, which do not infringe upon the freedom of others? "May a man, for instance, mutilate his body for profit? May he sell a tooth? May he surrender himself at a price to the highest bidder?" (*LE* 43). Kant regarded these acts as debasing and immoral, though they do not violate the freedom of anyone else. Within his legalistic ethics, however, he could not simply say that they were debasing and immoral; he had to find legalistic reasons for his moral judgment, and he tried to find those reasons in the maxims governing those acts. Kant defined a maxim as a subjective law underlying the intent of an act (*LE* 43). He proposed the following way to test the moral character of a maxim or intent: "If the intent of the action can without self-contradiction be universalized, it is morally possible; if it cannot be so universalized without contradicting itself, it is morally impossible" (*LE* 44).

The test of universalization stems from his legalistic conception of moral law. But the formal test of self-contradiction is not strong enough to rule out the maxim of selling or mutilating oneself for profit. It is as self-consistent as the maxim of improving oneself. By "self-contradiction" of a maxim, Kant means something else. In the case of self-regarding acts, which do not concern the freedom of others, he means the incompatibility of a maxim with the dignity of humanity. When we sell ourselves for profit, he says, we dishonor human nature in our own persons by turning ourselves into things

2. This point is well noted by Thomas Hill in "Kant on Imperfect Duty and Supererogation," *Kant-Studien* 62 (1971): 74.

(*LE* 43). In the case of other-regarding acts, he means the unacceptability of a maxim as a universal rule for the harmony of free wills (*LE* 44). The supposedly formal test of self-contradiction presupposes the material concept of harmony or dignity. It cannot be a formal test. Kant's idea of a formal test is like a rubber band. This flexibility and indeterminacy is required by his determination to squeeze the entire ethics into his legalistic theory of morality.

In his Copernican revolution in ethics, Kant tries to dissociate his formal test from all material concepts. In this formalist program, he cannot differentiate self-regarding acts from other-regarding acts, because such a differentiation requires substantive considerations. So he ignores the distinction between ethics and politics, the questions of virtue and the questions of justice, in the *Groundwork* and the second *Critique*. In the *Metaphysics of Morals*, however, he affirms this distinction in terms of external and internal freedom. He has abandoned his formalist program and reinstated his earlier substantive approach of the first *Critique*. The distinction between justice and virtue corresponds to the difference between the two Platonic Ideas he had recognized in the first *Critique:* the Idea of a virtuous person and the Idea of a republican constitution.

Kant now restricts the legalistic conception of law to the domain of justice and constructs his theory of virtue in terms of ends. In his theory of virtue, the notion of a universalizable maxim is no longer primary; it is derived from the notion of obligatory ends. The formula of universal law becomes only a formality. In the new ethics of ends, Kant calls practical reason the faculty of ends (*MM* 395) and defines ethics as "the system of the ends of practical reasons" (*MM* 381). This is a radically different view of practical reason from the one he had advocated in his Copernican revolution. He had stressed the formal character of pure practical reason, which is totally independent of material concepts of the good. But the concept of ends is a material concept par excellence in ethics, and his ethics of ends is the reversal of his Copernican revolution.

In his discussion of ethical virtues, Kant almost completely ignores his earlier formalism and appeals to the two obligatory ends of perfecting oneself and securing the happiness of others. He divides all ethical duties into (1) duties to oneself and (2) duties to others, and he subdivides the former into (3) perfect duties to oneself and (4) imperfect duties to oneself (*MM* 421–47). Perfect duties to oneself are further divided into those duties to oneself as an animal being and those duties to oneself as a moral being. The first perfect duty to oneself as an animal being is to preserve oneself in one's animal nature. Kant says that this duty forbids suicide, wanton self-abuse, and self-stupefaction through the immoderate use of food and drink. Suicide is the total destruction of oneself as an animal being, and the others are partial self-destructions. All of these are forbidden, because they contravene the duty of preserving oneself as an animal being, which is essential for the duty of perfecting oneself.

In his discussion of perfect duties, Kant mentions neither the maxim nor its universal form. Suicide is wrong not because of its maxim but because it goes against the duty of preserving one's natural being and because it destroys the natural basis of oneself as a moral being (*MM* 422–23). Following his discussion of suicide, he raises many casuistical questions. Is it self-murder to plunge oneself into certain death (as Curtius did) in order to save one's country? Should we regard the sacrifice of oneself for the good of humankind as a heroic deed? If one is given, as Seneca was given, the choice between suicide and an unjust death sentence, is suicide permissible? Bitten by a mad dog, a man already feels hydrophobia coming upon him. Since he is convinced that there is no cure for this malady, he decides to terminate his life as the only way to avoid spreading his misfortune to other people. Is he doing anything wrong? Kant answers none of these questions; he only presents them as questions to be considered.

There is no doubt about how he would answer those questions if he were still operating under the rigor of his formalism.[3] In fact, there are some Kant scholars who take these casuistical questions to mean that he does not allow suicide even for a victim of rabies.[4] They

3. The difference between Kant's accounts of suicide in the *Groundwork* and in the *Metaphysics of Morals* is well noted by Nelson Potter in "Kant on Ends That Are At the Same Time Duties," *Pacific Philosophical Quarterly* 66 (1985), 78–92.

4. Roger Sullivan, *Immanuel Kant's Moral Theory* (Cambridge, 1989), 202.

assume that Kant is still rigidly holding on to his formalism. If he were, he would not even permit these questions to be raised, because all of them concern the contingent circumstances for suicide, which are totally irrelevant under his formal practical principle. Why, then, does Kant raise these casuistical questions? The questions make sense only if we assume that he is reorienting his thought from formal to material considerations. All the casuistical questions are concerned with competing ends, and the choice of competing ends is a central function for ethics of ends. This was inconceivable under the formal conception of practical reason, because the choice of competing ends involves substantive considerations.

The rigor of formalism is not much in evidence even in Kant's discussion of the duty to oneself as a moral being (*MM* 429–37). He says that this duty is opposed to the vices of lying, avarice, and false humility (servility). He condemns lying as a vice, not because of any maxims, but because it obliterates the dignity of a liar as a human being and because it goes against the natural purpose of communication. By *avarice* Kant means stinginess. It is a vice that makes it impossible to provide adequately for one's true needs in life. Servility is a vice by which one denies one's dignity as a human being. It goes against the virtue of self-esteem. Kant handles all of these virtues and vices on substantive grounds; he never tries to back his views up with formal considerations.

Kant's conception of moral perfection and rational agency also changes. In the *Groundwork* he had identified moral agency with the good will and had insisted on its total independence from natural conditions:

> Even if, by some special disfavor of destiny or by the niggardly step-motherly nature, this will is entirely lacking in power to carry out its intentions; if by its utmost effort it still accomplishes nothing, and only good will is left (not, admittedly, as a mere wish, but as straining of every means so far as they are in our control); even then it would still shine like a jewel for its own sake as something which has its full value in itself. Its usefulness or fruitfulness can neither add to, nor subtract from, this value. (*GMM* 394, trans. Paton)

This view of the moral will, that is, that it should be independent of all natural conditions, is indeed radical, but it is dictated by Kant's formal conception of practical reason and its autonomy. Formal reason can never depend on anything external without relinquishing its autonomy, and natural conditions and natural dispositions are surely external to formal reason. In the *Dreams,* as we saw in chapter 1, Kant had held an equally radical view of the moral will. Since the morality of an action concerns the inner state of a spiritual being, he had said, a moral action can produce adequate results in the spiritual world, even when it fails to do so in the physical world (*KGS* 2:336). Moral intentions and actions have different efficacies in the two worlds. Their spiritual effects are governed by spiritual laws *(pneumatisher Gesetze),* and their physical effects by physical laws.

In the *Metaphysics of Morals* Kant no longer subscribes to a sharp separation between natural and moral orders, or between natural and moral persons. He freely admits the importance of a natural person *(homo phaenomenon)* for the existence of a moral person *(homo noumenon).* He says that the abuse of a natural person is morally wrong because it destroys the subject of morality (*MM* 423). As to moral perfection, he had said in the *Groundwork* that it had nothing to do with inclinations or dispositions. In fact, the more recalcitrant dispositions one has to fight against, the greater moral merit one is said to achieve. Now he regards moral dispositions as essential elements in the moral character of a person; the concept of moral perfection includes the concept of morally perfect dispositions, which are acquired through long practice. A morally perfect disposition *(Gesinnung)* is none other than moral virtue (*MM* 383).

This is Kant's substantive conception of moral agency, which underlies Onora O'Neill's argument of agency in her interpretation of the categorical imperative. She maintains that the various formulas of the categorical imperative should be interpreted in such a way that they cannot impair the capacity of human beings as moral or rational agents.[5] For example, the maxims of deceit and violence cannot pass the formal test of universalization, because their universal-

5. "Universal Laws and Ends-in-Themselves," *Monist* 72 (1989): 353–54.

ization would destroy the rational agency of people. She assumes that human beings can maintain their moral and rational agency only by securing a set of material conditions, such as food, health, and security.

To be sure, it is obvious that the moral agency of rational people requires the support of material conditions. But Kant's Copernican revolution in ethics flouts this commonsense truth. In his discussion of moral agents and moral will in the *Groundwork* and the second *Critique* he emphatically asserts the independence of moral will from the material conditions. Only in the *Metaphysics of Morals* does he acknowledges the importance of the natural dimension of human beings for their moral vocation. In her agency-oriented interpretation of Kant's ethics, O'Neill relocates the categorical imperative from the *Groundwork* and the second *Critique* to the *Metaphysics of Morals*.

Kant divides the duties to others into (1) the duties of love and (2) the duties of respect. Only in his discussion of the duties of love does he makes use of the formula of universal law. He proposes to consider why the maxim of benevolence should be accepted as a universal law. Since I want every other man to be benevolent to me, he says, I should also be benevolent to every other man (*MM* 451). This sounds like the repetition of his argument in the *Groundwork*, but it takes an unexpected direction. Because "all other men" with the exception of myself would not be "all men," Kant says, the law prescribing the duty of benevolence should include myself because it is a universal law. Thus he links the universality of the law to the universal idea of humanity (*MM* 451).

In this argument, Kant derives the universality of the maxim of benevolence from the universality of humanity. The selfish maxim of getting help from others but giving none to others is rejected because it is inconsistent with the universality of this law. Kant never says that such a maxim cannot be universalized, but he points out that it is incompatible with the idea of needy rational beings, united by nature in one dwelling place for mutual aid (*MM* 453). This argument is based on natural teleology and the kingdom of ends. He uses even the formula of universal law only to secure equality in the duty of mutual benevolence: "it permits me to be benevolent to my-self under the condition that I also am benevolent to everyone else" (*MM* 451, trans. Ellington). The formula of universal law is clearly understood as a substantive rule of equity for his theory of virtue, as it is for his theory of justice.

As far as the maxim of benevolence is concerned, it is based on the duty of all men toward one another, that is, the duty of promoting the happiness of each other (*MM* 450). In this Kant is only reaffirm-ing the principle of universal affection or benevolence from the *Observations*. His teleological ethics in the *Metaphysics of Morals* is as pre-Critical as his ethics was in the *Observations*. In his discussion of the duty of respect for others, he again reaffirms the principle of uni-versal esteem or respect from the *Observations*. The duty of respect is securely based on the dignity of human beings. Because of their dignity, they should never be used as mere means. We should never despise or mock other people, nor should we ever slander or abuse them. Pride is also a vice: it goes against one's proper esteem of others. Pride amounts to the demand of special esteem from other people, which goes against the equal dignity of all human beings. The duty of respect is far more important than the duty of love. The omission of the latter represents only a lack of virtue, but the omis-sion of the former is a vice. Even this point is a carryover from the *Observations*, and the comparative ranking of two duties or virtues cannot be made from a formal perspective.

Let us consider the relation of the concept of dignity to the moral law. In the second *Critique* Kant derived the respect for persons from the respect for moral law. Human beings have dignity because they can obey the moral law. This is the primacy of moral law over the dignity of human beings, which has led to the troublesome ques-tion whether immoral or amoral human beings (remorseless sin-ners, idiots, and children) have any dignity. Many Kant scholars have found it difficult to give a satisfactory answer to this question, but the question is forestalled by the position Kant takes in the *Meta-physics of Morals*, namely, that human dignity is assumed to be prior to moral law. The concept of human dignity now stands as one of the substantive ideas for the formulation of moral laws.

* * The Concept of the Highest Good

There is one serious defect in Kant's ethics of ends: he never demonstrates the existence of obligatory ends. Without giving any reason, he names two such ends, the perfection of oneself and the happiness of others (*MM* 385). This is a glaring gap in his theory of virtue. To be sure, he gives one feeble argument for the existence of obligatory ends. He says that there must be some obligatory ends for the possibility of the categorical imperative, that is, that "a categorical imperative would be impossible" without such ends (*MM* 385). He implies that the existence of the categorical imperative proves the existence of obligatory ends. This implied claim should be valid if the categorical imperative is defined in terms of obligatory ends, but Kant has never provided such a definition.

In the *Groundwork* he presented his notion of the categorical imperative within the framework of formal practical reason and the Copernican revolution in ethics. He could not admit the concept of ends in this definition, because it is not a formal but a substantive concept. So he gave his definition of the categorical imperative only in terms of maxims and relegated the notion of ends to the domain of hypothetical imperatives. The categorical imperative is end-independent; the hypothetical imperative is end-dependent. Hence the existence of the categorical imperative proves the existence of universalizable maxims but does not prove the existence of obligatory ends. In his new ethics of ends, Kant may be reconceiving the categorical imperative in terms of ends and may redefine it as an imperative of a categorical or obligatory end. In that case, he must demonstrate the existence of such an end before he can assert the existence of the categorical imperative.

Even if we accept the idea of obligatory ends, why should they be identified as the perfection of oneself and the happiness of others? This question is seldom discussed among Kant scholars, chiefly because he says so little for them to discuss. I know of only two plausible accounts. One can be traced back to the Wolffian ethics of perfection. As we noted in chapter 1, Christian Wolff says that the principle of perfection includes the perfection of oneself and the happiness of others. It is plausible that Kant has decided to reinstate this Wolffian principle. But this account is not quite satisfactory until and unless we can adduce Kantian reasons for its reinstatement. The other plausible account I have in mind appears to provide some rationale for its reinstatement. This account has been proposed by Nelson Potter, who believes that the concept of the highest good is the ultimate ground for Kant's theory of obligatory ends.[6]

The concept of the highest good contains two components: moral virtue and happiness. Let us ignore the commensurate relation between these two components, or, rather, let us leave it to the care of an omniscient and omnipotent governor of the universe, as Lewis White Beck says. Potter points out that our duties to these two components are different, depending on whether the highest good is ours or someone else's. In the case of the highest good for ourselves, we have no duty to seek our happiness, because we are by nature inclined to seek it; our only duty is to achieve our moral perfection. In the case of the highest good for others, we cannot seek their moral perfection, because it is not within our control. But we have the duty to promote their happiness, because we do not have the natural inclination to do it. Hence the duty to realize the obligatory ends is the same as the duty to promote the highest good.

This is Potter's thesis. Although it is ingenious, its scope is not broad enough for it to give a complete account of all obligatory ends. Potter's thesis makes my moral perfection alone my obligatory end, but Kant names as my obligatory end my entire perfection, including my natural perfection. We can fill this gap between Potter's thesis and Kant's own account by adopting John Silber's refinement of the concept of the highest good, according to which it can be understood as the conjunction of the moral good and the natural good.[7] Although Silber equates the natural good with happiness, we can do better by defining it as the realization of natural ends. Whereas the concept of happiness is highly indefinite, as Kant says, the concept of natural ends and their realization is much more definite.

6. "Kant on Ends That Are At the Same Time Duties," 84.
7. "The Moral Good and the Natural Good," *Review of Metaphysics* 36 (1982): 397–437.

In the last *Critique,* as we will see later, Kant says that the concept of happiness plays different roles for the ultimate ends of animals and rational beings (C_3 430–31). Happiness can fulfill the ultimate end of animals but not that of rational beings. In the *Idea for a Universal History,* as we saw in chapter 3, the ultimate destiny of human beings is to realize all their talents and capacities. Hence the realization of natural ends is a much broader and much richer Kantian conception of the natural good for human beings than merely achieving their happiness. This broader and richer conception of the natural good need not exclude happiness; happiness can be taken as one of the natural ends, or it can be defined as the realization of all ends. But we do not have the duty to seek happiness for ourselves because we are naturally inclined to do it. There are, however, some natural ends for whose development we have no natural inclination, even though they are our own. Hence they are the objects of our moral duties.

The redefinition of the natural good in terms of natural ends can also improve the concept of obligatory ends for others. Our duty to promote the happiness of others can take on many absurd implications if it is understood without any normative constraints. If my neighbor can find happiness only in alcohol and drugs, I will have the duty to provide those substances for him. If his natural good is understood in terms of natural ends rather than happiness, I will have the duty to take him to a rehabilitation center even against his will or at the expense of his happiness. As Kant says, we can do nothing for the moral perfection of others, but we can do many things for their natural perfection. Hence the concept of natural perfection or the natural good is a far better notion of obligatory ends for others than the concept of their happiness.

The concept of happiness is ambiguous: it can be taken empirically or normatively. In its empirical sense, happiness is a subjective mental state; in its normative sense, it is much more than that. One cannot be happy without fulfilling certain normative conditions. For example, a drug addict may be considered happy on the empirical level but should be considered unhappy on the normative level. Likewise, Oedipus Rex is happy in the empirical sense before he discovers his crimes but unhappy in the normative sense. The normative sense of happiness cannot be defined without presupposing a theory of natural and moral ends.[8]

If the concept of the highest good is defined in terms of moral and natural ends, it also contains the notion of a hierarchy of ends. This hierarchy obtains in the context of the individual as well as in the context of the community. For any individual, the concept of the highest good not only contains a complete summation of all ends but ranks those ends in terms of their priority. As Nelson Potter correctly points out, Kant's discussion of the obligatory ends for oneself is chiefly concerned with the question of priority for the various ends.[9] For example, to demean oneself for social advancement is bad, because it is to sacrifice the higher end of human dignity for the lower end of material gain. Kant's entire discussion of one's duty to oneself becomes much more intelligible and coherent if it is understood in terms of an unmentioned system or hierarchy of ends. This system of ends is dictated for each individual by the concept of the highest good.

The question of priority is also important for determining our duty to others. Though we have the duty to promote their happiness, we should not do so when that happiness can be obtained only at the expense of their moral virtue. We should respect the priority ranking of the moral and the natural good not only for ourselves but for others. This question of respecting the relative importance of the moral and the natural good is quite different from the question of the exact apportionment of happiness to virtue, although both concern the relation of the two goods within the concept of the highest good. One is a question of priority, while the other is a question of justice. Although we have no power and perhaps no right to handle the second question, we have no right to avoid the first one, because the priority of moral over natural good is dictated by the moral law.

In the context of the community, the concept of the highest good is the systematic coordination of the good of all its members. It

---

8. These two conceptions of happiness are well discussed by Richard Kraut in "Two Conceptions of Happiness," *Philosophical Review* 88 (1979): 167–97.

9. "Kant on Ends That Are At the Same Time Duties," 89–90.

should also contain the priority ranking of different goods. Without such a systematic coordination, we would have no reliable way of determining how much is demanded by our duty to others. If the happiness of others were the only measure for determining our duty to others, your neighbor might have the right to demand even your Rolls Royce if he were awfully unhappy with his Chevy. So there must be a way of determining the relative weights of ends for all members of a community. Such a collective system of ends is the kingdom of ends.

This is my elaboration and extension of Nelson Potter's thesis. If it is correct, it is the concept of the highest good that determines not only the obligatory ends but also their relative rankings. This is the ultimate Idea of pure reason, which Kant once identified as the Idea of "the necessary unity of all possible ends" (A328/B385). Kant's theory of virtue articulates a system of ends and duties derived from one ultimate Idea, namely, the concept of the highest good. This derivation can also be achieved by the method of eidetic construction in the same way the derivation of Ideas is obtained in Kant's theory of justice. The particular ends and duties are generated by articulating the ultimate Idea of the highest good in the context of empirical and historical conditions. Just like the story of juridical Ideas, the articulation of the ultimate ethical Idea is a story of its descent and of its progressive realization in this world.

We have already noted that the Idea of the highest good is equivalent to the Idea of the kingdom of ends. The two parts of Kant's *Metaphysics of Morals* present two versions of one and the same Idea: the kingdom of ends on the legal level and the kingdom of ends on the ethical level. The ethical kingdom of ends takes two forms: the kingdom of ends for one individual and the kingdom of ends for the whole community. All these different forms of kingdom of ends are only different specifications of one Idea of pure reason, the concept of the highest good. In Kant's ethics, the concept of the highest good occupies the same place that is given the Form of the Good in Plato's *Republic*. It is the ultimate source of all Ideas of practical reason for his theory of justice and virtue. By the process of eidetic construction, it becomes a system of all rights and duties and a system of all ends and goods.

* * The Descent of Platonic Ideas

I hope I have shown that the concept of the highest good is the central principle of the *Metaphysics of Morals*. This is indeed an unconventional way of reading Kant's text. The firmly established tradition has been to read the *Metaphysics of Morals* as an application of the moral theory laid out in the *Groundwork for the Metaphysics of Morals*. In fact Kant's own claim was that the *Groundwork* was meant to lay the foundation for the *Metaphysics of Morals*. Taking his words at face value, Kant scholars have tried to interpret the *Metaphysics of Morals* as a systematic application of the categorical imperative. Mary Gregor regards it as "a procedure which implies a patient search for criteria through which duties can be derived, step by step, from the categorical imperative."[10]

Instead of studying Kant's own application of the categorical imperative, Gregor says, most students of Kant's ethics totally disregard the *Metaphysics of Morals* and construct their own versions of a metaphysics of morals. As far as they are concerned, Kant might as well not have written the *Metaphysics of Morals*. But the neglect of this important work, Gregor maintains, has led to a gross distortion and misunderstanding of Kant's "formalism." If this work had been studied carefully, the prevalent views that the consequences, ends, and circumstances of our actions are morally irrelevant and that the freedom from logical contradiction is a sufficient test of a moral maxim could never have taken root.[11]

Gregor claims that the duties of justice and virtue are all derived from the categorical imperative. Her claim is ambiguous, because

10. *Laws of Freedom* (New York, 1963), xii. Bruce Aune follows a similar method in *Kant's Theory of Morals* (Princeton, 1979), 131–201.

11. Gregor, *Laws of Freedom*, xi. Onora O'Neill is one Kant scholar who has taken Gregor's advice to heart. She has made a sustained attempt to read the *Groundwork* in tune with the substantive ethics laid out in the *Metaphysics of Morals*.

the categorical imperative has many forms, and those forms are not equivalent. When Kant scholars talk about the categorical imperative without specifying any of its various forms, they usually mean the formula of universal law. This formula is surely on her mind, because she is trying to defend Kant's "formalism." Let us now see whether the duties of justice and virtue can be derived from this formula. I have already noted that the duties of virtue cannot be derived from the formula of universal law. The duties of virtue are dictated by obligatory ends, and the formula of universal law is only a formality that Kant retains in his discussion of obligatory ends.

The duties of justice may have a closer relation to the formula of universal law, since the principle of justice refers to a universal law. Some Kant scholars have maintained that the principle of justice follows directly from the first formulation of the categorical imperative.[12] The principle of justice, however, is too complex to be exhausted by the formula of universal law. It contains one important element that cannot be found in the formula of universal law, namely, the reference to freedom.[13] To account for this difference, Mary Gregor says that the principle of justice is similar to the second formulation of the categorical imperative. Like the formula of humanity, she says, the principle of justice fixes absolute limits to our freedom.[14]

In fact both formulations apply equally to the principle of justice, because the principle contains two different features. Following Gregor, Bruce Aune also connects the principle of justice to the formula of humanity as an end in itself, but he sees more than she does. Aune recognizes the need to link the principle of justice to the formula of the universal law of nature. This is his way of admitting that the first two formulations of the categorical imperative apply equally to the principle of justice.[15] The formula of universal law concerns the

12. Onora O'Neill, *Acting on Principle: An Essay on Kantian Ethics* (New York, 1975), 38–39, 72; Roger Sullivan, *Immanuel Kant's Moral Theory*, 247.

13. This point is well noted by Allen Buchanan in his review of *Acting on Principles*, in *Journal of Philosophy* 75 (1978): 325–40.

14. *Laws of Freedom*, 39.

15. Aune, *Kant's Theory of Morals*, 137–40.

form of the principle of justice, and the formula of humanity concerns its content, namely, freedom, or rather its limit. Thus, the two formulas are indeed in the relation of form and matter, as Kant says in the *Groundwork* (*GMM* 436). As form and matter, the two formulas control two different features of the principle of justice. These two features are complementary and inseparable, but contrary to Kant's claim, they are neither equivalent nor independent.

In Kant's theory of justice, the combination of the first and the second formulas, as form and matter, produces the third formula, the kingdom of ends, as Kant explains in the *Groundwork* (*GMM* 436). As we noted earlier, however, the kingdom of ends is only one special form of the concept of the highest good. Thus we come back to the conclusion that the concept of the highest good is the central principle of Kant's theory of justice, as central as it is to his theory of virtue. In his *Lectures on Ethics* Kant says that every ethical system is defined by its conception of the highest good (*summum bonum*) and that it is an ideal, indeed, "the highest conceivable standard by which everything is to be judged and weighed" (*LE* 6). This observation turns out to be absolutely true of his *Metaphysics of Morals*.

Most Kant scholars have not paid serious attention to the *Metaphysics of Morals*, not because they love to spin out their own metaphysics of morals, as Gregor maintains. Their chief reason for ignoring or neglecting it lies elsewhere. The *Metaphysics of Morals* refuses to stand on the foundation prepared by the *Groundwork* and categorically reverses Kant's Copernican revolution as executed in the Analytic of the second *Critique*. In the *Metaphysics of Morals* Kant does not apply or realize his formalist program but repudiates it and returns to his old program of substantive practical reason. He returns to the ethics of Platonic Ideas. But the world of Ideas he presents in the *Metaphysics of Morals* is not quite the same as the one he portrayed in the first *Critique*.

In the first *Critique* Kant mentioned only two ethical Ideas; in the *Metaphysics of Morals* he parades a whole battery of them. The former Ideas are transcendent; the latter, immanent. The transcendent Ideas were accessible only to pure reason; sensibility and inclination have no access to it. In the first *Critique* Kant believed that the natural, or empirical, elements of humanity were totally alien to the truth and demand of Ideas. Hence he stressed the split or even the conflict between the rational and the nonrational dimensions of human existence. In the *Metaphysics of Morals* he no longer stresses their split. When he makes the distinction between the phenomenal person (*homo phaenomenon*) and the noumenal person (*homo noumenon*) he duly recognizes their mutual dependence. Although dispositions are empirical or natural, he says, they are indispensable for moral perfection. The Ideas of pure reason are equally important for the rational and the nonrational dimensions of human existence, because these two dimensions become inseparable from each other in Kant's new theory of virtue.

In his theory of justice, Kant also stresses the intimate connection between the ideal and the real (empirical). He distinguishes between the two modes of possession, the sensible (or empirical) and the intelligible (*MM* 245). But the Idea of intelligible possession is not a transcendent Idea with no empirical content; it is defined in the context of empirical conditions. Insofar as the Idea of intelligible possession is a normative standard, it is totally different from the concept of empirical possessions. Insofar as it is a normative concept, its meaning cannot be given by sensibility; to that extent it is transcendent. But it is immanent in that its transcendent meaning is spelled out in the context of the natural world. Until the Idea of intelligible possession is given its empirical reference, it is no more than the primitive Idea of an innate right to external freedom. Even this Idea has an implicit reference to the world of nature; the concept of external freedom means the freedom in the natural world. Such an Idea is transcendent in its origin but is immanent in its operation and significance.

A world of immanent Ideas underlies Kant's *Metaphysics of Morals*. In the first *Critique* he had singled out two transcendent Ideas as the foundation of his practical philosophy: the Idea of virtue and the Idea of an ideal republic. In the *Metaphysics of Morals* he articulates the transcendent Idea of virtue in his theory of virtue and the transcendent Idea of an ideal republic in his theory of justice. These two theories present two systems of immanent Ideas that presuppose an intimate relation between the intelligible and the sensible worlds.

Such an intimate relation is quite different from the one Kant had presented in earlier writings, where he had stressed the transcendence of Ideas and the enormous chasm between the two worlds. As the Ideas are realized in the domain of culture and history, they descend from Platonic Heaven to the world of nature. It is their Platonic descent (*katagoge*) that coincides with their historical development as portrayed in Kant's philosophy of history. Here again his ethics is in harmony with his philosophy of history.

In Platonic tradition, the descent of Ideas means their application or realization in the phenomenal world. This is accomplished by the process of eidetic construction, which articulates transcendental Ideas in the context of empirical and historical conditions. Eidetic construction or articulation is the way of descent and realization for Platonic Ideas. Kant gives his account of their descent in the *Metaphysics of Morals*. Hence this treatise implements not the principles that he spelled out in the *Groundwork for the Metaphysics of Morals* but the ones he laid out in the *Inaugural Dissertation* and reaffirmed in the *Critique of Pure Reason*.

As we noted earlier, even his formalist ethics can be accommodated in Kant's Platonic scheme if it is given a constructivist account. This is the resourcefulness of my Platonic interpretation; it can bridge the gap between Kant's Platonic ethics and his formalist ethics. On the other hand, if we want to uphold Kant's formalist ethics as his only true teaching, we have to relegate his *Metaphysics of Morals*, together with his writings in the history of philosophy and his Platonic ethics in the first *Critique*, to the land of Kantian aberration. We have to say that these pieces mark the occasional retreats he made to this mysterious land during his Critical period.

By the standard demarcation of Critical and pre-Critical Philosophy, the ethics of Platonic Ideas belongs to his pre-Critical Philosophy. It begins in the *Inaugural Dissertation*, that is, eleven years before the publication of the *Critique of Pure Reason*. But Kant does not reject it in his Critical Philosophy; on the contrary, it is firmly endorsed in the first *Critique* and solidly fulfilled in the *Metaphysics of Morals*. Its presence is equally unmistakable in his philosophy of history, which was developed during his Critical period, and it also underlies his philosophy of religion. The *Groundwork* and the *Critique of Practical Reason* appear to be the only exceptions to his long-standing allegiance to Platonism. Even these two works do not completely abandon Platonism, as we have seen, and his formalist ethics covers only a brief period of four years (1785–88) in his long illustrious career.

The Platonic legacy in Kant's philosophy has largely been overlooked because most Kant scholars have followed the conventional wisdom that the spirit of criticism, the central force for his Critical Philosophy, is incompatible with Platonism. Hence the demarcation between the Critical and the pre-Critical periods in Kant's career has been a devastating blinder for Kant scholarship of the past two centuries. Too many of Kant's important works cannot neatly be classified into the dyadic division of Critical and pre-Critical Philosophy. Although the spirit of criticism is important for his Critical Philosophy, it serves only a procedural and instrumental function. The substantive and thematic force of Kant's philosophy comes from the Platonic conception of transcendental normative standards. They provide the ultimate goal for all his maneuvers; they give the unity and integrity to all his works. The spirit of criticism is only a dutiful handmaid to his grand Platonic vision.

To be sure, Kant ceaselessly wavers between formalism and substantivism. As we have noted many times over, he seems to believe that eidetic construction can provide the bridge between formalism and substantivism. Sometimes he squarely accepts Platonic Forms as substantive normative ideals; sometimes he tries to derive them from a higher source or unity, which he understands to be purely formal. This endless indecision is perhaps the most pervasive cause for the recurrent ambiguity and obscurity in his writings and the ultimate cause for countless confusions and interminable controversies in Kant scholarship.

6 The Third *Critique:* Post-Critical Kant

* * * * * * * * * * * * * * * * * *

The world of immanent Ideas was not introduced for the first time in the *Metaphysics of Morals*. Seven years earlier, in the *Critique of Judgment*, Kant had used it in his theory of reflective judgment. There are two species of reflective judgment, aesthetic and teleological. In the third *Critique* Kant had examined the nature and power of these two species. He examined the function of reflective judgment by contrasting it to that of determinative judgment (C_3 179). These two types of judgment are two different ways of relating a particular (object) to a universal (concept). If the universal is given, judgment only subsumes the particular under it. This is the role of determinative judgment. If only the particular is given, judgment has to find a suitable universal for it. This is the role of reflective judgment.

Reflective judgments supervene upon determinative judgments. This is an important point that can easily be overlooked. In his distinction of these judgments, Kant talks as though they were on the same level. He gives the impression that there are two ways of encountering objects: (1) to have a concept and then an object or (2) to have an object and then a concept. But he means to say that there are two levels of judgment. On the first level, all objects of sense must be subsumed under the categories. This is the determinative judgment for the recognition of the objects of experience, or empirical objects. For these objects, we can find suitable universals in reflective judgment. This is the second level, which goes beyond the categories.

Why do these two levels of judgment exist? Why is it that we do not stop at the first level but go on to the second? Kant never raises these questions. And these questions may not occur to his readers, because he presents his distinction between determinative and reflective judgments not as two levels of judgment but as two alternative relations between objects and concepts. When he explicates the nature of reflective judgment, however, he often uses the word *estima-*

tion (Beurteilung) as an equivalent of *reflective judgment. Estimation* means the estimation of value; reflective judgment is an evaluative judgment. In contrast, determinative judgments are descriptive and value-neutral. Hence the supervenience of reflective upon determinative judgment is our ascent from descriptive to evaluative judgment.

* * Aesthetic Judgment

Since reflective judgments are evaluative, they cannot be made without using normative standards. But Kant tries his best to analyze the nature of aesthetic judgment without using normative standards. Instead of a normative account, he first presents a psychological account of aesthetic experience. Let us see how far he can carry through this attempt. His analysis of aesthetic judgment is given under the four moments quality, quantity, relation, and modality. As to its quality, a judgment of taste is devoid of all interest (C_3 204). It is supposed to differentiate aesthetic judgment from the judgment of the agreeable, on the one hand, and from moral judgment, on the other. A judgment of the agreeable expresses the pleasure of empirical sensations. It is a function of empirical interest and its gratification. A moral judgment is governed by the interests of practical reason. A judgment of taste is free from both rational and empirical interests. The pleasure associated with aesthetic experience is neither the gratification of appetites nor the esteem for moral goodness.

As to its quantity, a judgment of taste is universal. By this, Kant does not mean that an aesthetic judgment is given as a universal proposition. On the contrary, he says that all judgments of taste are singular judgments (C_3 215). The universality of aesthetic judgments is their universal communicability, which is the same as their acceptability to everyone. If my judgment "This rose is beautiful" is true for me, I have the right to expect that it is also true for everybody else. Kant says that this is the basic difference between the judgment of taste and the judgment of the agreeable. Whatever pleasure I may have in eating slimy slugs, I have no right to expect everybody else to share my judgment of this delicacy. A judgment of the agreeable is never universal, because it is empirical.

Kant's proof for the universality of aesthetic judgment is quite complicated. He begins by posing the question whether the feeling of pleasure precedes or succeeds the estimation *(Beurteilung)* of the object (*C₃* 216). This question could have been put in a Socratic form: Does the judgment of beauty give pleasure because it is a judgment of beauty, or is it a judgment of beauty because it gives pleasure? Or even more simply: Does something give pleasure because it is beautiful, or is it beautiful because it gives pleasure? Kant's answer to these questions again distinguishes the judgment of taste from the judgment of the agreeable. In the latter, the judgment follows the feeling of pleasure: the agreeable objects are agreeable because they give pleasure. In the former, the feeling of pleasure follows the judgment: the beautiful objects give pleasure because they are beautiful. The feeling of pleasure is the essence of judgment for the agreeable; it is only the consequence of judgment for the beautiful.

What is the essential feature of aesthetic judgment if it is not the feeling of pleasure? If the feeling of pleasure is only a consequence or effect, what is its cause? For these questions, Kant gives an incredible answer: "Hence it must be the universal communicability of the mental state, in the given presentation, which underlies the judgment of taste as its subjective condition, and the pleasure in the object must be its consequence" (*C₃* 217, Pluhar 61). He is saying that a judgment of taste gives pleasure by virtue of its communicability. In support of this point, Kant says that the communicability of a mental state is always a source of pleasure and that this point can be proven by the empirical and psychological propensity of human beings for sociability (*C₃* 218). Since communicability and sociability are essential features of aesthetic experience, human beings would never experience aesthetic pleasure if they were to live in complete isolation from each other. "Someone abandoned on some desolate island would not, just for himself, adorn either his hut or himself; nor would he look for flowers, let alone grow them, to adorn himself with them" (*C₃* 297, Pluhar 163–64).

This is an implausible claim. The assertion that communicability is the source of aesthetic pleasure, or that no one in solitude can experience aesthetic pleasure, contradicts our aesthetic experience. But

Kant does not stop with this implausible assertion: he goes on to explain how the communicability of aesthetic experience is constituted. He locates its constitution in the free interplay between imagination and understanding (C_3 217). He says that communication always involves the use of cognitive faculties and that the communicability of aesthetic judgment is derived from the harmonious interaction of imagination and understanding. Their interplay is free because it involves no concepts or rules. This is his well-known doctrine of the harmony of cognitive faculties as the basis of aesthetic judgment and experience.

Kant's account of aesthetic pleasure delineates its causal chain. The feeling of aesthetic pleasure is the consequence of its universal communicability, which in turn is the consequence of the free interplay of imagination and understanding. This causal chain underlies what Richard Aquila calls Kant's causal account of aesthetic pleasure and experience.[1] The causal account may also be called the psychological account, because it locates the source of aesthetic pleasure in the interplay of imagination and understanding. But there is one serious objection to this account. The interplay of imagination and understanding is not confined to the domain of aesthetic experience. In the first *Critique* Kant had said that their cooperation was a universal requirement for all our experience. If so, even our experience of the agreeable must also involve the interplay of imagination and understanding.[2] This is the most serious defect in Kant's psychological theory of aesthetic harmony.

Kant has to provide the differentia that can transform the harmony of imagination and understanding from its old role as a universal requirement for all experience into its new role as the unique essence of aesthetic pleasure and experience.[3] He gives the differentia as follows:

1. "A New Look at Kant's Aesthetic Judgments," in *Essays in Kant's Aesthetics*, ed. Ted Cohen and Paul Guyer (Chicago, 1982), 87–114.
2. This is Ernst Cassirer's criticism of Kant's psychological account of aesthetic experience (*Kant's Life and Thought*, trans. James Haden [New Haven, 1981], 314).
3. This is Paul Guyer's criticism. Guyer also makes the same point in regard to the idea of proportion that Kant uses for describing the relation of imagination and understand-

When imagination is used for cognition, then it is under the constraint of the understanding and is subject to the restriction of adequacy to the understanding's concept. But when the aim is aesthetic, then the imagination is free, so that, over and above that harmony with the concept, it may supply, in an unstudied way, a wealth of developed material for the understanding which the latter disregarded in its concept. (C₃ 316–17, Pluhar 185)

The interplay of imagination and understanding involves no concepts for aesthetic judgment, whereas the use of concepts is indispensable for their interplay in cognition. The differentia is the absence of concepts. It is this negative differentia that is supposed to be accountable for the genesis of aesthetic pleasure. The negative characterization may seem positive when it is called the free play of cognitive faculties. But their freedom is negative rather than positive; it is defined by the absence of rules and concepts. This is a paradoxical development in Kant's theory. Rules and concepts are not required for aesthetic judgments, whereas they are required for determinative judgments. There is one more paradox in this account of aesthetic pleasure: if aesthetic judgment involves no concepts, how can understanding, which is the faculty of concepts, participate in it? What can understanding contribute to our experience of aesthetic pleasure without using its concepts? Kant says nothing about the role of understanding in aesthetic judgment, although he says a great deal about the role of imagination. Understanding appears to do nothing for aesthetic judgment, though its cooperation with the imagination is said to be vital for the generation of aesthetic delight.

Let us set aside these baffling questions for a while and move on to the remaining two moments of aesthetic judgment. As to its relation, Kant says, aesthetic judgment is purposive without purpose (C₃ 236). Ernst Cassirer says that a knowledge of the eighteenth-century usage of *purposiveness* is necessary for a correct understanding of Kant's assertion. The meaning of *purposiveness* is not limited to

---

ing in aesthetic judgment (*Kant and the Claims of Taste* [Cambridge, Mass., 1979], 295, 322–23).

the notion of a purpose; its general meaning is the harmonious uni-
fication of parts in a whole.[4] It is the concept of a harmonious order;
it is the relation of parts and whole. When the harmonious order is
a living entity, its purposiveness (harmonious order) expresses a real
purpose. When it is not such an organic entity, its purposiveness
expresses no real purpose. It serves no organic function. That is purposiveness without purpose, which is also called the formal, or subjective, purposiveness in contrast to the real, or objective, purposiveness of organic beings.

Aesthetic purposiveness is only formal; it has the form of purposiveness but not its content (no organic functions). Kant says that the
formal purposiveness is the cause of aesthetic pleasure. The form
(harmonious order) of beautiful objects and the design of artworks
occasion the harmonious interplay of imagination and understanding (C_3 225). To put it another way, the harmony of imagination and
understanding only reflects the harmonious order of aesthetic objects. By this assertion, Kant adds one more link to the causal chain
of aesthetic pleasure. The harmonious interplay of imagination and
understanding is neither the ultimate nor an independent event but
a function of the harmonious order in the objects of beauty, that is,
their aesthetic form. Kant associates the idea of aesthetic form with
the idea of models and archetypes (C_3 232). He says that the objects
of taste or art are "exemplary"; that is, they exemplify a model or
archetype. With the notion of archetypes, he introduces normative
elements into aesthetic judgment.

Kant distinguishes empirical and a priori standards (C_3 249). An
example of an empirical standard is the average size of animals, trees,
houses, or mountains. An empirical standard is established by an
empirical investigation. But an a priori standard does not depend on
any empirical conditions; examples are the standards of virtue, civil
liberty, and justice. Aesthetic standards are also a priori; hence they
are called archetypes. They are different from both the standards of
the agreeable and the moral standards. The standards of the agreeable
are empirical; aesthetic standards are a priori. Although moral stan-

4. Cassirer, *Kant's Life and Thought*, 287.

dards are also a priori, they still differ from aesthetic standards. The latter are indeterminate; the former, determinate. The determinate standards can be stated in the form of definite rules and principles, but the indeterminate cannot (C_3 239). The indeterminacy of aesthetic standards derives from the fact that these standards involve no concepts. They can be exemplified only by the objects of imagination.

Because aesthetic judgments involve a priori standards, Kant says, they have exemplary validity or necessity (C_3 239). The fourth moment of aesthetic judgment, modality, is the idea of exemplary necessity. But the notion of necessity has a special meaning for aesthetic judgment. It is not the necessity of a rule that can be stated as a universal proposition, because aesthetic judgments are singular. Nor does it mean that every aesthetic judgment is necessarily true, because aesthetic judgment can be false. The necessity of aesthetic judgment is only exemplary. When a person makes an aesthetic judgment, Kant says, he or she offers it as an example of an ideal standard (C_3 239). If the person's judgment correctly exemplifies the ideal standard, then he or she has the right to demand that it be accepted by everybody else. This is so, because everyone shares the same ideal standard. If they do not, they ought to. This is the power of normative necessity. Normative standards dictate the normative necessity that underlies the exemplary necessity of aesthetic judgment.

This is Kant's theory of aesthetic judgment or experience under four moments. As I have already indicated, Kant begins his theory of aesthetic judgment as a psychological account and then introduces normative elements in the latter half. Since his theory contains both psychological and normative elements, it is systematically ambiguous. Kant's psychological account can be taken either as an empirical and descriptive theory or as a normative and prescriptive one. For example, the harmony of imagination and understanding can be understood in either a normative or a descriptive mode. The normative approach will explain their harmony as based on the aesthetic norms, but the empirical or descriptive approach will take their harmony as an empirical fact and then determine aesthetic norms in reference to it. That is, aesthetic norms can be defined as whatever can generate the harmony of imagination and understanding, in which case those norms will be empirical rather than a priori.

Even the idea of universal communicability can be taken in two ways. Whether you and I can communicate about our aesthetic experiences can be an empirical question. On the other hand, if your aesthetic judgment has exemplary necessity, it should be communicable to everyone else. And this is a normative assertion. The same distinction applies to the idea of agreement. Some agreements are empirical facts; they depend on empirical conditions. Two people may agree or disagree on the taste of slugs, and their agreement or disagreement is a contingent fact. On the other hand, there are normative, or ideal, agreements; they obtain under ideal conditions (C_3 214-16). Those conditions can be specified only by normative standards, and only normative agreements have the exemplary necessity of aesthetic judgment (C_3 239).

Kant's idea of common sense *(sensus communis)* is equally open to two different interpretations. He introduces this idea as the ultimate basis for explaining the necessity of aesthetic judgment (C_3 238). He says that we can have the same aesthetic pleasure because we have the same cognitive faculties of imagination and understanding. This is an empirical or psychological description of common sense. Kant also gives a normative view of common sense; he describes it as a principle (C_3 238) and as the power of estimation (C_3 293). Common sense makes a priori aesthetic judgments by its formal rules of estimation (C_3 290). Common sense is common to everyone, because we share its a priori standards. This is a normative description of common sense rather than a descriptive or empirical one.

Kant's theory of aesthetic judgment and experience is systematically open to these two interpretations. What Aquila calls the causal account belongs to the descriptive or psychological interpretation of his theory. The causal account is unsatisfactory because it diverges phenomenologically from our aesthetic experience. Aquila says that "it reduces the *intentionality* of aesthetic feeling to a merely causal relation involving that feeling."[5] The causal account is also incompat-

---

5. "A New Look at Kant's Aesthetic Judgments," 95.

ible with Kant's claim for the apriority of aesthetic judgment: an empirical account cannot provide the ground for a priori judgments. Hence the normative account remains the only acceptable alternative. But the normative account presupposes normative standards, and Kant has to explain what they really are.

* * Aesthetic Ideas and Normative Standards

Only after the Deduction of Aesthetic Judgments does Kant identify these normative standards with aesthetic Ideas. He defines an aesthetic Idea as "a presentation of the imagination which prompts much thought, but to which no determinate thought whatsoever, i.e., no [determinate] *concept*, can be adequate, so that no language can express it completely and allow us to grasp it" (C_3 314, Pluhar 182). Such an Idea is said to be indeterminate. The indeterminacy of aesthetic Ideas can resolve some of the perplexities we have encountered in Kant's theory of aesthetic judgment. We noted earlier that Kant could not explain the role of understanding in aesthetic judgment if it truly involves no rules or concepts. Aesthetic Ideas do not belong exclusively to imagination, because they are Ideas. They require the participation of the understanding in aesthetic experience, but its cooperation with the imagination involves no rules because aesthetic Ideas are not concepts.

The presence of aesthetic Ideas can explain not only the need for the cooperation of imagination and understanding but also the aesthetic pleasure that arises from their harmony. Kant observes that mechanical regularity produces boredom rather than pleasure. If aesthetic pleasure were solely owing to the harmony of imagination and understanding, mechanical regularity would perhaps be more effective than anything else for producing aesthetic delight, because it can effect a perfect harmony between imagination and understanding. But the complete harmony in such a case produces no aesthetic pleasure, because it exemplifies no aesthetic Ideas.

The presence of aesthetic Ideas is even more important for the sublime. Whereas the experience of beauty involves the harmony of imagination and understanding, the experience of the sublime derives from the discrepancy between sensibility and Ideas of reason (C_3 257). Such natural phenomena as thunder and lightening generate the experience of the sublime, not by producing the harmony of imagination and understanding, but by showing the inadequacy of sensibility for the representation of Ideas. Sensibility and imagination can never provide any empirical representation that can fully correspond to the Idea of the sublime and the truly awesome. This discrepancy between sensibility and intellect, which is the source of the sublime, is accountable only in terms of aesthetic Ideas.

Aesthetic Ideas are quite different from the Ideas of pure reason. The latter, which are called rational Ideas, are purely intellectual. Kant stresses the difference between rational and aesthetic Ideas. No intuition can be adequate for rational Ideas, and no concept can be adequate for aesthetic Ideas. The latter, which can be exemplified (provide examples) only by sensibility, they are called the indemonstrable or unexpoundable Ideas (C_3 343). This is a remarkable development in Kant's theory of Ideas. In his earlier writings he had never acknowledged any Ideas other than rational ones, and he had not allowed sensibility and imagination access to them, because they are totally transcendent. But aesthetic Ideas are accessible to sensibility; they are immanent in the world of phenomena. The immanent Ideas are not restricted to the aesthetic domain. In the *Metaphysics of Morals,* as we noted in the preceding chapter, some ethical and political Ideas also function as immanent normative standards in the kingdom of ends. Let us now see how Kant employs immanent Ideas in his theory of art and natural teleology.

In Kant's view, art is a product of genius, and he defines artistic genius as the power to exhibit aesthetic Ideas (C_3 313). The productive power of artistic genius derives from aesthetic Ideas. Kant makes the same point by characterizing genius as a talent for producing works of art without determinate rules (C_3 307). If genius were to follow determinate rules, there would be no creativity and originality in its production. But Kant notes that the absence of rules alone cannot account for the originality of genius, since the absence of rules can also produce nonsense and trivia. Genius owes its originality to aesthetic Ideas, but those Ideas cannot be rendered into rules, because they are indeterminate. They are the guiding spirit and inspiration for genius (C_3 308).

Aesthetic Ideas are indispensable not only for the production of artworks but also for our appreciation of and communication about them (C_3 328). Kant says that we cannot talk about the aesthetic themes of music and poetry without reference to aesthetic Ideas. Even the differences between various arts can be explained in terms of their different ways of articulating aesthetic Ideas. No doubt, the experience of art involves the physical sensations, the emotions of all kinds, and even the kinetic sense of the body. But none of these empirical components can add up to aesthetic experience unless they are brought under the control of aesthetic Ideas (C_3 331–32). Above all, it is the quality of aesthetic Ideas that determines the "spirit" *(Geist)* of a work of art (C_3 313).

In Kant's view, the role of Ideas is equally important for natural teleology. He begins his analysis of teleological judgment by recounting Plato's story in the *Phaedo* of Socrates' conversion (C_3 363). As we saw in chapter 2, this is the same story that inspired and encouraged Leibniz to reject the mechanistic view of the natural world and accept the principle of final causality. According to Anaxagoras, it is not the dead matter but the living mind that orders all things in nature. If the mind has the power to do this, Socrates says, it is so by virtue of Ideas. This is what Kant takes to be the essence of Plato's theory of Ideas:

> For the concept of natural purposes leads reason into an order of things that is wholly different from that of a mere natural mechanism, which we no longer find adequate when we deal with such natural products. And hence the possibility of such a product is to be based on an idea. But an idea is an absolute unity of presentation, whereas matter is a plurality of things that cannot itself supply a determinate unity for its combination. Therefore if the unity of the idea is to serve as the very basis that determines a priori a natural law of the causality [responsible] for a product with such a form in its combination, then the purpose [the idea] of nature has to be extended to *everything* that is in this product of nature. (C_3 377, Pluhar 256)

Final causality is inseparable from Ideas; it is the causality of Ideas. In the first *Critique* Kant had restricted the causality of Ideas to the domain of practical reason. Now he is extending it to the entire natural order. That is what Socrates did under the inspiration of Anaxagoras. The principle of mechanical causation cannot account for even a single blade of grass, because it involves the Idea of purposes (C_3 378, 409). What, then, is the ultimate purpose of nature? Kant believes that it is the production of humankind (C_3 435). But what is the purpose of human existence? It is the realization of the highest good. For this realization, human beings have to exercise their freedom and become moral agents, prescribing for themselves the unconditioned moral laws. But human existence is not limited to its moral dimension; its completion requires the development of its cultural dimension. If human beings were no more than products of nature, Kant says, their ultimate purpose would be fulfilled in their happiness. But they are rational agents of talent and skill, and so their destiny can be fulfilled only in establishing the kingdom of culture (C_3 430). The kingdom of culture realizes the concept of the highest good. Culture is a unique product of freedom; it is the ultimate purpose of natural teleology (C_3 431).

This is the same view of natural teleology that Kant presented in his philosophy of history. As we saw in chapter 3, he maintained that the ultimate purpose of nature was to produce human history. The production of human history is the production of human culture, which is for the realization of the highest good. In his ethical and historical writings, Kant had restricted the role of Ideas to the world of human beings. Hence the phenomenon of humankind had appeared to be an anomaly in the world of dead matter. By extending the domain of teleology to the entire physical world, he brings human existence into harmony with natural order. Both fall into a universal scheme of purposiveness under the governance of Ideas.

* * The Fusion of Two Worlds

Kant's conception of nature has changed drastically. He began his long career with a mechanical conception of nature. This was the picture of nature as dead matter that had filled Pascal's heart with dread. Kant has changed this chilling view of nature into a teleological view. He now regards nature as not only alive but beautiful. When he distinguishes between the subjective purposiveness of natural beauty and the objective purposiveness of natural teleology, he gives the impression that natural beauty belongs only to human sensibility whereas natural teleology objectively exists in nature. Contrary to this impression, he regards beauty as a pervasive attribute of nature. He begins his discussion of beauty with the beauty of natural objects. He is deeply impressed with the fact that nature is adorned with an abundance of beauty: "How are we to explain why nature has so extravagantly spread beauty everywhere, even at the bottom of the ocean, where the human eye (for which, after all, this beauty is alone purposive) rarely penetrates?" (C_3 279, Pluhar 142; see also C_3 380).

Nature is alive and beautiful by virtue of Ideas. Since the world of Ideas is the intelligible world, the living and beautiful nature is the fusion of the intelligible and sensible worlds. The intelligible world is no longer understood as merely supersensible or transcendent. It is now fully immanent and even sensible, and its immanence is evident in the relation of reflective and determinative judgments. As we have already noted, determinative judgments are descriptive, and reflective judgments are evaluative. In the first two *Critiques* Kant had separated them by assigning determinative judgments to the first *Critique* and evaluative judgments to the second *Critique*. In the third *Critique* he brings them together: reflective judgments supervene upon determinative judgments. The world of value is immanently real in the sensible world. This is not to say that Kant denies the existence of the supersensible world. He indeed affirms and reaffirms the existence of God as the only way to explain natural beauty and teleology. But the scope of the intelligible world is not restricted to the existence of God but extends to the realm of Ideas. Although God remains in the supersensible world, the Ideas have descended to the phenomenal world. The world of beauty and natural teleology is the fusion of phenomena and noumena.

The fusion of the intelligible and the sensible worlds is also evident in the perfect harmony of imagination and understanding in the creative power of artistic genius. In the first *Critique* Kant had advocated a clear-cut division of labor between imagination and understanding. Imagination is a faculty of sense; understanding is a faculty of thought. Imagination provides the matter of experience; understanding, its form. The form of synthesis is given in the pure concepts of understanding, which are also called the rules of synthesis. Hence the understanding was called the faculty of rules. In artistic creation, Kant now holds, understanding freely cooperates with the imagination without rules (C_3 316–17). This happy union of imagination and understanding without the restriction of rules is the essence of artistic freedom and the power of genius.

The same happy union obtains in the constitution of reflective judgment. In the first *Critique* the distinction of a priori and a posteriori propositions had been Kant's first step in building his theory of experience. Does the same distinction apply to reflective judgments? Kant never raises this intriguing question. Before answering this question, we should note the distinction between a priori judgments and their a priori elements. The a priori elements of judgment are the concepts, Ideas, or even intuitions of the a priori origin. The a priori judgments are the judgments of a priori truths. The a priori elements neither carry truth values in their own right nor automatically constitute a priori judgments. The fact that a priori aesthetic Ideas are used in making aesthetic judgments does not guarantee that those aesthetic judgments have a priori truths. Likewise, the fact that the a priori concept of cause is used in making causal judgments does not mean that those judgments have a priori truths. Although the concept of causation is a priori, the causal judgment or principle may be true only a posteriori.

The a priori origin of a concept does not automatically translate into the a priori truth of a judgment. For this reason, Kant had to devise a transcendental proof for the a priori truth of the causal principle, although he was sure of the a priori origin of the concept of cause and effect. Although Kant recognizes the role of a priori Ideas in the third *Critique*, he never claims that they produce a priori judgments. In fact, he never uses the distinction of a priori and a posteriori reflective judgments. In my view, reflective judgments can be characterized (1) as neither a priori nor a posteriori or (2) as both a priori and a posteriori. To the extent that they involve a priori aesthetic and teleological Ideas, they are a priori, but to the extent that they do not carry the same mark of universality and necessity that the causal principle is supposed to carry, they are not a priori. The distinction between a priori and a posteriori judgments becomes irrelevant to aesthetic judgments. Instead of making this old distinction, Kant stresses the unity of a priori and a posteriori elements in one reflective judgment.

The central theme of the last *Critique* turns out to be the idea of unity and harmony. All Kant's works prior to this one had been permeated by the opposite idea; they were studded with distinctions and oppositions, such as sense versus intellect, imagination versus understanding, receptivity versus spontaneity, the a priori versus the a posteriori, phenomena versus noumena, the sensible versus the supersensible. Most important of all was the opposition of formal and substantive rationality. All these distinctions and oppositions reflect Kant's systematic dualism, which he had devised to fight against the materialistic view of natural science. If he had accepted natural science as the only source of all truth, he would have developed a monistic view of reality. As we have already seen, he has tried to make room for the world of norms and values while acknowledging the truth of natural science. This has led to his dualism of the sensible world of phenomena and the intelligible world of noumena. This is the opposition of the world of fact and the world of value, which expresses the pervasive tension and discord in the scientific ethos of modern Europe.

The discord of Kant's old dualism is overcome by the power of reflective judgment, which knows no distinction between formal and substantive reason. It cannot admit even a clear split between imagination and understanding. Nor is it any longer important to maintain the uniquely Kantian distinction between understanding and reason. Kant had formerly justified this distinction by linking it to the distinction between concepts and Ideas. Understanding is the faculty of concepts, and reason is the faculty of Ideas. In aesthetic experience, however, Ideas are equally accessible to both understanding and reason. They are accessible even to the imagination. The separation of faculties has been replaced by their union, and their union is none other than the faculty of reflective judgment.

The faculty of reflective judgment replaces Kant's old universe of discord with his new universe of concord. Throughout the last *Critique* Kant stresses the idea of harmony—the harmony of faculties in reflective judgments, the harmony of nature and culture, the harmony of the sensible and the supersensible. Kant felt this sense of harmony in his own soul and experienced one of the happiest periods of his life. He expressed his satisfaction with the last *Critique* as follows: "Here I saw my most diverse thoughts brought together, artistic and natural production handled the same way; the powers of aesthetic and teleological judgment mutually illuminating each other. . . . I rejoiced that poetic art and comparative natural knowledge are so closely related, since both are subject to the power of judgment."[6]

By "the power of judgment" Kant meant the power of reflective judgment. The sense of harmony Kant experienced by the power of reflective judgment could not be contained in his soul for long, for the tension and conflict between the world of dead matter and the world of the living spirit was not his private agony but the cultural syndrome of the entire age. As Cassirer says, the last *Critique* touched the nerve of the entire spiritual and intellectual culture of his time more than any other of his works.[7] Goethe and Schiller were captivated by the last *Critique*. It was not any particular doctrine of this book but its ethos and spirit of unity that became the source of inspiration for many Romantic followers of Kant.

Goethe recognized the existence of eternal ideals. But they are in nature. They are neither abstract nor transcendental, but concrete and real. To fulfill these ideals is to realize human perfection in and through nature. This was how Kant portrayed the destiny of human history in the *Idea for a Universal History*. Moreover, Goethe's no-

6. As quoted in Cassirer, *Kant's Life and Thought*, 273. Cassirer does not give the textual source.

7. *Kant's Life and Thought*, 273.

tion of eternal ideals in nature was basically the same as Kant's notion of immanent Ideas. Goethe stressed the importance of individual and cultural variations of eternal ideals. As Robert Solomon says, this aspect of his outlook was no doubt influenced largely by Lessing and Herder.[8] But it was also in line with Kant's concept of immanent Ideas. In Kant's theory, these Ideas are contextually defined and articulated. The world of art does not operate with one transcendent Idea of beauty. The transcendent Idea takes different shapes for different ages and for different cultures. Not only each culture but also each artistic genius operates with its own aesthetic Ideas. The individuality and particularity of aesthetic Ideas extend down to individual works of art; each exemplifies its own aesthetic Idea. Hence different works of art and different artistic geniuses manifest different spirits of art, because the spirits of art are determined by aesthetic Ideas, which are unique to each creative genius and to each of his or her works.

Schiller accepted Goethe's notion of human perfection in and through nature.[9] Having grown up with the systematic Kantian dualism, he eventually found the ground of wholeness and integrity in Kant's aesthetics.[10] Schiller recognized three basic drives in human nature: the material instinct *(Stofftrieb)*, the formal instinct *(Formtrieb)*, and the play instinct *(Spieltrieb)*. The material instinct, also called the sensible or empirical instinct, is subject to the laws of nature, whereas the formal drive is subject to the laws of freedom. These two correspond to sensibility and rationality in Kant's conception of an individual. They are in perpetual conflict and strife. But the play instinct brings them into harmony; it heals the systematic fissure in the human soul, making it sound and whole.[11] It also leads to Schiller's third *Reich*, the aesthetic state. The principle of this social order is the principle of taste and beauty, which alone "brings

8. *History and Human Nature* (New York, 1979), 142–47.

9. This point is well discussed by Solomon in ibid., 153.

10. This point is well discussed by Eva Schaper in *Studies in Kant's Aesthetics* (Edinburgh, 1979), 100–103.

11. Schiller, *On the Aesthetic Education of Man*, trans. Elizabeth Wilkinson and L. A. Willoughby (Oxford, 1967), esp. letters 12–16.

harmony into society, because it fosters harmony in the individual.[12] This was Schiller's Romantic conception of an aesthetic utopia: it began with the harmony in the individual and spread to the harmony of the whole society.

In Kant's theory, aesthetic sensitivity not only heals but also brings the eternal Ideas down to the world of sensibility. That is the way Schiller and other Romantics appropriated Kant's doctrine of immanent Ideas. They wanted to bring the world of supernature down to the world of nature or to elevate the world of nature to the world of supernature. Either way, it appeared to achieve the union of nature and supernature. This sense of unity seemed to revive and revitalize the European sensibility, which had been stifled under the relentless pressure of scientific materialism and rationalism.

∗ ∗ The End of Critical Philosophy

If the last *Critique* is as radically different from Kant's previous writings as I have presented it to be, it should not even be regarded as a part of his Critical Philosophy. In fact, I will try to show that the last *Critique* was not a part of his original design for Critical Philosophy. In support of this thesis, I will advance the following evidence. In the winter of 1770–71 Kant became dissatisfied with his *Inaugural Dissertation* and decided to abandon his original plan of improving and refining it. Instead he started a new project called *Die Grenzen der Sinnlichkeit und der Vernunft* (The boundaries of sensibility and reason), which eventually materialized as his Critical Philosophy.

In a letter of June 1771 to Marcus Herz, Kant described his new project as an investigation of the basic concepts and laws of the sensible world, together with a sketch of the essential aspects of the theory, taste, metaphysics, and morality (*KGS* 10:121–24). This new project appears to have foretold the three parts of Critical Philosophy; taste, metaphysics, and morality appear to have been the three respective topics for the three *Critiques*. In a letter of February 1772 to Herz, however, Kant described his projected work as having two

12. Ibid., letter 27, par. 10.

parts, theoretical and practical. The theoretical part was to treat general phenomenology and metaphysics; the practical part, general principles of the feeling of taste and sensuous desire and the first foundations of morality (*KGS* 10:129).

The feeling of taste did not yet constitute an independent department, contrary to Kant's claim later, in the last *Critique*. He recognized no distinction between the pleasure of aesthetic experience and the pleasures of inclination. In the same letter to Herz, he also described his forthcoming book as "Critique of Pure Reason," which "will deal with the nature of theoretical as well as practical knowledge—insofar as the latter is purely intellectual. Of this, I will first work out the first part, which will deal with the sources of metaphysics, its method and limits. After that I will work out the pure principles of morality" (KGS 10:132, Zweig 73).

Kant's habit of dividing philosophy into the two basic divisions of theory and practice antedates his Critical period. In the *Prize Essay* he recognizes two different types of first principles in philosophy, the first principles of metaphysics and the first principles of ethics (*KGS* 2:273–301). In the *Dreams of a Spirit-Seer* he recognizes two orders of creation, the order of physical objects and the order of spiritual beings. One is governed by Newton's law of nature; the other, by the moral law of general will (*KGS* 2:315–83). In the *Inaugural Dissertation* he reaffirms his notion of two orders in his distinction of phenomena and noumena (*KGS* 2:385–419). The latter is a spiritual order governed by moral principles; the former is a natural order governed by physical principles.

The format of the *Observations*, of 1764, is quite different from that of the other pre-Critical treatises. Instead of a systematic treatise, it presents a collection of informal observations. Moreover, it is devoted to the practical branch of philosophy. Although the aesthetic concepts of the beautiful and the sublime are the central categories in the *Observations*, Kant never separates them from ethical categories. On the contrary, he employs the concepts of the beautiful and the sublime in his discussions of both aesthetic and ethical properties. He recognizes no important distinction between taste and desire. He lumps them together in the domain of feeling, which is supposed to belong to practical or moral philosophy. He is still operating under the influence of Shaftsbury and Hutcheson, who had advocated the unity of all feelings and desires.

In the *Critique of Practical Reason* Kant goes beyond Shaftsbury and Hutcheson and recognizes two sources of feeling, the phenomenal and the noumenal. The phenomenal source is our desires and inclinations, which produce pleasure and pain. These feelings are governed by empirical laws. The noumenal source is the moral law, which provokes the feeling of awe and the sublime. This feeling transcends the empirical domain and reflects the dignity of human beings as rational agents. Although Kant emphatically stresses the difference between these two types of feeling, he does not yet see the need to make a special place for aesthetic feeling. As far as the second *Critique* goes, aesthetic feeling is still one species of empirical feeling.

In his architectonic review of the first *Critique* Kant reaffirms his two-part program: "Metaphysics is divided into that of the *speculative* and that of the *practical* employment of pure reason, and is therefore either *metaphysics of nature* or *metaphysics of morals*" (A841/ B869). In the preface to the second edition of the first *Critique* he reaffirms this binary demarcation of theoretical and practical philosophy (Bx). In the preface to the second *Critique* he recognizes two faculties of the mind and two sets of a priori principles, theoretical and practical. This dyadic division is reaffirmed as the systematic basis for his entire Critical Philosophy (C_2 12).

Kant announces the completion of his Critical program in the conclusion of the second *Critique*, where he makes his moving observation about two wonders, "the starry heavens above me and the moral law within me" (C_2 161–62). The first is located in the external world, and the second, in the inner self. These two represent Kant's two worlds, phenomena and noumena, the domain of natural necessity and the domain of moral freedom; they are the objects of his inquiry in the *Critique of Pure Reason* and the *Critique of Practical Reason*, respectively. In the conclusion of the second *Critique*, Kant sums up his accomplishments not only in that volume but in his entire Critical Philosophy. Hence it reads like the coda for his Critical program as a whole.

The first two *Critiques* contain recurrent references to each other. The aim of the first *Critique* is to limit the domain of knowledge so as to secure the possibility of belief, which is the domain of the second *Critique*. The theory of moral law and freedom in the second *Critique* is formulated within the ontological framework of the first *Critique*. The dialectical chapters of these two *Critiques* especially read like a well-orchestrated antiphony. In contrast to this inseparable mutual reference, these two *Critiques* make absolutely no reference to the third *Critique*.

Kant begins the last *Critique* by reaffirming his binary division of philosophy: "Our cognitive power as a whole has two domains, that of the concepts of nature and that of the concept of freedom, because it legislates a priori by means of both kinds of concept. Now philosophy too divides, according to these legislations, into theoretical and practical" (C_3 174, Pluhar 13). If this division of philosophy is correct, the first two *Critiques* cover the entire domain of philosophy, leaving no room for another critique. So Kant feels the need to make a special plea for writing another critique. He now claims to see an enormous chasm between the phenomenal and the noumenal worlds. This so-called chasm was never regarded as a problem in the first two *Critiques:* in fact, it was the ontological foundation for the Critical program. He now looks upon it as the most serious problem in his philosophy, because the chasm makes it impossible for practical reason to translate its ends from the domain of freedom to the domain of nature (C_3 175–76).

In neither the *Groundwork* nor the second *Critique* had Kant ever regarded the chasm as an obstacle for practical reason. Why, then, does it suddenly appear as an obstacle? As long as practical reason operates only with formal concepts and principles, it does not have to cross the chasm between the phenomenal and the noumenal worlds. Formal concepts and principles are not derived from the noumenal world; they are constructed by formal practical reason in this world. But the chasm is a serious obstacle for the material (substantive) conception of practical reason. Material concepts and principles are located in the noumenal world and have to be brought down to the phenomenal world for their realization. Kant's recognition of the chasm between the two worlds becomes inevitable with his reversion from formal to material practical reason. With the acceptance of aesthetic and teleological Ideas, he has indeed returned to his old substantive conception of practical reason.

In the last *Critique* Kant proposes to use the faculty of judgment to bridge the chasm between phenomena and noumena. This faculty can establish the ground of unity and mediation for the two worlds, he says, because it lies between understanding and reason. In the first two *Critiques* Kant had recognized two rational faculties, understanding and reason, and had designated phenomena as the province of understanding and noumena as the province of reason. Now he says that the faculty of judgment is a third intellectual faculty lying between understanding and reason. So he proposes a new triadic division of faculties: the faculty of knowledge, the faculty of feeling (pleasure and pain), and the faculty of desire.

This triadic division represents a clear departure from his previous view, in which the faculty of feeling (pleasure and pain) was not yet separated from the faculty of desire. In the first two *Critiques* judgment had not been a separate faculty, but only a function. The two rational faculties of understanding and reason had had their respective functions. Judgment had been the function of understanding; inference, the function of reason. To elevate judgment to the status of a faculty, Kant distinguishes reflective from determinative judgment (C_3 179–80). Determinative judgment determines an object of cognition and belongs to understanding. Reflective judgment does not determine an object but only appreciates its beauty and finality, and thus, Kant claims, it is an independent faculty.

Kant's aim is not merely to establish the independence of reflective judgment but to demonstrate its role for mediating between the sensible and the intelligible worlds and overcome their enormous chasm. How does the faculty of reflective judgment mediate between the two worlds? Kant makes no effort whatsoever to answer this question. This is the most baffling feature of the third *Critique*. After mentioning mediation as the most urgent problem for his entire philosophy at the beginning of the third *Critique*, he seems to forget it altogether for the remainder of the volume. Werner Pluhar says that the task of mediation is accomplished by affirming the third supersensible as the ground of natural beauty and teleology.[13] Two supersensibles had already been affirmed in the first two *Critiques*, and the third *Critique* is to perform the role of mediation by affirming a third supersensible. This interpretation makes little sense, though it may be gleaned from Kant's scattered remarks about the proposed mediation.

It appears that Pluhar has forgotten the original problem of mediation. As he notes, Kant had asserted the existence of two supersensibles in the first and the second *Critiques*, creating the chasm between phenomena and noumena. According to Pluhar, the third *Critique* designates the third supersensible as the mediator between the first and the second supersensibles. There is no need to mediate between the first and the second supersensibles, because they are one and the same; what needs mediation is the chasm between the sensible and the supersensible, phenomena and noumena. This chasm cannot be mediated by adding the third supersensible to the first two.

If anything, the addition of one more supersensible to the first two should aggravate the original problem. There are other accounts of the mediation for the two worlds, but they are not very different from Pluhar's. For example, Francis Coleman says that "just as the supersensible is the *tertium quid* that harmonizes the dictates of Nature with the commands of morality, so artistic genius, Kant implies, is the link between the world of appearances and the world of freedom."[14] But the supersensible cannot be the *tertium quid* for bridging the two worlds, because it is one of the two worlds. To be sure, Kant reaffirms the supersensible as the ground of unity for nature and freedom, but he never explains how it mediates between the two worlds of phenomena and noumena. If it indeed mediates between the two worlds, there can be no chasm between the two, and Kant's original problem cannot even arise.

Cassirer correctly notes that Kant does not give us "even a hint"

---

13. Translator's introduction to Immanuel Kant, *Critique of Judgment*, lxii–lxiii, cii–civ.

14. *The Harmony of Reason: A Study in Kant's Aesthetics* (Pittsburgh, 1974), 163.

for explaining the mediation between the two worlds.[15] In desperation, some commentators have suggested that the faculty of reflective judgment performs its function of mediation by being partially
similar to the faculty of sensibility and partially similar to the faculty
of pure intellect, or that the world of art and natural teleology can
mediate between the two worlds of phenomena and noumena because it resembles both worlds to some extent. But no one can explain how the notion of resemblance turns into the function of
mediation.

Cassirer has perhaps given us the best hint for resolving the riddle
of mediation. Instead of looking for the ground of mediation in the
supersensible, he suggests, we should look upon the world of art as
pointing to "a new unity of the sensible and the intelligible, of nature
and freedom."[16] Let us assume that instead of mediating the two
worlds, the faculty of reflective judgment fuses them into one. This
is not to close our eyes to the textual fact that in the last *Critique*
Kant still talks about the demarcation of phenomena and noumena
and appeals to the supersensible in his account of aesthetic and teleological judgments. But we should be careful in understanding
Kant's concept of the supersensible: it can mean the supersensible
existence (God) or the supersensible Ideas. In the third *Critique* the
existence of God is still supersensible, but Ideas are no longer supersensible. In our experience of the beautiful and the sublime, we can
no longer see the old demarcation of the intelligible and the sensible
worlds. The transcendental ideals are immanently real. Even the
faculty of judgment is not the third rational faculty but an intimate
joint operation of sense and intellect, imagination and understanding, ideas and feelings. Because the third *Critique* fuses the two
worlds into one, there is no longer any need for their mediation.

The separation of the two worlds is the central theme of Kant's
Critical Philosophy. But the last *Critique* fuses the two worlds into
one; it terminates the Critical period and begins a new one, which
I propose to call the post-Critical period. In the first two *Critiques*

15. *Kant's Life and Thought*, 331.
16. Ibid., 331–32.

sensibility was constricted to the world of phenomena, the objects of sense and desire. The world of noumena, the transcendental ideals and principles, was only postulated by the intellect. This created a serious gap and severe strain between intellect and sensibility, between what can be thought and what can be felt. This gap is a typical syndrome of scientific consciousness, and Kant's formalism was its inevitable outcome. Once this gap is eliminated, the domain of sensibility becomes coextensive with the domain of intellect, and practical reason can get out of the barren world of formal imperatives and move into the rich world of substantive ideals. This rich world is the domain of the highest good, which cannot be complete without including all substantive norms and standards and all material ends and purposes.

The concept of the highest good that is to become the central practical principle for the *Metaphysics of Morals* is already prepared in the last *Critique*. It is no longer the thin concept of apportioning happiness to virtue but a far richer concept of all ends and values, including the beauty of nature and the refinement of culture. In the last *Critique* Kant relocates his theory of value from the formal to the substantive ground. If the conception of formal reason is regarded as the foundation of the enterprise of Critical Philosophy, the last *Critique* does not really complete it but supersedes it. This point has gone unnoticed, chiefly because the third *Critique* is still called a critique. It is a standard pedantic habit to be led by the name of a book instead of recognizing what is really written between its covers.

The fact that the third *Critique* repudiates the central teaching of the first two should not come as a surprise to those who already know that even the second *Critique* repudiated Kant's ethical theory of the first *Critique*. As we saw in chapter 4, Kant wrote the *Critique of Practical Reason* in response to his critics' complaint that his ethical theory in the *Groundwork* was incompatible with his ethical theory in the first *Critique*. In the latter work, he had performed his Copernican revolution only for theoretical philosophy and retained the Platonic Ideas of his *Dissertation* for practical philosophy. Evidently, Kant had a change of heart about the ethics of Platonic Ideas after the publication of the first *Critique* and extended his Copernican revolution to ethics. So he wrote the *Groundwork*, wherein he presented his novel idea of formal practical reason. In order to defend this novel idea, he had to write the *Critique of Practical Reason*.

Although Kant wrote the second *Critique* because he changed his mind, it was still within the spirit of his Critical Philosophy. In fact, it expands and extends the spirit of critical formalism from theoretical to practical philosophy. By a strict standard of critical formalism, the first *Critique* was not completely critical; it should not have left the domain of practical philosophy under the control of supersensible Ideas. To that extent, the first *Critique* was partly Critical and partly pre-Critical, if the spirit of formalism is taken as the essence of his Critical Philosophy. The Copernican revolution in ethics was meant to rectify this imperfection and inconsistency and achieve the total perfection and consistency of Critical Philosophy.

The role of the last *Critique* is quite different. It neither improves nor perfects Critical Philosophy. On the contrary, it eliminates the basis of Critical Philosophy by repudiating formalism and by installing the unity of the sensible and the supersensible and of nature and freedom. Kant never succeeds in eliminating the ponderous presence of Critical Philosophy; the third *Critique* still retains many traces of his Critical formalism. But his philosophical reorientation is so drastic that the *Critique of Judgment* can no longer be regarded as a continuation or completion of Critical Philosophy. In that regard, his change of heart in the last *Critique* is different from his change of heart in the second *Critique*. The latter was within the dualistic scheme of Critical Philosophy; the former annuls and transcends that dualistic scheme.

Without these changes of heart, Kant would have given us only one *Critique*, the *Critique of Pure Reason*. Even this work came from his change of heart. He had taken his metaphysical stand for the first time in the *Inaugural Dissertation*, quite late in his long, checkered career. His metaphysical stand was to accept Platonism and its two-world view. When he changed his mind about theoretical knowledge, he had to write the *Critique of Pure Reason*. When he changed his mind about the first *Critique*, he had to write the *Critique of Practical Reason*. When he changed his mind about both the first and the second *Critiques,* he had to write the *Critique of Judgment.* Throughout the course of these changes, each of which was drastic enough to be called a philosophical revolution, his commitment to Platonism remained firm and intact. The *Inaugural Dissertation* and his three *Critiques* were his different attempts to account for the relation of Platonic Forms to the world of phenomena, especially how those ideal entities constitute the basic conditions for human cognition and existence.

If my account is correct, the three *Critiques* do not constitute a harmonious trilogy, as they have long been taken to do in Kant scholarship. On the contrary, they constitute three successive revisions in his philosophy. Moreover, none of the three *Critiques* marks a more important event in Kant's illustrious career than the *Inaugural Dissertation* does. It was in this modest treatise that he made the momentous philosophical commitment to Platonism. This was his Platonic revolution, or rather its beginning. Kant devoted the rest of his life to the tortuous task of elaborating and articulating the original position he had taken in the *Dissertation.* Kant's Platonic revolution has turned out to be a perpetual revolution, and even his so-called Copernican revolution can best be appreciated only as an event in this perpetual revolution.

7 Kant's Platonic Constructivism and Hegel's Neoplatonic Historicism

* * * * * * * * * * * * * * * * * * * *

For two centuries, in one way or another, Western philosophy has lived off the Kantian legacy. It is about time for us to consider its strength and its weakness. Its weakness lies in Kant's incurable penchant for cheating. Let us review some of the notable incidents: (1) his illusive maneuver of deriving the twelve categories from the forms of judgment (chapter 2); (2) his dubious claim that all moral laws can be derived from the formal principle of consistency (chapter 4); (3) his contention that the first and second formulas of the categorical imperative are related as form and matter and yet are equivalent and independent (chapter 4); (4) his pretense that the *Metaphysics of Morals* is only an application of the moral principle laid out in the *Groundwork* (chapter 5); and finally (5) his proposal that the third *Critique* bridges the chasm between the two worlds created by the first two *Critiques* (chapter 6).

This is not simply a series of flimsy arguments, which abound in metaphysics. These have nothing to do with metaphysical subtlety. To be sure, Kant has concocted his share of metaphysical theories (e.g., his idea of the *Ding-an-sich*, or his idea of space and time as the forms of intuition), and he had tried to support them with some unconvincing arguments, which, however, cannot be denounced as fraudulent claims. But his cheating game, which we have witnessed in our investigation, is much more blatant. It makes fraudulent claims that openly violate the commonsense logic of natural reason. But these claims are so ingeniously disguised that they have misled not only his unwary readers but Kant himself. Unfortunately, as we will soon see, this shady side of Kantian legacy has had such an enduring impact on his posterity that continental philosophy has often appeared to be a continuous game of massive deception and delusion.

Kant's strength lies in his Platonic constructivism. But his conception of Platonic Forms is quite different from the conventional understanding of Plato's teaching. He understands them as the most general normative Ideas, highly abstract and indeterminate, and he states his conception of indeterminate Ideas as early as in the *Inaugural Dissertation* (1770) and as late as in the third *Critique* (1790). To be sure, he often says that the Ideas of practical reason are determinate and that this is the important difference between them and the aesthetic Ideas. But this is a misconception on his part that is required for his equally mistaken moral rigorism. Because he assumes that moral laws should never allow exceptions, he feels that they should be based on the determinate Ideas of practical reason. As we saw in chapters 4 and 5, however, if we want to discard his formalist constructivism in favor of his Platonic constructivism, we have to concede that the Ideas of practical reason are as indeterminate as the aesthetic Ideas.

The indeterminacy of Platonic Ideas is the essential prerequisite for constructivism. If they were determinate, they would leave no room for our construction. The art of construction is to render an indeterminate Idea more and more determinate, thereby making it more and more relevant to our concrete situations. This is the process of articulation and concretion. By this process Platonic Forms descend to the phenomenal world, and by this descent the transcendent Forms become immanent. Kant recognizes the immanent Ideas in every phase of human culture. In his philosophy of history he shows how the abstract Ideas are particularized differently for different historical epochs. In his *Metaphysics of Morals* he shows how the same Idea of the highest good is realized differently in different spheres of ethics and politics. In the third *Critique* he holds that each great work of art is animated by its own unique aesthetic Idea. This transition from the indeterminate to the determinate Ideas is the essence of Platonic constructivism.

* * The Two Programs of Platonic Construction

In the first *Critique* Kant tried out two versions of Platonic constructivism, eidetic and ontic. In the eidetic version, definite concepts are constructed from indefinite ones; in the ontic version, the objects of experience are constructed in accordance with the concepts. If ontic constructivism is successful, it can secure the ontological foundation for the truth of Kant's a priori principles. If the transcendental subject can construct the objects of experience in accordance with the categories, those objects can provide the truth conditions for the a priori principles generated from the categories. There can be no better way to secure the a priori truths of those principles. But the very idea of constructing the objects of experience in accordance with the pure concepts is no more than a metaphysical fairy tale and thus cannot withstand the reality test.

The program of eidetic construction is much more plausible than the program of ontic construction. It is perhaps the best way to account for the genesis of our concepts. Hume tried to explain their genesis by his empiricist thesis that all our ideas are copies of sense impressions. But there are too many concepts whose origin cannot be traced back to impressions, and yet not all the nonempirical concepts have to be placed in Platonic Heaven or in the pure understanding. Most of them can be constructed from a few a priori or primitive concepts or Ideas. For example, we can construct many different concepts of substance (e.g., the concept of an organic or an inorganic substance) from the purely logical concept of substance as an entity that can serve as a grammatical subject and never as a predicate. Although the different concepts of substance are constructed, there is no way to derive the logical concept of substance by construction or from empirical sources. As Hume says, it cannot be a copy of any impression. In that case, it must be a priori and primitive.

To be sure, the word *construction* cannot be found in Kant's lexicon, but the Kantian term *synthesis* is its equivalent. In Kant's own text, however, the term *synthesis* is restricted largely to the domain of ontic, or objectival, construction, and he never openly advocates the notion of eidetic, or conceptual, construction. I have proposed the latter notion as the best way for reading some of the most opaque and mysterious passages in Kant's writings. For example, as we saw in chapter 2, he claims that the categories are produced from the forms of judgment by introducing transcendental content (A79/

B104–5), but he never explains how the introduction of transcendental content produces the categories. By imputing the notion of eidetic construction to him, we can take his claim to mean that the transcendental content is used in the construction of the categories from the forms of judgment.

By *transcendental content* Kant means the content of pure intuitions, namely, space and time. By adding the spatial and temporal dimensions to the concept of a purely logical or grammatical subject, we can construct the concept of an empirical substance. In chapter 2 we identified this process of eidetic construction with Kant's doctrine of transcendental schematism. Although this identification reveals schematism to be a commonplace phenomenon in human cognition, it appears to be a great mystery to Kant, who tries to describe it without employing the notion of eidetic construction. So he plays up the mystical dimension of schematism by calling it "an art concealed in the depth of the human soul, whose real modes of activity nature is hardly likely ever to allow us to discover, and to have open to our gaze" (A141/B181–82, trans. Kemp Smith).

Let us again consider the three formulas of the categorical imperative (see chapter 4). While claiming their independence and equivalence, Kant also says that the first two are related as form and matter and that the third is the combination of the two. This assertion is a sheer absurdity. If the first and the second formulas are related as form and matter, they can be neither independent nor equivalent. In Kant's lexicon, form and matter are complementary to each other. Two complementary things can never be independent or equivalent. If the third formula is the combination of the first and the second formulas, the former cannot be independent of the latter. In chapter 4 I reinterpreted the relation of those three formulas as that of three moments in the construction of law. The first formula secures the universality of law; the second takes into account the objective of law; and the third formula considers the law in the context of the whole community.

This is a process of Platonic construction, which is radically different from Kantian formalist construction. The former begins with the Platonic Idea of Law, whereas the latter depends solely on the notion of formal consistency. If we do not accept the Platonic account of the three formulas for the categorical imperative, we can maintain the integrity of Kant's formalist ethics only by resorting to a systematic cheating game. We have to derive all the substantive moral maxims from the empty formula of universal law. But we can succeed in this Kantian endeavor only by surreptitiously introducing substantive considerations in the name of formal consistency. And then we have to show that those maxims are identical to those we can derive from the second and third formulas, which are clearly substantive. We can produce this marvelous result of coincidence only by a dialectical sleight of arguments.

As a standard practice, one can be a champion of Kantian ethics only by being either a master of this dialectical trickery or its victim, or both at the same time. We can redeem Kantian ethics from this longstanding dialectical trickery only by restating it in terms of Platonic constructivism. Although our Platonic reading of Kant dissolves most of Kant's dialectical mystifications, it leaves one major problem unresolved: he has given not one program of Platonic construction but two competing programs. It appears that we have to choose between his ontic and eidetic programs.

According to the ontic program, the transcendental subject constructs the causal relations by organizing the manifold of intuition in accordance with the category of cause and effect. The causal relations do not exist apart from this ontic construction, nor do the empirical causal laws. Kant says that they are only specifications of the a priori causal principle. This is an idealistic picture of the physical world; its structure is completely determined by the transcendental subject. The eidetic program, on the other hand, recognizes the independent existence of causal relations and their laws; they are not constructed by the transcendental subject. The a priori causal principle is necessary only for the recognition of causal relations. The transcendental subject performs not the awesome function of constructing the physical objects and their relations but only the modest function of recognizing those objects and their relations. In order to perform this function, it has to construct the empirically suitable concepts from the pure concepts of understanding. The eidetic program presents a realistic picture of the physical world by limiting the role of the transcendental subject to the epistemic domain.

* * The Fusion of the Two Programs

Do we really construct the objects and their relations, or do we only recognize what they are? This is the most vexing question in Kant. Plato provides us with the best way to resolve this question: we can fuse Kant's two programs into one. According to Plato, the phenomenal world is an indefinite dyad (*Philebus* 16c–18c). Let us look, for example, at the phenomena of sounds and noises. They are indeterminately many, but they can be organized into a musical scale of five or seven tones. Another example is the range of the human voice that is used in speaking. It is composed of indefinitely many kinds of vocalization, but they can be organized into a system of a few vowels and consonants. The organization of phonemes or a musical scale is a process of constructing objects, which also requires the construction of concepts. We cannot distinguish one vowel from another, or vowels from consonants, without constructing the concepts of vowels and consonants.

By *indefinite dyad* Plato means something that can be more or less than what it is. For example, the size of a mountain can be greater or smaller than it is. Likewise, its weight, its greenness, or its beauty can be more or less than it is. Each of the properties that characterize the nature of the phenomenal world is an indefinite dyad. Each can be either increased or decreased. The color spectrum is perhaps the best example of an indefinite dyad. It comprises an indefinite number of colors and shades. If we have to have a word for each of the colors and shades that can be discriminated, we will be swamped in an immense, chaotic lexicon of color words. To avoid such a semantic chaos, we divide the entire color spectrum into five or seven different colors. This operation involves both eidetic and ontic constructions.

By this theory of construction, the nature and order of the phenomenal world should be understood on two different levels. For example, the color spectrum has its own nature before its construction and gains a new order after its construction. Before the construction, its nature is so diverse and so indeterminate that it can never be fully recognized by the human mind. After the construction, its chaotic original nature is simplified and ordered by a system of concepts invented by the human mind. Although the simplified order is a human invention and convention, it is still ontologically dependent on the original nature of the color spectrum. If the original nature were to have no distinction of colors and shades, their distinction could not be introduced by the invention of color words alone. The conceptual organization of the color spectrum is not a total construction, with no basis to build on, but a partial construction, or rather a reconstruction, of its original nature.

The notion of an indefinite dyad may not be alien to Kant; it may be lurking behind his enigmatic adage, "Percepts without concepts are blind; concepts without percepts are empty." By this adage he wants to stress the interdependence of concepts and percepts; human knowledge becomes possible only by combining percepts with concepts. But this Kantian thesis contains a paradox: If percepts are blind by themselves, and concepts are empty in their original nature, how is it possible to produce knowledge by combining those two? The conjunction of blind percepts and empty concepts should produce only blind emptiness or empty blindness.

We can avoid these paradoxical problems only by refusing to take the blindness of percepts in its literal sense. Percepts can be blind in two quite different senses. They can be regarded as blind (1) if they allow no distinctions whatsoever and (2) if they allow more distinctions than the human mind can cope with. Let us make an analogy to information processing. It is possible to produce the same result of information chaos either by putting no information whatsoever into a cybernetic circuit or by overloading it with too much information. If Kant's blind percepts are taken as the total absence of distinction and information, they can never be a source of knowledge, regardless of whether they are combined with concepts. On the other hand, if they are taken to contain too many distinctions and too much information, they can be organized into knowledge by a system of concepts, which simplifies their limitless complexity.

I have tried to restate Kant's view of percepts as a special version of Plato's view of indefinite dyads. The same Platonic reading can be given to his favorite expressions, "the manifold [*Mannichfaltige*] of intuition" or "the manifold of appearance." These expressions stress the multiplicity of sensation and phenomena. What sort of multiplicity does Kant have in mind? He says that the objects of sensibility can be divided (decreased) or added (increased) indefinitely on both the quantitative ("extensive magnitude") and the qualitative ("intensive magnitude") levels. These two features of sensibility form the ontological basis for his two a priori principles, the Axioms of Intuition and the Anticipations of Perception (A162–76/B202–18). These two principles state the very essence of Platonic indefinite dyads.

Let us now see how Kant's two programs of construction can be unified in a Platonic mode. Take the pure concept of unity, the first of Kant's twelve categories. We use this category in our distinction of one color from another, one sound from another, one rock from another, one frog from another, one musical style from another, or one historical period from another. We do not use the same concept of unity for all these distinctions. Each one requires a different articulation of the pure concept of unity. But we can say that all these different conceptions of unity are constructed from the same pure concept of unity. This is the eidetic construction. Moreover, when we apply these different conceptions of unity to different empirical domains, we can find no clear-cut boundaries between different entities. The unity, or identity, of an empirical object is never perfect, because it is located in the world of indefinite dyads or indeterminate continua. Hence we introduce new orders into the phenomenal world by our individuation and construction. This is a partial ontic construction rather than a total one.

These two constructivist operations, ontic and eidetic, are required for the application of not only the category of unity but all the other categories as well. To make this point clearer, let us see how the two programs of construction should work for the pure concept of cause and effect. A few months ago a hailstorm shattered the windshield of my car. This is a typical case of causation: the hailstorm was the cause, and the shattered windshield was the effect. But the hailstorm was not the only cause of the disaster. If I had parked my car in a garage, the hailstorm could not have damaged the windshield. If the windshield had been made of much stronger material, it could have easily withstood the hail storm. If the direction of the wind had been different, the storm might not have done the same damage to the windshield. Its destruction could also have been avoided if the storm had been subject to a much weaker force of gravitation. There was no one definite cause of the disaster; it was produced by an indefinite number of events and forces whose multiplicity can never be fully enumerated.

Whenever we talk about a causal chain, we select only one or a few out of an indefinite multiplicity of causes. Moreover, different causal chains may require different conceptions of causation. The conception of causation in the biological domain is different from the conception of causation in the mechanical domain. Even in the same mechanical domain, quantum mechanics employs a causal concept different from the one used in classical or statistical mechanics. Kant can say that all these different conceptions of causations are constructed by articulating the same pure concept of cause and effect. This is the eidetic construction. When these concepts are applied to the world of phenomena, the latter is reorganized in accordance with the former. This is the partial ontic construction or reconstruction. The two constructions are two phases of one continuous operation.

By the Platonic reading of Kant's constructivism, we can give a better account of the relation between the a priori causal principle and the empirical causal laws. As I have already noted, Kant says that the empirical laws are the specifications of the a priori principle. In that case, the empirical laws should have the same sort of a priori truth that the a priori principle does. But Kant still insists that the truth of an empirical law is not a priori but a posteriori. We can eliminate this discrepancy in Kant's account by substituting *empirical concepts* for *empirical laws* in his statement. We should say that the empirical concepts of causation are the specifications of the a priori concept of causation. Moreover, the question of truth for these concepts is an empirical one, because there is no a priori way of securing their truth.

With the fusion of eidetic and ontic constructions into one operation, the distinction between the pure concepts of understanding and the Ideas of pure reason becomes insignificant. Let us consider the Idea of the world as the totality of phenomena. This Idea already contains the pure concept of totality, one of the twelve categories. Just like the pure concept of cause and effect, the Idea of the world can be articulated in many different ways and on many different levels. The Idea of a biological world is different from the Idea of a mechanical world, which is still different from the Idea of a quantum mechanical world. The Idea of a biological or mechanical world is again different from the Idea of a moral or historical world. All these different Ideas can be constructed from one Idea of pure reason, and their application to the phenomenal world is the construction of different worlds.

The idea of constructing different worlds on different levels resolves one of the most embarrassing problems in Kant's philosophy, namely, the relation between nature and freedom. In the first *Critique* Kant accepts the causal principle for all phenomena and endorses a deterministic view of the physical world. But he also endorses the Idea of moral freedom, which is clearly incompatible with his deterministic view of the phenomenal world. He tries to explain away their incompatibility in his theory of dual perspective. From the perspective of phenomena, all human actions are causally determined and necessitated. But they are free from the perspective of noumena. One and the same action is free and determined; it is free transcendentally but determined phenomenally. This dual-perspective account is surely one of the best-known mystifications in Kant's philosophy.

Kant's theory of transcendental freedom is so mysterious that we do not know what it really means. We have no idea of what it means to be free from the perspective of noumena. Kant repeatedly says that we have no idea of what we are talking about if we apply categories such as cause and effect to the world of noumena, which transcends space and time. If causal statements can make no sense without reference to the space-time framework, the concept of freedom should be equally unintelligible outside the phenomenal domain.

For the two concepts are logically inseparable; the concept of not being causally determined is the minimal basic semantic requirement for the concept of being free. Hence we have no better idea of what it means to be free in the world of noumena than we have of what the concept of causation means in that world. This is the semantic embarrassment for Kant's doctrine of transcendental freedom, and it becomes even more embarrassing when he tries to link the noumenal freedom to the phenomenal determinism, because we do not know how to make this link semantically either.

All these embarrassments can be avoided by rejecting Kant's presupposition that a human being should be either totally free or totally determined. This presupposition has led to his doctrine that the noumenal self is totally free but the phenomenal self is totally determined. But it is impossible to combine these two entities into one coherent human agency. Kant can get out of this embarrassment by replacing his original presupposition with another, namely, that a human being is partially free and partially determined. This revised presupposition is in tune with the idea that there are many levels of causation, requiring different conceptions of causation. The different levels of causation can contain different degrees of ontic indeterminacy. That is, not all the empirical causal laws are uniformly rigid and absolutely determinate; some of them, for example, the causal laws in quantum mechanics and biology, allow greater room for causal indeterminacy than others.

This concept of indeterminate causation goes hand in hand with the concept of partial freedom: human freedom is not absolute but limited. In our everyday life we operate on this concept by assuming that different people have different degrees of freedom. We assume that an immature, stupid person is not free to the same extent that a mature, wise person is free. For this reason, in the court of law, people who differ significantly in intelligence and maturity are not held to the same level of accountability. Even one and the same person can be less free on some occasions than on other occasions. According to Kant's doctrine, distinctions such as these cannot be permitted, because except for idiots and the insane, everyone is supposed to be absolutely free. Let us try to understand the concept of partial freedom in an analogy to the concept of partial unity or identity. The unity or identity of a human being over time is never total but only partial; it is mixed with multiplicity and diversity. Likewise, human freedom is never total but only partial; conversely, we are never totally but only partially determined.

Although the concept of partial freedom is incompatible with Kant's concept of transcendental freedom, it is consistent with his concept of practical freedom. As we saw in chapter 3, he defines practical freedom as the power to act in accordance with Ideas of reason. This power cannot be uniform for all human beings; it should be a function of their intelligence and wisdom. It should change even for the same person over his or her lifetime, because the level of a person's intelligence and wisdom is subject to change. For the same reason, the different levels in the development of human culture should provide different levels of freedom. This is consistent with what Kant says in his *Conjectural Beginning of Human History*, where he recognizes different levels of culture and different forms of human freedom that correspond to different cultural levels.

The different levels of culture belong to different levels of construction, and all of them are produced by the articulation of the Ideas of reason, according to Kant. These different cultural levels provide different levels of partial freedom. But Kant cannot account for these cultural constructions as long as he is straitjacketed by his picture of a totally deterministic universe. Nor can he make the connection between moral and cultural freedom. Thus he has given his commentators every reason to relegate all his astute writings in the philosophy of history to the limbo of dogmatic philosophy. Platonic constructivism alone can help us to recover his philosophy of history from this limbo of indignity and appreciate his profound understanding of history.

* * Varieties of Normative Construction

Platonic fusion of Kant's two constructivist programs works much better for his normative philosophy than for his philosophy of nature and natural science. This is largely owing to the difference between the normative world and the physical world. Although not many people can readily accept the idea of constructing the objects of nature, they have no trouble believing that the objects of culture are constructed by human beings. We can not only construct a concept of contract but make a contract in accordance with the concept. We can form a concept of a state and then build a state in accordance with the concept. The first step is an eidetic construction, and the second step is an ontic construction. In normative construction, Kant's two programs of construction, eidetic and ontic, are obviously two interconnected phases in one continuous process.

The idea of normative construction is not Kant's invention. It is much older than Kant, and there are a few other modes of normative construction besides his Platonic construction. It is about time for us to grasp the essential features of his Platonic construction by clarifying its salient differences from the other modes. The obvious alternative to Platonic constructivism is Kant's own formalist program. It pretends to construct normative rules and standards by using only the logical principle of contradiction. We have already seen that it is no more than a program of dialectical trickery. The principle of logical consistency is the minimum requirement in any normative construction, and Kant has tried to pass this minimum requirement off as a sufficient one.

The program of positivist construction differs from Platonic construction; the former denies the existence of transcendental normative standards accepted by the latter. In the positivist program, normative standards come into being only by the grace of their construction. They can be created by any one of the various legislative agencies, for example, a king, a dictator, an assembly elected by the people or appointed by a king, or a prophet relaying the message of the gods. All normative standards are immanent; they are embodied in the laws and customs thus created. Even the normative rules and standards governing the legislative agencies are embodied in the positive law and convention. There are no normative standards that transcend the positive institutions.

The program of positivist construction was advocated by Thomas Hobbes almost a century before Kant proposed his Platonic program. According to Hobbes, there is nothing just or unjust before the social contract is made and the law is proclaimed by the sovereign. It makes no sense to criticize some law as unjust, because the standard of justice is set by the law itself. There can be no external constraint on the Hobbesian sovereign, whose sovereignty is truly absolute and unlimited. No one has a right to say whether the sovereign is making a good or bad law if such a statement has to appeal to some normative criterion lying outside the positive law of his or her making.

The program of positivist construction does not always have to accept an absolute sovereign. It can operate with a limited sovereign, for example, one who has no power to make laws abrogating the customary rights sanctioned by the religious tradition. Whenever the sovereign exceeds or abuses its power, it can be criticized. But the criticism does not appeal to any transcendental normative standards but relies on the custom or convention that limits the sovereign's power. Whether the program of positivist construction is entrusted to a limited or an absolute sovereign, it recognizes no transcendental normative standards. This is the unique hallmark of positivist construction.

We can also limit the legislative power of a sovereign. We can do this by subjecting it to a general principle, for example, that all laws should be made under the general principle of securing the greatest happiness for our republic. Is such a program of construction still positivistic? The answer depends on how the general principle should be construed and how the greatest happiness of our republic should be understood. If the sovereign alone has the power to interpret this principle, its construction is positivistic. No one has the right to question whether the sovereign's legislation is or is not in accord with the general principle. Since such a power of interpretation can be capricious, let us try to set up some criterion for measuring the happiness of our republic. We can measure the happiness of our republic scientifically by measuring and aggregating the happiness of all citizens. This empirical approach is still compatible with positivistic construction.

The project of measuring and aggregating the happiness of all citizens may turn out to be much more complicated than an empirical procedure. First of all, we have to know what constitutes happiness. There is a positivistic way of settling this question: happiness can be defined as the satisfaction of desires or preferences, which can be taken as empirical data. But we may feel that the satisfaction of desires or preferences does not always contribute to happiness and that some desires and preferences are destructive of happiness. We may even say that the concept of happiness is a normative ideal. But this normative ideal can be understood as either an objective entity or a subjective feeling. If it is the latter, you have no right to question the legislative behavior of our sovereign by appealing to your private idea of happiness. If the idea of happiness is objective, you do have such a right. But our legislative program ceases to be positivistic because we have accepted a transcendental normative standard.

The role of general principles can take us beyond the positivist program of construction and lead us to the question of natural law. Let us now see what kind of constructivist program can be devised on the basis of natural law. But there are so many different theories of natural law. For the sake of simplicity, let us group them into two ideal types: the bedrock and the skyscraper version. The bedrock version of natural law recognizes the existence of only the most general principles required for legislation. Moral and political laws should be constructed by articulating these general principles. This version of natural law is endorsed by Thomas Aquinas in his distinction between its primary and secondary precepts. He says that the secondary precepts are derived from the primary precepts by practical reason. This is his way of saying that the particular rules and precepts are constructed from the most general precepts and principles.

The primary precepts, or the general principles, play exactly the same role that Platonic Forms do. They are transcendental normative standards. The construction of particular rules from general principles requires the same procedure of normative construction as that of Platonic construction. Hence the bedrock version of natural law is reducible to Platonism. But the skyscraper version is quite different: it conceives of natural law as a complete system of eternal rules and standards for the government of human behavior. Oliver Wendell Holmes depicts this type of natural law as "a brooding omnipresence in the sky."[1] Such a complete system, if accessible, should be the most ideal model for constructing a system of positive law. According to the skyscraper version of natural law, the process of normative construction is a process of replication.

The difference between these two versions of natural law has to do with particulars. The particular rules and precepts are given in the skyscraper version but not in the bedrock version. Hence the skyscraper version is more powerful than the bedrock version. But this extra power is not its asset but its liability; it is an obvious object of suspicion and distrust. It is hard to believe that the particularity of rules and precepts, which is always attributable to empirical circumstances, is inscribed in the timeless code of natural law. This is the incredible combination of eternity and particularity, incredible enough to discredit the skyscraper version of natural law. Its elimination leaves only two viable programs of normative construction, Platonic and positivistic.

Let us now compare these two survivors. The positivist program admits no transcendental normative standards and no external constraint on the legislative sovereign. This is both an advantage and a disadvantage. It allows no external criticism, which may be a disadvantage. Nor does it allow any normative dispute, and this may be an advantage. If there is any normative dispute, it can always be resolved by the legislative sovereign. The advantage and disadvantage of positivist constructivism are reversed for Platonic constructivism. Because it admits transcendental normative standards, it can foster normative disputes on any positive law. These disputes arise not simply because some positive law is outright wrong by some transcendental normative standards but because these standard are highly general and indeterminate. For example, there can be an indefinite number of ways for articulating the Idea of Freedom in the construction of positive law, because its articulation is made in the world of indefinite dyads. There is no sure way of deciding which is the best way, and any dispute about it cannot be resolved conclusively by anyone.

1. *Southern Pacific Ry. v. Jensen,* 244 U.S. 205, 222 (1916).

Platonic constructivism is an open invitation to endless disputes, as it is manifested in many aporetic endings of Plato's dialogues. In ancient Greece, in fact, Platonism was closely associated with skepticism; Plato was sometimes regarded as the father of skepticism.[2] Platonic skepticism largely reflects the indeterminacy and indefinability of normative standards. Because of the indeterminacy of normative standards, all Platonists are by their nature prone to skepticism. Conversely, all normative skeptics are incipient Platonists. One usually develops normative skepticism by questioning the merit of positive normative standards, and it makes little sense to question positive norms without presupposing some transcendental normative standards. One cannot adopt such a questioning posture as long as one acknowledges only the positive norms. To be sure, even a positivist may develop some questions and disputes about the interpretation of some positive law, but normative positivism can always provide positivist answers for those questions. Hence positivism cannot, by itself, lead to normative skepticism.

There is an inner tension in skepticism, because it is suspended between positivism and Platonism. The tension can be resolved by accepting Platonism. This is why a skeptic is an incipient Platonist. The skeptical tension can also be resolved by reinstating positivism, which is difficult for many skeptics because they have become skeptical by losing their faith in positivism. A third way to resolve the skeptical tension is through subjectivism. Because nothing definite can be said about the normative standards, the skeptics may feel, they must be no more than the figments of our imagination. They are only subjective ideals. The subjectivity of normative standards, however, should eliminate the ontological ground for making any truth claims in normative discourse, because they can be neither true nor false. This is the unwelcome consequence of subjectivism.

As long as we believe in the objectivity of normative standards, we assume that the discovery of truth will guide our normative discussions. That naive assumption should be rejected if there is neither

---

2. This point is well discussed by Julia Annas in "Plato the Sceptic," ed. Annas, *Oxford Studies in Ancient Philosophy*, suppl., 1992, 43–72.

truth nor falsehood in normative assertions. What, then, is the purpose of engaging in a normative discussion? Its purpose is not discovery but persuasion; we try to impose our normative ideas on others by persuasion and sometimes even by deception. This view was popular with the Greek Sophists, as it is with the emotivists of today. But this account of normative discourse is phenomenologically untrue, as J. M. Balkin has clearly shown.[3] If our normative ideas are truly private, they cannot even become an object of our discussion, because every discussion must have a common ground. Subjectivism inevitably leads to normative solipsism; true subjectivists can never talk with each other.

Plato was indeed concerned with the problem of indeterminacy, which comes with the acceptance of transcendental normative standards. In the *Republic* and the *Laws* he tried to resolve this problem by entrusting the legislative function to the wise. But this resolution has the danger of turning the wise legislator into an autocratic sovereign. With such a transformation, Platonic constructivism can easily degenerate into a positivist program. Thomas Aquinas tried to solve the same problem by means of his doctrine of legislative authority. Although natural law is known to all human beings, he held, human law (the positive law) should be made only by legitimate authorities. But how can we determine who should have the legitimate authority to make the positive law? Aquinas did not say that natural law contains a precept for deciding this question. For him, it was a practical question that should be settled by the authority of an established institution.

It is the practical dimension of normative reason that introduces the problem of indeterminacy and contingency. The Platonic program of normative construction is not a theoretical but a practical enterprise; it is the project for translating and transposing eternal normative ideals to the contingent world of practice. Plato and Aquinas tried to resolve the practical question of normative indeterminacy by their notions of legitimate authority, that is, the authority of wise people for Plato and the authority of established institutions for Aquinas. But authority has to be embodied in a particular person or institution, which is a contingent fact. And a contingent fact is always a hotbed of uncertainty. The modern West has tried to cope with this problem by devising the institution of democratic or popular sovereignty. This institution may not work for three reasons. First, it may be democratic or popular only in name, while its real power is exercised by an oligarchy. Second, even if its real power is exercised by the people, they may not know what is truly good and just for themselves. Third, the ruling majority may oppress the minority.

Hegel thought that a better way of dealing with the normative indeterminacy in the contingent world would be to extend Kant's constructivism and not only derive moral laws from one ultimate principle but deduce even the institutions that make and embody those laws from one highest source. This ambitious program of construction is Hegel's Neoplatonic constructivism. It can also be called the dialectical constructivism, because it is a method of construction by the dialectical logic of assertion (synthesis), opposition (antithesis), and reconciliation (synthesis).

* * Neoplatonic Construction

Before getting to Hegel's Neoplatonic program of normative construction, let us note the basic difference between Platonism and Neoplatonism. Platonism is a drive for unity; it is an answer for the question of the One and the Many. Each Platonic Form is meant to account for the unity of phenomenal objects; for example, the Form of Horse accounts for the unity of all horses in the phenomenal world. The same drive for unity can be extended to the world of Forms; the plurality of Forms should be explained by their unity. This can be achieved by deriving all Forms from one ultimate Form, which is called the One by Neoplatonists. But even this move does not secure the unity of the entire reality, because the soul and the material world still remain outside the domain of the One. This final problem can be resolved by deriving the soul and the world also from the One. The universe and everything in it is derived from the One. This is the Neoplatonic doctrine of Emanation.

In his late dialogues, Plato himself advocated the idea of deriving the complex Forms from the simple ones; this was the original source of the Neoplatonic impetus for deriving everything from the One. But Plato's ontology remained irreducibly pluralistic. First, he accepted the plurality of the ultimate Forms; second, he admitted the independent existence of the soul and the material world. In his philosophy, the soul, the Forms, and the space-time matrix are the three irreducible elements. He is a confirmed pluralist, and Neoplatonism is a systematic attempt to convert his pluralism into an absolute monism. This conversion has produced two quite different versions of Neoplatonism: one by Plotinus in the *Enneads,* the other by Proclus in the *Elements of Theology.* The Plotinean version is highly mystical; the Proclusean version is logical and mathematical. Hegel was captivated by the logical version.

Hegel's derivation scheme begins with the concept of Being, which is as empty as the concept of Nothing, and comprises three stages. The first stage produces his Logic, a system of concepts and Ideas. In the second stage the Logic externalizes itself and produces Nature. The third stage creates Spirit by annulling the external relation of Idea and Nature. The development of Spirit also takes place in three stages: (1) the Subjective Spirit, (2) the Objective Spirit, and (3) the Absolute Spirit. Moral and political normative standards are generated in the development of the Objective Spirit, which reaches its full realization in the rational state. All of these developments are governed by Hegel's dialectical logic, the logic of opposition and reconciliation.

Although the same dialectical logic governs all three stages in the development of the Absolute, Hegel uses two different methods in his exposition: a logical method in his *Science of Logic* and a phenomenological method in his *Phenomenology of Spirit.*[4] The logical method is a method of dialectical genesis. By the dialectical power of

4. *Phenomenology of Spirit,* trans. A. V. Miller (Oxford, 1977), cited in the text as *PhS; Hegel's Science of Logic,* trans. W. H. Johnston and L. G. Struthers, 2 vols. (London, 1929). The abbreviated version of his Logic is given in the first part of the *Encyclopedia of Philo-*

opposition and reconciliation, it generates a system of concepts and Ideas, beginning with the concept of pure Being, the lowest and barest concept, and ending with the absolute Idea, the highest and richest concept. Hegel's phenomenological method is a method of phenomenological analysis. It analyzes the collective human consciousness and its historical development as a series of phenomena. This method of phenomenological analysis articulates all the dialectical movements that have produced the different stages of human history. Hence it is the method of reconstruction, while the logical method is the method of construction. The former reconstructs what has been constructed by the latter.

Which of these two methods is more basic in Hegel's philosophy? To answer this question, let us compare the two methods. The logical method works with concepts and Ideas; the phenomenological method analyzes objects of consciousness (phenomena, or *Vorstellungen*). The logical method is internal; it remains within the domain of thought from the beginning to the end. The phenomenological method, on the other hand, is external. A phenomenon *(Vorstellung)* is external to thought. In the logical method, thought moves without reference to objects; it operates purely by its own internal dynamics. In the phenomenological method, thought operates on objects. The latter method presupposes the linkage of thought to being, whereas the former method requires only the linkage of thought to thought.

The extralogical dimension of the phenomenological method is indicated by the indexical sign *this,* which establishes the initial relation of thought to an object in the first chapter of the *Phenomenology*. The extralogical dimension is not restricted to this one episode; it appears again and again in the course of phenomenological exploration. But the indexical sign never appears in the logical method, because it is totally devoid of extralogical reference. In Hegel's *Science of Logic,* as Michael Theunissen correctly notes, there is no analysis

---

sophical Sciences in Outline. This so-called smaller, or lesser, Logic has been translated by William Wallace and published as *The Logic of Hegel* (Oxford, 1873).

of extralogical reality.[5] Because his Logic is totally self-contained and does not depend on any extralogical elements, Hegel regards it as a true science. On the other hand, his *Phenomenology* is an imperfect science; it presupposes the existence of extralogical elements. By Hegel's standard, a perfect science has to be free of all presuppositions. For this reason, Hegel regards the *Phenomenology* as a preliminary or introduction to his *Science of Logic* (*PhS,* par. 48). Hence the logical method is primary, and the phenomenological method is secondary.

Let us first consider Hegel's logical method of construction. For an illustration of its generative power, we should examine the first triad of Hegel's Logic, the triad of Being, Nothing, and Becoming.[6] The concept of pure Being is logically opposed to the concept of pure Nothing. By the logical principle of negation, the former generates the latter. But their logical opposition is not the whole truth: the two concepts are also identical. The concept of pure Being is totally indeterminate; so is the concept of pure Nothing. In fact, Hegel says, these two totally indeterminate concepts are indistinguishable from each other. The distinction and opposition of these two concepts belong to the abstract understanding, which knows only partial truths. The logical combination of these two concepts produces the concept of Becoming. The concept of Becoming is the synthesis or combination of the concepts of Being and Nothing, or the dialectical resolution of their opposition or conflict.

The concept of Becoming is richer and higher than the concepts of Being and Nothing. This is the magical power of Hegel's Logic; it can produce richer and higher concepts from poorer and lower ones. His Logic manifests its power of genesis at three different moments: (1) the assertion of Being, (2) the generation of Nothing by the negation of Being, and (3) the generation of Becoming by the combination of Being and Nothing. This is the well-known triad of thesis, antithesis, and synthesis. It is the process of self-diremption and reunion; one concept becomes two, and the two become one

5. *Sein und Schein: Die kritische Funktion der Hegelschen Logik* (Frankfurt, 1978), 138.
6. *Logic of Hegel,* 158–69; *Hegel's Science of Logic,* 1:94–120.

again. It is also the process of opposition (antithesis) and reconciliation (synthesis). It accomplishes two tasks in one process: the rejection of partial truths and their elevation to a higher truth. For
example, it rejects and annuls the concepts of Being and Nothing,
because neither of them has the whole truth. But it also preserves
their partial truths as two moments of a whole truth in the higher
and richer concept of Becoming. At every step of this generative process the Absolute becomes richer and truer, until it becomes the
Absolute Spirit.

Let us carefully consider Hegel's contention for the generative
power of his Logic. In its first triad, first the concept of Being generates the concept of Nothing by logical opposition, and then the
contradiction of these two concepts is resolved by generating the
concept of Becoming. The logical power of generation is the power
of opposition, contradiction, and reconciliation. But these logical
powers cannot obtain in the domain of concepts. There can be no
contradiction between the concept of Being and the concept of
Nothing. A logical contradiction can obtain, not between concepts,
but only between propositions. There is no contradiction between
the concept of being white and the concept of not being white. But
there is a contradiction between the propositions "This horse is
white" and "This horse is not white." Propositions do not arise until
concepts are applied to objects. The application of concepts to
objects is the basic requirement for producing contradictions, but
the pure concepts of Hegel's Logic are not yet related to any objects.
In fact, there are no objects in Hegel's world until they are generated
by the dialectical logic.

For a better understanding of Hegel's logical method, we should
distinguish between the dialectic of concepts and the dialectic of
propositions. In the *Science of Logic* he presents the dialectic of Being
and Nothing as a dialectic of concepts.[7] It is an interplay of two concepts, pure Being and pure Nothing; these concepts are not yet
applied to any object. In the Logic of the *Encyclopedia*, Hegel presents the same dialectic as a dialectic of propositions. He applies the

7. *Hegel's Science of Logic*, 1:94–95.

two concepts to the Absolute and produces the following propositions: (1) "The Absolute is Being" and (2) "The Absolute is the
Nought."[8] The Absolute is the object, to which the concepts of Being and Nothing are applied. But where does the Absolute come
from? It cannot be the Absolute that is supposed to be generated by
his Logic, because its generation is supposed to take place after the
completion of Logic. His Logic can have the Absolute only by taking over the final outcome of his *Phenomenology*, which ends with
the Absolute Spirit. In that case, his Logic presupposes his *Phenomenology*, and the logical method depends on the phenomenological
method. The former cannot avoid the extralogical reference any better than the latter can. The logical method can never be better than
the phenomenological method.

The logical method can avoid the extralogical reference only by
abandoning the dialectic of propositions and returning to the dialectic of concepts. The latter dialectic produces no contradictions, because it does not apply concepts to objects. It can only combine the
concepts of Being and Nothing. But their combination is no more
possible if they are logically opposed than is the combination of the
concepts of being white and being not white. Hegel says that the concepts of Being and Nothing are also identical because both of them
are totally indeterminate. If they are identical, then their combination is not a combination. It is logically impossible to generate the
concept of Becoming by the dialectic of combination. The dialectic
of concepts has no generative force whatsoever, because it cannot
produce contradictions. Without contradictions, there can be no logical moves in Hegel's Logic. Without logical moves, his Logic will forever be stuck at its starting point, the concept of pure Being. In this
regard, the Hegelian Neoplatonism is radically different from any
other version of Neoplatonism. No other Neoplatonist has ever located the generative power of concepts and Ideas in the logical power
of contradiction.

The external relation of thought and being is essential for generating contradictory propositions. The phenomenological method

8. *Logic of Hegel*, 158–61.

generates contradictions because of its externalism. Because the existence of phenomena is independent of our thought, we can give only partial accounts, which are contradictory of each other. We can give two conflicting accounts of the solar system, geocentric and heliocentric, because its existence is independent of our thought. If the solar system had been created in accordance with our thought, our thought would not be a partial account of it, but the only complete account. For this reason, Kant says, divine thought is totally free of contradictions because it creates its own object.

The external relation of thought and being should be accepted as the ultimate ground for dialectical moves if those moves are to be based on logical contradictions. But Hegel destroys this ultimate ground for dialectical moves in his Logic by eliminating all external relations of concepts to objects. Hence his logical method is totally vacuous. Moreover, he shows no pretense of generating normative ideals by his logical method. His *Science of Logic* contains no transcendental normative standards. He recognizes only the positive normative standards generated by the Objective Spirit, which constitute the *Sittlichkeit* of a community. But he claims that every system of positive norms has its own rationality, and he tries to demonstrate their rationality by the phenomenological method.

∗ ∗   The Phenomenological Method

Hegel's account of positive norms is scattered all over his works: his *Phenomenology,* his Philosophy of Spirit, the third and final part of his *Encyclopedia,* and his *Philosophy of Right.*[9] His method of analysis and exposition in these works is phenomenological. He does not try to logically deduce social and cultural phenomena, for example, civil society, to be investigated; instead he accepts them as social phenomena for his analysis and explication. His method is reconstructive rather than generative. And yet he wants to demonstrate that positive norms are constructed by the development of the Absolute and its rationality and that they constitute the essence of a rational

9. *Philosophy of Right,* trans. T. M. Knox (Oxford, 1977), cited in the text as *PhR*.

state. Let us now see what sort of rationality Hegel attributes to the normative dimension of human culture.

As we have already noted, positive norms are generated by the Objective Spirit. Since we cannot go over the entire dialectical development of the Objective Spirit, let us selectively examine a few of its representative features. We should begin with Hegel's account of the normative standard governing the differentiation of two sexes. He says that the Objective Spirit differentiates itself into two sexes. One is the Spirit endowed with knowledge and volition in the form of free universality; the other is the Spirit endowed with knowledge and volition in the form of concrete individuality and feeling. The former is the male; the latter is the female. The male is powerful and active; the female is passive and subjective (*PhR*, par. 166). They are unequal by nature. Because the male sex is the sex of universality, it is destined for public life. By contrast, because the female sex is the sex of particular feelings, it is the internal enemy of the universal. Its natural place is the family, the private institution of immediate feelings. Women have no place in a rational state; they can only pervert the public world: "Womankind—the everlasting irony [in the life] of the community—changes by intrigue the universal end of the government into a private end, transforms its universal activity into a work of some particular individual, and perverts the universal property of the state into a possession and ornament for the Family" (*PhS*, par. 475).

This is supposedly the way two genders are generated by the Objective Spirit, and it is alleged to be a logical account by Hegel's dialectical logic. But there is nothing logical about it. It gives no reasons why the Objective Spirit differentiates itself into two genders rather than one, three, four, five, or any other number of genders. Nor does it give any reasons why the female should be passive and subjective, and the male powerful and active. It only describes what has happened in Hegel's own society and does not even recognize the historical fact that the gender differentiation has produced different results in some other societies, especially in matriarchies.

In civil society, Hegel says, the Objective Spirit differentiates itself into three social classes: (1) the agricultural class, which is substantial or immediate; (2) the business class, which is formal or reflective; and (3) the universal class of civil servants (*PhR*, par. 202). Here again Hegel does not explain why the Objective Spirit differentiates itself into three classes rather than two or four. Moreover, the triadic schema of substance, form, and universal cannot be found in Hegel's Logic. He has probably made it up by compounding two dyadic schemata. The dyadic schema of universal versus particular differentiates the universal class of civil servants from the agricultural and business classes, which are the particular classes. The latter two classes are differentiated from each other by the schema of form versus substance. The agricultural class is substantial, the business class formal.

The class of civil servants may be said to represent universal interests, and the other two classes, particular interests (*PhR*, par. 205). The relation of universal and particular classes is similar to the relation of two genders; the male-female distinction is associated with the distinction of universality and particularity. In that case, the dialectic of classes should follow the dialectic of genders. The class differences should turn out to be the same as the gender differences. That is, the universal class should be powerful and active; the particular classes, passive and subjective. For these reasons, Hegel should conclude that only the universal class of civil servants is suited to handling the public affairs of the state and that the other two classes can only pervert the state if they are allowed to participate in its affairs.

In the dialectic of social classes, however, the difference between universal and particular carries no special weight. Hegel now assigns the critical role to the categories of form and substance. He says that the relation of the agricultural and the business classes is the relation of form and substance. The agricultural class lives and works directly on the soil, and its mode of subsistence "owes comparatively little to reflection and independence of will, and this mode of life is in general such that this class has the substantial disposition of an ethical life which is immediate, and resting on family relationship and trust" (*PhR*, par. 203). The business class has a different mode of life and production. Because its task is the adaptation of raw materials rather than their production, Hegel says, it is forced into a life of reflection and intelligence.

Does the economic relation of these two classes justify Hegel's characterization of it as the relation of form and substance? This question is open for dispute. Hegel uses the relation of form and substance only metaphorically in describing the relation of the agricultural and business classes. Because the agricultural class works closely with natural resources, Hegel calls it the class of substance. *Substance* means natural substance. Because the business class works on those natural resources in commerce and industry, he calls it the class of form. The business class adds the form to the substance produced by the agricultural class.

The relation of the two classes may be regarded as analogous to the relation of form and substance if the function of the agricultural class is limited to the production of raw materials and the function of the business class is limited to working on those raw materials. In Hegel's own day, however, this sort of division of labor did not obtain between the two classes. Most agricultural products, such as grains, vegetables, and fruits, were not raw materials but finished products. At the same time, the business class did not always depend on the agricultural class for the supply of raw materials. For the most part, the business class had its own way of acquiring raw materials, for example, by developing the mining and forestry industries. For these reasons, Hegel's characterization of the two classes is simply arbitrary.

The categories of form and substance cannot even be found in Hegel's Logic, though they are important for his dialectic of social classes. The categories closest to these are the categories of form and content.[10] Why does Hegel not use this pair of categories rather than form and substance? He may have thought that the relation of form and substance better described the relation of the two classes. The relation of form and content, however, is much more integral than the relation of form and substance. Form and content are inseparable from each other, but form can be added to substance, which can exist independently. At any rate, Hegel conjures up a pair of categories that are not given in his Logic to describe the relation of the two

10. *Logic of Hegel*, 242.

classes. This conjuring trick further aggravates the arbitrariness of his categorial maneuver.

To describe the relation of the classes as that of form and substance is only a preliminary for determining their respective natures. According to Hegel, the class of substance never develops its intelligence and reflection and thus becomes unfit for public affairs. On the other hand, the business class is well suited for significant political roles. The fact that this class is not a universal but a particular class does not affect its political standing. In Hegel's dialectic, it is impossible to tell when a pair of metaphysical terms such as *universal* and *particular* will or will not carry any significance, or what sort of significance they will carry if they do. This is the essence of arbitrariness in his dialectical logic.

Hegel notes that the agricultural class used to be the universal class (*PhR*, par. 203). In traditional societies, he notes, agriculture was associated with "forms of universality," the modes of self-assertion for rationality. If the status of being a universal class is not fixed for any particular class forever, what logical process is there for its determination? This question is neither raised nor answered by Hegel. He only says that agriculture is no longer venerated as it was in the olden days. Since then the agricultural class has undergone many modifications, which have adversely affected "the development of its power of reflection" (*PhR*, par. 203n).

Although the demotion of the agricultural class is an established fact, how is it to be explained by Hegel's dialectical constructivism? There are two ways. One is to say that the agricultural class has deteriorated in modern Europe because it has ceased to be the universal class. The other way is to say that this class is no longer the universal class because it has deteriorated. In the former account the status of being a universal class determines the transformation of a social class. This is a logical account; the logical category of universality determines the social transformation. In the latter account the status of being a universal class is determined by social transformation. This is not a logical but a sociological account. Hegel's dialectical logic is meant to give a logical account in its dialectic of social classes, but it gives only a sociological account, which is proto-Marxian.

A sociological account only describes the status quo. Hegel's dialectic of social classes exalts the business class because it has become the dominant class, and it denigrates the agricultural class because it has lost its old power. For the sake of argument, let us grant Hegel's proto-Marxian claim that the two classes have differential intellectual developments because of their different modes of production. The sort of intelligence required for industry and commerce may indeed be different from the sort required for farming. But that is quite different from saying that the development of reflection and intelligence is a special privilege of the business class that is not available to the agricultural class. Although the business class tends to develop a special form of technical intelligence, there is no more reason to believe that this special form of intelligence is essential for participating in the rational state than there is to believe that a special form of intelligence required for professional pickpockets is essential for participating in it. The sort of intelligence required for participating in a rational state is the practical wisdom of becoming well informed about the affairs of the state and making right judgments about handling those affairs. It is a matter of general intelligence and education and has nothing to do with any special form of technical intelligence.

Hegel talks as though the level of intelligence for the agricultural class had drastically deteriorated through some terrible misfortunes. The simple fact is that the rural nobility had lost its economic and political dominance to the commercial and industrial estates, and Hegel assigns the honorific title of universality to whatever class or group attained the dominant status. When he cannot assign the title of universality to the dominant class, he makes up a new honorific title of the formal class and endows it with a greater power and glory. His dialectic of social classes is flexible and arbitrary enough to allow him to say whatever is needed to justify the reigning institutions. Hence his dialectical logic is the logic of rationalization; it rationalizes the status quo.

Hegel never questions the premise that the rational state is the state of estates. The estates represent the particularity of the state, and the Idea of the state consists in its universality. In this dialectic of universality and particularity, he recognizes the estates as the basic constituents of the state. Many scholars have pointed out that it makes much better sense to regard the people as the basic constituents of the state. In that case, the people should be identified as the particularity of the state, and he would never have scorned the idea of popular sovereignty.[11] Should the category of particularity be imposed on the people or the estates? How does Hegel decide this critical question for his entire dialectic of the state?

Hegel decides the question by accepting the existing social facts. He simply accepts the fact that the Prussian state is composed of three estates. Because the Prussian state is not a democratic institution, he never considers the people to be the ultimate basis of the state. Instead he ridicules the idea of popular sovereignty and gives the general populace no important political role. They have no voice even in the legislature. He also glorifies the feudal institution of corporations in the name of universality because those feudal institutions are still strong and operative in the Prussian monarchy. For the same reason, he exalts and glorifies the hereditary monarchy (*PhR*, par. 279). The empirical facts are the sole bases for his categorial impositions, and all his dialectical moves are for the sole purpose of rationalizing those empirical facts.

If rationalization is the essence of Hegel's dialectical construction, it gives a new meaning to his notorious dictum, "The real is the rational." Now it can be taken to mean that whatever is real can be rationalized. Hegel can rationalize not only the Prussian monarchy but also Napoleon Bonaparte as the World Spirit on horseback. In his dialectical construction, he claims to demonstrate the logical necessity for the development of social institutions. But he only dresses contingent facts and relations in the verbal garb of dialectical necessity.

No doubt Hegel tries his best to cover up this dialectical trickery with his opaque language and dubious rhetorical maneuvers. No greater hoax has been perpetrated than his dialectical logic in the name of logic. If Hegel were to say in the manner of Plotinean mys-

11. This point is stressed by Klaus Hartmann in "Towards a Systematic Reading of Hegel's Philosophy of Right," in *The State and Civil Society*, ed. Z. A. Pelczynski (Cambridge, 1984), 114–36.

tical utterance that all social institutions had been generated from the One or God, there would be no ground for the charge of fraud. But he says that he is giving a logical account, and that is a blatant hoax. His grand game of hoax is a Kantian legacy. Kant's cheating game, which is more or less localized in his writings, becomes a global plague in Hegel's Neoplatonic constructivism.

* * Neoplatonic Historicism

The logic of rationalization inevitably leads to normative positivism; it can rationalize any existing social and political order. All positive norms, which are supposedly generated by the Objective Spirit, constitute the *Sittlichkeit* (system of ethical standards) of a community. Every *Sittlichkeit* has its own historical tradition, which generates its own reason for existence. Thus Hegel's normative positivism is linked to his historical relativism. What ethical norms will prevail in any society is determined by the historical development of the Absolute. Hegel's historicism cannot admit any transcendental normative standards. In that regard, it is radically different from Kant's, which recognizes the Ideas of pure reason as eternal archetypes.

As we saw in chapter 3, Kant believes that to realize the kingdom of ends is the ultimate goal of history. This transcendental end contains a transcendental norm, the Idea of a republican constitution. But this political ideal cannot be realized overnight in some ideal state; it can be realized in different forms at different stages of human history. Hence different political systems have different normative standards, but they are all derived from the same transcendental standard. Although Kant's historicism can take the form of historical relativism, it is compatible with universalism because its relativity is restricted to situation-relativity. Although the positive norms are relative to their respective situations, they can be compared in terms of their ultimate archetype. The Kantian relativism provides a transcendental normative perspective.

Many scholars have thought that Hegel had his own transcendental norms. For example, he said that the struggle against slavery involved the question of eternal human rights, and this statement appears to presuppose a transcendental norm of human right. On the basis of this remark, Allen Wood says that Hegel's philosophy has some kernel of universal norms.[12] But his reading is too charitable for the text he cites, which appears in the following context:

> As regards the historical side of this relationship, it can be remarked that ancient peoples, the Greeks and Romans, had not yet arisen to the Notion of absolute freedom, since they did not know that man as such, man as this universal 'I', as rational self-consciousness, is entitled to freedom. On the contrary, with them a man was held to be free only if he was born free. With them, therefore, freedom still had the character of a natural state. That is why slavery existed in their free States and bloody wars developed in which the slaves tried to free themselves, to obtain recognition of their eternal human rights.[13]

To say that the slaves struggled to obtain "recognition of their eternal rights" seems to imply that they already had their eternal rights and that they were only seeking the recognition of those rights by others. But that cannot be true. If Hegel is right, the slaves who lived before the age of freedom did not even have the concept of freedom. They were still living in a natural state, which knew only natural freedom, the freedom of wild beasts. Even wild beasts have the right to retain their freedom, and to regain it when they lose it. Ancient slaves' struggle to obtain freedom could not have been any different from wild beasts' struggle to regain their freedom when they are caged. The right to natural freedom is obviously an eternal right, because it eternally obtains in every natural state.

Hegel also appears to appeal to some universal standard when he says that the modern state is better organized or more organic than the feudal state (*PhR*, pars. 278n, 286n). But in this comparison, made in his discussion of the modern state, he is using the standard of rationality for the modern state. As a historical relativist, he should say that the feudal state had its own standard of rationality, which was quite different from the modern standard. These two standards

---

12. *Hegel's Ethical Thought* (Cambridge, 1990), 98.
13. *Hegel's Philosophy of Mind*, trans. A. V. Miller (Oxford, 1971), 174 (sec. 434n).

of rationality are different because the modern and the feudal states serve different functions. To compare the two states on the basis of the standard of modern political rationality does not make any better sense than to compare them on the basis of the standard of feudal rationality.

In the Hegelian historicism, some scholars have said, what comes later is better than what comes earlier, and what comes at the end of history is the best. This assertion hides an ambiguity that can be spelled out by the following questions: Is it the case that the last stage of history is the best because it is the last stage, or is it the case that the last stage comes at the end because it is the best? Does the historical sequence automatically determine the normative ranking of different historical stages? The affirmative answer to these questions can substitute the word *better* for *later* and the word *worse* for *earlier*. To say that Nazi Germany came later than the Weimar Republic because the former was better than the latter is surely absurd.

Those scholars must mean to say that the last stage of history is the best because it is the fullest realization of the Absolute. They seem to take as their axiom that the complete realization of a goal is better than an incomplete one. But this axiom is true on the condition that the goal to be realized is a good one. If it is a bad one, like that of the Third Reich, its complete realization would be worse than its incomplete realization. How, then, do we determine the goodness or badness of a goal to be realized? Does Hegel offer a transcendental standard for this determination?

Although we do not know how to answer this question, we know at least that the ultimate end of history for Hegel is the realization of the freedom of the Absolute. But his conception of freedom should not be confused with the standard normative conception of individual freedom, because it is the freedom of the Absolute. The freedom of the Absolute is none other than its self-determination; it is the autonomy of the Absolute Spirit. Every event in history has as its goal the realization of freedom, because it arises from the self-determination of the Absolute. For example, the master-slave struggle is an expression of freedom. The master achieves his freedom in his enjoyment of the fruits of the slave's labor; the slave, in his mastery over nature. The Stoics have their freedom, and so do the Skeptics. All represent different ways of realizing the freedom and autonomy of the Absolute.

In the political world, Hegel indeed recognizes the freedom of individuals as a unique achievement of Western Europe. There is plenty of textual evidence in support of a liberal interpretation of his political philosophy, as Shlomo Avineri has demonstrated.[14] But Hegel firmly relegates the freedom of individuals to civil society, which must be sublated in the state. What really counts in Hegel's theory of politics is not the freedom of citizens but the freedom of the state, because the freedom of the state is the freedom of the Absolute. The state is the Absolute Incarnate. In practice, the freedom of the state is further equated with the freedom of the officeholders of the state, and the freedom of citizens is reduced to the freedom to trust that the officeholders will act in the universal as well as in particular interests. This form of freedom is said to belong to a higher stage of history than the freedom in civil society. In Hegel's theory, every stage of history has its own form of freedom. Freedom as the ultimate goal of history is a blank check on which the Absolute can write whatever it or Hegel pleases.

Hegel's Idea of freedom as the ultimate end of history is very much like Kant's notion of autonomy. As we saw in chapter 4, Kant rejected transcendental norms whose acceptance he regarded as incompatible with the autonomy of practical reason. Thus began his Copernican revolution in ethics; he decided to generate all moral maxims from formal practical reason. Formal reason cannot accept any external constraint without losing its autonomy; it must determine itself from itself. Hegel emphatically endorses Kant's idea of autonomy: "But the essence of the will is to determine itself from itself; for practical Reason gives itself laws."[15] Although Kant's formal reason is autonomous, it is still finite. By removing its finitude, Hegel

---

14. *Hegel's Theory of the Modern State* (Cambridge, 1972).

15. Hegel, *Lectures on the History of Philosophy*, trans. E. S. Haldane, 3 vols. (London, 1892), 3:459.

transformed it into the Absolute Spirit. Hence there is a remarkable similarity between the two.

Like Kant's formal reason, Hegel's Absolute Spirit cannot accept any external constraint in the construction of moral laws and social institutions. It can appeal only to the logical principle of contradiction, which is Hegel's counterpart to Kant's principle of self-consistency. In Hegel's program of dialectical construction, the principle of contradiction plays exactly the same role that the principle of self-consistency plays in Kant's program of formalist construction. It also defines the development of freedom and autonomy in the Absolute: to be free and autonomous is to be free of contradictions. This is the internal characterization of its freedom and autonomy. Their external characterization in terms of external constraint cannot be given, because there is nothing outside the Absolute. It has to generate everything from nothing.

Nothing comes out of nothing, however. Hegel's dialectical program is as vacuous as Kant's formalism. His charge of emptiness against Kant applies to his own dialectical logic with far greater vengeance. He tries to hide its vacuity by pretending to deduce the prevailing norms and customs from the concept of the Objective Spirit. Once his rhetoric of rationalization and mystification is exposed, we can see that those norms and customs stand on no other ground than nothing. Not only does his historical relativism cover up his normative positivism by rationalization but it turns out to be normative nihilism. Normative nihilism is always inseparable from normative positivism. If there really are no transcendental normative standards, then the only available normative standards are the positive ones.

8 From Construction to Deconstruction: Marx and Derrida

* * * * * * * * * * * * * * * * * * *

Constructivism is one of the great inventions by Plato's genius, but he has never been accorded the credit. Although the *Timaeus* and its myth of divine construction were well known and popular among the medieval Christians, Plato's theory of human construction was not known to them. His constructivism is given in his late dialogues, which did not become available to the Latin West for a long time. In fact, Platonism and constructivism have rarely been associated throughout the history of Western philosophy. Even the origin of constructivism in the modern West was not directly influenced by Plato's writings. It drew its inspiration from the idea of geometrical construction, which was an important element in the genesis of modern physics. This was no accident. Plato's own constructivism had also been inspired by the Pythagorean tradition of geometrical constructivism.

The modern tradition of constructivism has gone through three stages. It began informally with Hobbes and Vico in the seventeenth century, and Kant made two attempts to formalize and systematize it in the eighteenth century. In the first *Critique* he tried to discover a system of categories as the basis for his constructivist program. In the second *Critique* he tried to base the construction of all moral laws on the single principle of logical consistency. The second method was the formalist program, which was much simpler and much more systematic than the first method. In fact, nothing could be simpler than the formalist program. Hegel's ambition was to construct everything, from pure logic to the whole universe, from this single principle. This was the third stage of constructivism, in which the agency of construction was shifted from the finite human subject to the infinite divine subject.

In continental philosophy, constructivism became an overriding concern with Kant; in that regard, he really introduced a revolution. What is known as Kant's Copernican revolution in philosophy is his constructivist revolution. But what is not equally well known, though it is equally important, is his deconstructivism. Deconstruction is the reverse of construction; what is constructed can be deconstructed. In the *Critique of Pure Reason* Kant not only presents his constructivism but also deconstructs the Leibnizian metaphysics in chapter 3 ("The Ground of the Distinction of all Objects in General into Phenomena and Noumena") of the Analytic of Principles.

Since Kant, deconstruction has been integrally connected with construction, though it has not been known by the same label. Hegel deconstructed Kant's transcendental logic before constructing his own dialectical logic. Feuerbach deconstructed Hegel's absolute idealism, and Marx deconstructed both Feuerbach and Hegel. Nietzsche was referring to his own version of deconstruction when he said that he was doing philosophy with a sledgehammer. Kierkegaard had a religious hammer for deconstructing Hegel. Heidegger wanted to deconstruct the entire tradition of metaphysics, and deconstruction has become everything with Derrida.

Because deconstruction is the reverse of construction, the former should raise exactly the same normative problems as those we have encountered with construction. Time and again we have noted that the most basic question for constructivism is the question of normative standards. This question divides construction into two modalities, the positivist mode and the transcendental mode. The latter presupposes transcendental normative standards; the former does not. These same two modalities should also obtain for deconstruction: either it has to accept transcendental normative standards or it has to become positivistic. Moreover, the positivistic program of deconstruction should inevitably lead to deconstructive nihilism, just as the positivistic program of construction leads to normative nihilism. I will try to demonstrate these points by examining the two best-known examples of deconstruction: the Marxist and Derridian programs.

* * Marxism and Deconstruction

Marx's critique of capitalism and ideology is his program of deconstruction. What normative standards does he use in his critique?
This question has called forth many different responses, because his
view of normative standards is perhaps the most obscure feature of
Marxism. Before considering some of those responses, let us first
accept Alvin Gouldner's distinction between Scientific and Critical
Marxism.[1] The scientific Marx wants to build his social theory on
the "scientific" method and accepts positive facts as the only legitimate basis for his scientific socialism. He is a normative positivist
who refuses to recognize any normative standards because they are
empirically inaccessible. But the question of normative standards is
important for the critical Marx, who cannot give a critique of social
order without presupposing them.

One group of scholars does not recognize the critical Marx; for
these scholars, the scientific Marx is the real, or official, one. This
group is well represented by Robert Tucker and Allen Wood. Tucker
says that Marx regarded all morality as ideology. For Marx, the idea
of transhistorical or eternal normative standards was only an ideological myth. Since there were no such standards, it made no sense to
ask whether wages paid to labor were just or unjust. Each economic
system produces its own standard of justice. By the capitalist standard, wage labor was perfectly justified.[2] It made no sense to base
moral judgments on what takes place within capitalism on external
normative standards. Allen Wood endorses this view of the scientific
Marx. He says that Marx neither called exploitation an act of injustice nor condemned capitalism for injustice.[3] The capitalist indeed
appropriates the surplus value of labor, and that is exploitation. But
it is not an injustice but an essential feature of the capitalist mode of
production.

Nevertheless, the presence of the critical Marx is evident even in

1. *The Two Marxisms* (New York, 1980).
2. *Philosophy and Myth in Karl Marx* (Cambridge, 1972), 16–19.
3. "The Marxian Critique of Justice," in *Marx, Justice, and History,* ed. Marshall
Cohen et al. (Princeton, 1980), 3–41.

the scientific Marx. As Ziyad Husami says, his "scientific" writings are loaded with moral condemnations; he characterizes the capitalist exploitation as robbery, usurpation, embezzlement, plunder, booty, theft, snatching, and swindling. Husami blames Tucker and Wood for closing their eyes to these explicit descriptions.[4] Even Tucker recognizes the critical dimension of the scientific Marx: *Capital* is a work not only of analysis and description but also of condemnation and protest.[5] Indeed, its subtitle is *A Critique of Political Economy*. There is no way to separate the scientific Marx from the critical Marx. So we cannot avoid the question of normative standards for his critical enterprise.

Many scholars have said that Marx uses the socialist ideal as his normative standard in his critique of capitalism. This raises another question: What right does he have to use this normative standard? In reply, he may say that it is the best normative standard. Before he can say this, however, he should be able to compare different normative standards. But such a comparison cannot be made without appealing to some transcendental norms, and the acceptance of transcendental entities is incompatible with Marx's historical relativism and scientific materialism. Some scholars have tried a futurist justification for Marx's use of the socialist ideal, namely, that it should be used because it is the ideal destined to replace the ideal of capitalism. But the use of future ideals constitutes an external critique of capitalism as much as the use of transcendental normative standards does. In Marx's historical relativism and normative positivism, there is no way to justify any form of external critique. Each stage of human history has its own system of normative standards; it cannot be meaningfully assessed by using the normative standards of another age.[6]

If all forms of external critique are incompatible with Marx's historicism, his critique of capitalism should be taken as an internal cri-

---

4. "Marx on Distributive Justice," in ibid., 42–79.
5. *The Marx-Engels Reader*, ed. Tucker (New York, 1972), xxvi.
6. George Brenkert stresses the incomparability of different moralities in Marx's and Engels's writings in "Marx, Engels–Relativity of Morals," *Studies in Soviet Thought* 17 (1977): 201–24, esp. 212–13.

tique. Allen Buchanan advanced the idea that Marx's critique of capitalism is based on capitalism's own normative ideals of freedom and equality.[7] Although wage labor is alleged to be a transaction in freedom and equality, it is nothing like such a transaction. The poor workers do not sell their labor freely, but under coercion. They cannot bargain with capitalists from a position of equality, because there is a glaring inequality in their bargaining powers. There is a systematic discrepancy between the reality of capitalism and its ideological picture. To expose this discrepancy is the purpose of Marx's critique.[8]

Do the normative ideals of freedom and equality as described by Buchanan really belong to the ethos of capitalism? I am inclined to give a negative answer to this question. The ideas of perfect freedom and equality constitute the socialist ideal. Let us suppose that poor John makes a contract with a rich capitalist, James, to sell his labor at six dollars an hour. Buchanan may say that this contract is made under coercion and that John is not really free. He may say, that is, that John and James do not make their contract from positions of true equality. These statements make no sense whatsoever for anyone who accepts the positive norms of capitalism. But the same statements make sense and become respectable to those who subscribe to the socialist ideal. Buchanan's internal critique is really an external critique; it appeals to external normative standards.

The true internal critique must be based on only the internal normative standards. It should try to detect and expose the discrepancy between those standards and the prevailing social practice, as well as the inconsistency among those standards. Their inconsistency and discrepancy fall under the Marxist principle of contradiction, the counterpart to Hegel's principle of contradiction. Hegel and Marx share this principle because their historical relativism does not allow them to appeal to external normative standards in their social critique. The principle of self-consistency is the ultimate internal nor-

7. *Marx and Justice* (Totowa, N.J., 1982), 54.

8. Philip Kain has characterized the technique of internal critique in somewhat different terms than Allan Buchanan's. According to Kain, its purpose is to expose the discrepancy between surface phenomena and the inner essence of capitalism. For further details, see Kain, *Marx and Ethics* (Oxford, 1988), 155–60.

mative standard. Although we may find fault with many aspects of capitalism by this principle, we can never make a radical critique of it and show that its basic normative principles are unjust or iniquitous.

In order to make a radical critique of capitalism, we have to appeal to some transcendental normative standards. In fact, Marx often takes the socialist ideal as his transcendental normative standard. It is the ideal of a totally free society that eliminates all forms of oppression and social domination and allows all its members to do whatever they want to do. Such an ideal society cannot allow even the division of labor and professional specialization. Philip Kain identifies it with Schiller's ideal of the aesthetic state.[9] This ideal stands as the common standard for his critique of not only capitalism but all social orders. It is also the common standard for measuring social progress at any stage of human history. Such a transcendental normative standard, of course, is incompatible with the scientific Marxism. This is the normative gap between the scientific and the critical Marxism.

Because of this normative gap, there are two ways to understand Marx's deconstructivist program. One way is to accept the socialist ideal as the transcendental normative standard for his social critique. The other is to reject such a transcendental entity as totally unscientific and reduce all his critical remarks to an internal critique, which is sometimes called the immanent critique. The immanent critique was favored in the critical theory developed by the founding fathers of the Frankfurt School largely because they were concerned with the "scientific integrity" of Marxism. But Habermas was dissatisfied with its relativistic and positivistic implication. He tried to restore the transcendental dimension of critical theory by proposing the ideal dialogue as its instrument.[10] In such a dialogue, all participants are given complete freedom to express and exchange their views. Consensus reached by such an ideal dialogue is to be taken as true. The truth thus attained, Habermas believed, can transcend his-

9. Ibid., 185.
10. "What Is Universal Pragmatics?" in Habermas, *Communication and the Evolution of Society*, trans. Thomas McCarthy (Boston, 1979), 1–68. For a critique of Habermas's proposal, see T. K. Seung, *Intuition and Construction* (New Haven, 1993), 85–88.

torical relativity. If social critique is conducted by this method, it should have transcendental significance.

* * Procedural Critique

In the normative domain, the function of an ideal dialogue is to solve what Habermas calls the normativity problem. This problem is settled by the force of tradition in a traditional society; hence it is not a problem at all. For the modernity, however, tradition no longer commands the institutional force to provide stable normative standards, because its authority has been shattered by rational critique. Habermas says that "modernity can and will no longer borrow the criteria by which it takes its orientation from models supplied by another epoch; *it has to create its normativity out of itself.*"[11] The problem of normativity is the problem of how to create normative standards out of pure rationality. This is the problem of modernity par excellence, according to Habermas.

There are two ways to settle the normativity problem: the procedural and the substantive. The substantive way is to settle the normative issues in terms of their substance; the procedural way is to devise a formal procedure to settle those issues without appealing to any substantive standards. Habermas's notion of an ideal speech belongs to the procedural method; he only provides a set of procedural conditions that should govern an ideal dialogue and does not even mention any substantive normative standards. The participants in such a dialogue should have freedom of expression and equality of participation. They should have the freedom to present the three validity claims truth, rightness, and truthfulness, as well as the freedom to criticize and evaluate the validity claims of others. Finally, they should have the freedom to defend their validity claims against their critics. This is roughly the character of an ideal dialogue, and its objective is to reach a rational consensus. Whatever is agreed upon

11. *The Philosophical Discourse of Modernity,* trans. Frederick Lawrence (Cambridge, Mass., 1987), 7.

by everyone in such a dialogue will be accepted as the solution of the normativity problem.

If the method of ideal speech works out well, Habermas can have the advantage of circumventing the unwieldy problem of confronting the substantive normative issues. But this advantage cannot be gained so easily, because the constitution of an ideal speech involves its own normative questions. All the conditions that Habermas stipulates for an ideal dialogue, such as freedom of speech and equality of participation, are normative ideals. Hence he cannot avoid the question whether these normative standards should be taken as positive or transcendental. If they are taken as positive standards, they will differ from society to society. Habermas never considers such a possibility; instead he clearly assumes that the ideal conditions of an ideal dialogue are invariant everywhere. That assumption is impossible unless we accept transcendental normative standards for the constitution of an ideal dialogue.

There is one normative standard that goes beyond the constitution of a dialogue. It is the standard of truth. The ultimate purpose of an ideal dialogue is not simply to have an ideal debate but to reach the truth. The dialogue or debate is only a means to this ultimate end. Like any other normative standard, the idea of truth can also be taken either as a positive or a transcendental norm. This duality is fully reflected in Habermas's definition of truth as a rational consensus. It can be taken either as a positive fact or as a transcendental ideal. If consensus is taken as a positive social fact, it is subject to change as other social facts are. On the other hand, if it is taken as a transcendental ideal, it transcends all agreements that may obtain in any society. On some occasions, Habermas clearly favors the ideal conception of consensus by recognizing the importance of a critical standard for questioning and evaluating any actually reached consensus.[12] Such a critical standard must be transcendental.

As soon as we recognize the conception of consensus as a critical

12. "Wahrheitstheorien," in *Wirklichkeit und Reflexion*, ed. H. Fahrenbach (Pfullingen, 1973), 258.

or transcendental standard, we cannot avoid the difficult question, What is the relation between consensus and truth if both are understood as transcendental normative standards? This question can be answered by asserting the priority of truth over consensus, or that of consensus over truth. The priority of consensus over truth means that truth is defined by a rational consensus; that is, whatever is agreed upon by everyone in an ideal dialogue is true by definition, and there is no truth apart from such a consensus. Truth is reducible to consensus. The priority of truth over consensus says the opposite: truth is irreducibly prior to consensus. The existence of truth does not depend on the existence of consensus. On the contrary, truth is the only ground for a rational consensus in an ideal dialogue; a rational consensus can be reached on something only when everyone sees it as true.

Habermas's conception of truth as a rational consensus is his way of endorsing the priority of consensus over truth. According to this conception, there can be no truth apart from consensus, and this is the reduction of truth to consensus, which presents some serious anomalies. These anomalies can be divided into two groups, those concerning dialogues and those concerning monologues. Let us first consider the monological anomalies. If we accept Habermas's definition of truth as consensus, we cannot talk about truth outside the context of a dialogue, but all of us think and talk about truth in our monologues. How can Habermas account for my thought that "One and two make three" is true when I entertain this thought in my monologue? He may say that my thought can be translated into the thought that "One and two make three" will be an object of a rational consensus in an ideal dialogue. There are two objections to this response.

First, when I entertain my thought about one and two making three, I have no idea of an ideal dialogue or its consensus. Therefore, the proposed translation is a mistranslation. Second, how would I know that my thought would be an object of a rational consensus? I may say that my thought will be accepted by every rational being because it is true. I may even claim that anyone who does not see the truth of my thought is irrational. In that case, rational consensus is defined in terms of truth, contrary to Habermas's definition of truth in terms of consensus. If I had no irreducible notion of the truth, I would have no idea whether my thought about one and two making three would be an object of agreement or disagreement in an ideal dialogue. My only recourse would be the empirical method of finding out whether anyone agrees or disagrees with me about my thought.

These difficulties constitute the monological anomalies of Habermas's theory of truth. Let us now consider its dialogical anomalies. In an ideal dialogue, every participant is supposed to present only truthful claims. If a truthful claim is defined as one that will be agreed on by everyone, the participants can state only those claims that they believe will be endorsed by everyone else. Should the participants state their views because they believe they are likely to be accepted by everyone else, or should they state them because they believe they are true, even though they may not be accepted by anyone else? Given his consensus theory of truth, Habermas has to accept the former alternative and reject the latter. But this is not only counterintuitive; it places an unnatural constraint on what the participants can and should say in an ideal dialogue.

Imagine two ideal dialogues. Although both have the common requirement that the participants can present only truth claims, they stipulate two different conceptions of truth: truth as consensus and truth as an independent notion. In the dialogue governed by truth as an independent notion, the participants can say whatever they believe to be true, without the burden of figuring out whether their claims will be the object of a rational consensus. In the dialogue governed by the consensus theory of truth, the participants cannot have this luxury. Whenever they want to make a truth claim, they have to figure out whether their claim will be an object of truth before they have the right to state their view. This is the unnatural constraint imposed on the participants by the second dialogue. Because of this constraint, it is far less ideal than the first dialogue.

Habermas may say that the participants have to be governed by the notion of truth as consensus because they have no other notion of truth. But the participants may reply that their notion of truth is prior to their notion of consensus. The transcendental idea of truth may even transcend the ideal of rational consensus for the reason that the scope of agreement or consensus is much broader than the scope of truth; we can agree on fictions as well as on truth claims. Our agreements on the latter can be stated in a statement such as the following:

TC: We agree that this claim is true.

If truth is reducible to consensus, this statement should be translated into the following:

AC: We agree that this claim is a matter of agreement.

AC is clearly different from TC. AC is an agreement claim, and TC is a truth claim. We can preserve the difference between the two only by admitting the transcendental notion of truth, which cannot be translated into the notion of agreement or consensus. With this admission, we should also recognize the possibility that even a rational consensus reached by a dialogue conducted under the most ideal conditions may sometimes fail to reach the truth. In that case, the notion of truth is transcendent in a special sense: it may transcend all agreements reached by an ideal dialogue. There may be some truths that may never be discovered even by ideal dialogue.

The consensus theory of truth is not Habermas's invention; he borrowed it from the American pragmatist Charles Peirce, who tried to resolve the question of truth by linking it to the notion of consensus. But I have never seen a decent explanation of why a rational consensus can always secure the truth. There are two ways to establish the link between consensus and truth. One way is to reduce truth to consensus by definition; in that case, the link between consensus and truth is the relation of identity. Since truth is identical with consensus, to achieve consensus is to achieve truth. We can never get one without the other. The other way is to preserve the irreducibility of truth to consensus and define the ideal conditions for consensus as those that can secure the truth. Any dialogue that cannot secure the truth fails to be an ideal dialogue, and its consensus cannot be a rational one. This second approach attests to the priority of truth over consensus. In that case, the notion of an ideal consensus can be defined only in terms of truth.

The notion of truth is a substantive normative standard; the notion of consensus is a procedural one. The relation of consensus to truth is the relation of a procedure to a substantive issue. An ideal dialogue and its consensus constitute a procedure for settling the substantive issues of truth claims. Habermas's proposal for the ideal speech is his attempt to restate critical theory in procedural terms and thereby avoid the troublesome substantive normative issues. In this regard, his motivation is similar to John Rawls's motivation for devising the original position as a formal procedure for deriving his two principles of justice. In fact, Habermas's ideal speech is Rawls's original position without the veil of ignorance.

The problem of how to find the right principles of justice is the most controversial issue in the normativity problem. Those principles are highly contestable substantive normative standards, and it is exceedingly difficult to establish their validity directly in terms of their substantive merit. In order to circumvent this intractable problem, Rawls has devised the notion of justice as a pure procedure: the principles that can be accepted unanimously by rational individuals in the original position will be adopted as the principles of justice.[13] But Rawls has to specify the conditions for the constitution of the original position and to justify those conditions. Elsewhere I have shown that those conditions cannot be justified without appealing to some substantive normative standards of justice.[14] For this reason, the procedural approach to normative issues cannot avoid the substantive normative problems. for the same reason, Habermas cannot set up his procedural project without accepting some substantive normative standards. Moreover, his critical theory cannot gain the transcendental dimension unless those normative standards are transcendental.

* * Derridian Deconstruction

Whereas the issue of normative standards has been a lively one for Marxist critical theory, it has seldom been raised for Derridian

13. Rawls, *A Theory of Justice* (Cambridge, Mass., 1971).
14. Seung, *Intuition and Construction*, 24–25.

deconstruction. In fact, few Derridians have recognized the normative dimension of their enterprise. But they cannot avoid the problem by merely refusing to recognize it. It is their turn to face the
inevitable question: What sort of normative standard is required for
Derridian deconstruction? It is exceedingly difficult to answer this
question because so many things have been claimed in the name of
deconstruction. In some circles the word is taken to be synonymous
with *negative criticism*. But this is a careless handling of a highly technical term; it neglects and ignores the unique features of the Derridian enterprise.

What are those unique features? Although they are difficult to
enumerate, they seem to be based on one central idea, namely,
Derrida's doctrine of *differance*, his basic principle of all signifiers, or
what he calls "writing." He repudiates our commonsense view that
every word or signifier has a definite and stable meaning. This view
is the heart of what he calls the metaphysics of presence, that is, the
dogma that some definite and stable meaning is present in every signifier. Against this dogma, he stresses the mutability and multiplicity of meaning. The meaning of every signifier is perpetually unstable and inevitably polysemous because it is a constantly changing
assemblage of grafts and associations. It is a Heraclitean flux.

Although Derrida's Heraclitean view has disturbed or even shocked
many people, it is by no means a novel doctrine. Consider the meaning of the word *freedom*, for example. Its polysemy is obvious. It
has so many different senses: political freedom, economic freedom,
moral and religious freedom, and even freedom in the metaphysical
sense. And each of these different senses has been defined and used
in so many different ways that it is impossible to catalog them all.
The diversity of its meanings is matched only by its mutability; each
of its meanings is subject to perpetual alteration. Instead of setting
forth a radically novel thesis, Derrida's doctrine only appears to capture the most basic and commonplace truth about human language.

Derrida locates the source of semiotic flux in the play of *differance*. His doctrine of *differance* is an adaptation of Saussure's semiotic theory. Derrida accepts Saussure's basic thesis that the signifiers
gain their meanings by establishing binary distinctions such as hot

and cold, inside and outside, speech and writing, presence and absence, subject and object. To establish these binary distinctions is as much the central function for Derrida's play of *differance* as it is for Saussure's play of difference. Derrida also shares Saussure's view that all binary distinctions are arbitrarily established conventions.[15] This goes against our commonsense understanding that every binary distinction reflects an essential distinction in the nature of things. For example, there is an essential difference between hot and cold, and this ontological demarcation underlies the semantic distinction between the two words *light* and *darkness*.

The doctrine of essential difference is based on essentialism, the doctrine of essence, the most stringent form of logocentrism. Since there is no essential nature of things, Derrida holds, there can be no essential or true meaning of a signifier. For example, the word *woman* has a plethora of meanings, but none of them can give the essence of woman or establish her identity. Every one of them is only a simulacrum.[16] Derrida says that the word *woman* is an expert mountebank or an acrobatic artist, who performs the art of perpetually replacing and supplementing one simulacrum with another. Likewise, every binary demarcation is only a simulacrum, subject to replacement and alteration. Hence every binary demarcation is the most unstable and vulnerable frontier for the play of *differance*.

Derrida introduces one more radical element into his doctrine of *differance*, namely, the notion of double writing. According to this doctrine, the binary distinction does not merely demarcate two opposing terms, but fuses them together into one. In *pharmakon*, for example, the two opposing terms *remedy* and *poison* are fused into one; the *pharmakon* contains the opposition of remedy and poison. Even the idea of *differance* is supposed to contain the ideas of both identity and difference at the same time.[17] The play of *differance*

15. Derrida, *Margins of Philosophy*, trans. Alan Bass (Chicago, 1982), 10, hereafter cited in the text as *Margins*.

16. Derrida, *Spurs*, trans. Barbara Harlow (Chicago, 1979), 49–51, hereafter cited in the text.

17. Derrida, *Speech and Phenomena*, trans. David Allison (Evanston, 1973), 82, cited in the text as *Speech*.

appears to be the exact opposite of Saussure's play of difference. The latter is the operation of distinction and demarcation; the former is the operation of union and combination.

This is only half of the story. Derrida's play of *differance* performs both operations simultaneously. The Derridian operation establishes not only the distinction and demarcation between two opposing terms but also their union and combination. In the opposition of hot and cold, for example, the play of *differance* not only separates these two from each other but makes each of them a combination of the two. This double motion is the essence of double writing. By this double motion, *hot* comes to mean not simply hot but partly hot and partly cold; *cold* comes to mean not simply cold but partly cold and partly hot. There is no such thing as purely hot or purely cold. Whatever is called hot is partly cold, and vice versa. Understood in this manner, every binary distinction is not a single but a double distinction, or what J. M. Balkin calls a nested opposition.[18] Derrida calls such a complex system of signification a double participation, which does not simply "mix together two previously separate elements [but] refers back to a *same* that is not identical, to the common element or medium of any possible dissociation."[19] The Derridian polysemy should not be mistaken for the ordinary conception of polysemy, an accidental assemblage of diverse meanings, because it is a virulent and necessary juxtaposition of opposite meanings.

Whereas Saussure's play of difference is a single operation, Derrida's play of *differance* is a double operation. This is the basic difference between them. But both stem from Hegel's dialectical logic, which constructs a series of binary oppositions such as Being and Nothing, Quality and Quantity, Essence and Existence, Reality and Appearance. The dialectical conflict of these opposing terms is the life and heart of Hegel's dialectical logic. This dialectical dimension of Hegel's logic is missing from Saussure's play of difference. The binary distinctions and oppositions established by Saussure's play of difference are relatively stable and free of conflict. Derrida reintro-

18. Balkin, "Nested Oppositions," *Yale Law Journal* 99 (1990): 1669–1705.

19. Derrida, *Dissemination*, trans. Barbara Johnson (Chicago, 1981), 127, hereafter cited in the text.

duces dialectical conflict into Saussure's doctrine of binary distinction and makes it even more radical than Hegel's Logic by packing the dialectical opposition into each of the opposing terms.

This is roughly Derrida's semiotic theory in outline. Now let us see how this theory functions as the basis for his deconstruction. At the outset, we should note that there are different modalities of deconstruction. Although we cannot enumerate all of them, we should recognize three prominent ones: (1) the deconstruction of effacement, (2) the deconstruction of contradiction, and (3) the deconstruction of rectification. Derrida uses all three modes in his deconstruction of phonocentrism, the metaphysical view that speech is a better form of communication than writing. It is sometimes called logocentrism, because the Greek word *logos* means speech. This view is encoded in the categorial hierarchy of speech over writing, which has been the favorite target for Derrida's sustained critique throughout his career.

In his *Speech and Phenomena*, Derrida deconstructs phonocentrism as presented in Husserl's theory of sign. He first lays out Husserl's position: that speech is a better form of communication than writing because the meaning of only the former is fully and immediately present to the speaker (*Speech*, 77–78). Then he shows that Husserl cannot even maintain the distinction between speech and writing. His argument is as follows. The distinction between speech and writing presupposes a clear demarcation between presence and absence, or the present and the past. But such a clear demarcation cannot obtain. By Husserl's own account of temporality, the present and the past are inextricably fused. In a paraphrase of Husserl's doctrine, Derrida says, "But this pure difference, which constitutes the self-presence of the living present, introduces into self-presence from the beginning all the impurity putatively excluded from it. The living present springs forth out of its nonidentity with itself and from the possibility of a retentional trace [the past and the absent]. It is already a trace" (*Speech*, 85).

By effacing the distinction between present and absent, Derrida undermines Husserl's phonocentrism. This is a deconstruction of effacement. But Derrida deconstructs Plato's phonocentrism in a different manner (*Dissemination*, 63–171). First, he states Plato's position as it is given chiefly in the *Phaedrus* and in other dialogues, and then he gives his deconstructive reading. In the *Phaedrus*, Socrates relates the story of the origin of writing: a god named Theuth gave the Egyptian king Thamus writing as a *pharmakon* for both memory and wisdom (*Dissemination*, 75). But the Greek word *pharmakon* is devilishly ambiguous, meaning both remedy and poison. By his description of writing as a *pharmakon*, Plato presents the nature of writing as both good and evil. This contradiction also obtains with the god who brings the gift of writing. On one hand, Theuth is a god of a lower rank, an engineer and a clever servant who has been sent as a messenger to King Thamus. On the other hand, he calls himself the son of the god-king, the eldest son of Ra, who is the sun-god or god the creator (*Dissemination*, 86–87). Theuth is at once a lowly messenger and a highly exalted deity, just as the *pharmakon* is at once remedy and poison.

The self-contradictory character of Theuth intensifies the self-contradictory character of his gift, the *pharmakon* of writing. By the interplay of these contradictory meanings, Derrida says, Plato's text destroys itself. Here and there, Derrida uses a much milder language than that of self-contradiction. He mentions the unstable ambivalence and ambiguity of Plato's text (*Dissemination*, 93, 139). Ambivalence or ambiguity is not an outright self-contradiction. But his main argument is that Plato's text is self-contradictory. In his summation of this argument Derrida says, "This 'contradiction,' which is nothing other than the relation-to-self of diction as it opposes itself to scription, as it *chases* itself (away) in hunting down what is properly its *trap*—this contradiction is not contingent" (*Dissemination*, 158).

The contradiction is not even contingent. Derrida at least concedes that this is not surely obvious to any casual reader, because the double writing of a text is usually hidden in the chain of its significations. In the opening sentence of his essay he says, "A text is not a text unless it hides from the first comer, from the first glance, the law of its composition and the rules of its game" (*Dissemination*, 63). Textual contradiction is concealed from those who fail to recognize the law of composition. This is the law of double writing. As soon as this universal semiotic law is recognized, every text should display its chain of significations as a chain of contradictions. This mode of reading should be called a double reading, a hermeneutic counterpart to a double writing. It secures the self-destruction of every text. This is the deconstruction of contradiction.

This mode of deconstruction is not only a necessary movement but also an internal movement. Derrida insists that the author has no control whatsoever over the deconstructive movement of a text. Nor should this movement be attributed to Jacques Derrida, the reader or interpreter; it is powered by the semiotic force of its own double writing, or Derridian polysemy. It is strictly an internal operation. Derrida says, "The movements of deconstruction does not destroy structures from the outside."[20] Every text destroys itself by its own inner contradiction, which is generated by its own double writing. This is Derrida's semiotic counterpart to Hegel's thesis that every position contains the germ of its own inner contradiction.

Derrida gives his third deconstruction of phonocentrism in *Of Grammatology*. He maintains that speech can function as a means of communication only by virtue of the essential characteristics it shares with writing, such as its semiotic autonomy (a sign can have its meaning in independence of its user) and iterability (it can be replicated indefinitely). Written signs, which can function in total independence of their authors, define the essential characteristics of all signifiers. Spoken and written words, along with other forms of communication, are only special forms of writing in this special sense, which Derrida calls "arche-writing" (*Grammatology*, 56). The phonocentrists have devalued writing and regarded speech as the most privileged form of communication only because they have misconstrued the true character of speech and writing and of human language in general. They have mistaken the accidental property of speech (the presence of the speaker) for its essential property. Derrida's deconstruction rectifies this error; it is a deconstruction of rectification.

20. Derrida, *Of Grammatology*, trans. Gayatri Spivak (Baltimore, 1974), 24, cited in the text as *Grammatology*.

* * The Derridian Predicament

These are the three relatively well-known modes of deconstruction. Unfortunately, they present a serious problem for Derrida and his followers. The first two modes are highly negative. The deconstruction of effacement can eliminate all binary distinctions, the common basis for all human languages. The deconstruction of contradiction may leave all languages intact, but it will drive all statements and texts into one common dumping ground of effacement or self-contradiction. Either of these two modes can engulf us all in a semiotic vortex, which sometimes does not even allow the distinction between contradiction and noncontradiction and sometimes admits both (*Dissemination*, 221). We can avoid this dreaded fate only by limiting the scope and target of deconstruction. But such limitation is unfaithful to Derrida's doctrine of double writing, which is not meant to capture the semiotic power of extraordinary words such as *pharmakon*. On the contrary, this doctrine is asserted as the universal principle of all signifiers.

Derrida emphatically claims that the principle of double writing governs the behavior not only of *pharmakon* but of all binary oppositions: "speech/writing, life/death, father/son, master/servant, first/second, legitimate son/orphan-bastard, soul/body, inside/outside, good/evil, seriousness/play, day/night, sun/moon, etc." (*Dissemination*, 85). It appears that we can escape its universal domination only by arbitrarily restricting the scope of our double reading. In fact, such restriction has been the standard practice of deconstruction in Critical Legal Studies (CLS). J. M. Balkin says that deconstruction is a neutral instrument that can be used for demolishing either side of any argument, for example, racism as well as anti-racism. But we limit its destructive power by carefully choosing our targets, because we do not want to deconstruct everything.[21] The Derridians always exempt their own writings from the universal rule of double writing. Although they deconstruct their opponents' writings by reading

21. Balkin, "Tradition, Betrayal, and the Politics of Deconstruction," *Cardozo Law Review* 11 (1990): 1613–30.

them as double writing, they would rather read their own as single writing. This has been the Derridian game of duplicity.

Pierre Schlag says that Balkin's account of legal deconstruction correctly captures what has been going on in CLS. He insists that the dominant paradigm for the CLS deconstructive practice has been unfaithful to the general principle of Derridian semiotics. The master of this practice is supposed to be a radically free subject who deploys deconstruction as a set of analytical techniques. He supposedly decides what to deconstruct and what not to deconstruct, when to begin and when to end the deconstruction, and above all, what purposes are to be served by deconstruction.[22] This dominant paradigm imports something totally alien and corrosive to the Derridian world of deconstruction, namely, a radically free subject, which Schlag calls the Sartrean worm.[23] He denies the very existence of such a free subject.

Pierre Schlag is correct about the radically free subject: it is a Sartrean legacy that has been disowned by most French intellectuals, structuralists and poststructuralists alike. Especially the Derridian world of semiotic autonomy cannot accommodate it without disrupting its entire fabric. The recognition of a free subject has to replace Derrida's well-known motto "There is nothing outside the text" with "Le Hors de texte, c'est moi," as suggested by Schlag. According to Schlag, as soon as the subject stands outside the text and controls its deconstruction with its free will, deconstruction violates Derrida's basic premise, loses its unique Derridian character, and turns into just one more practice or technique among others. Worst of all, it is transformed into an instrument of logocentrism.

As long as Derrida's doctrine of double writing is accepted as the universal semiotic principle, then even if there are truly free Sartrean subjects, they cannot restrict the scope of double reading without the Sartrean bad faith. If we know that every text is a double writing, we can refuse to read it as such only by lying to ourselves. As we noted earlier, Derrida says that the double writing of a text is not

22. "'Le Hors de Texte, C'est Moi': The Politics of Form and the Domestication of Deconstruction," ibid., 1641–42.

23. "The Problem of the Subject," *Texas Law Review* 69 (1991): 1693.

something injected into it by a reader and that even its author has no control over it. It is the inevitable nature and fate of every text. Hence even the Sartrean subjects, if they have the decency not to compromise truth for the sake of expediency, cannot ignore the double writing of a text and read it as a single writing. Of course, the Sartrean subjects may not care about truth at all.

In the deconstructions of effacement and contradiction, even the Derridian subjects cannot keep their consciences totally free of guilt. They have to accept and abide by the doctrine of double writing as a universal semiotic principle. To accept such a universal principle is to endorse the double writing as an essential feature of all signifiers. This is to endorse the doctrine of essence at least for one case, and that is a capitulation to the metaphysics of presence and its essentialism. This is the Derridian irony. After all those attacks on the metaphysics of presence, Derrida has to concede that his deconstruction can be powered only by essentialism. To make the Derridian irony doubly ironical, he had claimed the double writing as a universal essence of all writings by a tricky manipulation of the *pharmakon*. In Plato's text, the magic power of having a pair of contrary meanings such as remedy and poison belongs not to all signifiers but only to a few exceptional ones. They have this magic power, not by accident, but for a good reason. They stand for those extraordinary things that can powerfully influence human life in the direction of good or evil or both.

The deconstruction of rectification has one advantage over the other two modes. It produces positive results. It is a positive mode of deconstruction, while the other two are negative modes. But this advantage has a high price tag. As we have seen, Derrida claims that speech and writing share the same essential characteristics, which are captured by his notion of arche-writing. They differ only in their accidental characteristics; they are materialized in different media of communication. These claims cannot be made unless the distinction between the essential and the accidental properties of speech and writing is accepted. But this distinction is the heart of essentialism, perhaps the most stringent form of logocentrism and the metaphysics of presence.

For this reason, the deconstruction of rectification belongs to the metaphysics of presence. In fact, it has been one of the favorite metaphysical ploys in Western philosophy. Marx tried to rectify the Hegelian hierarchy of mind over matter by its inversion. For the sake of rectification, Nietzsche inverted the Christian hierarchy of the other world over this world, and slave morality over master morality. He called these inversions the transvaluation of values. The Christian slave morality itself had emerged by inverting the pagan morality of ancient Greece and Rome for rectification. Plato constructed his two-world view by inverting the natural philosophy of ancient Greece, which favored matter over mind. Aristotle brought down the eternal Forms from Platonic Heaven to this world by inverting Platonism. Hume inverted the hierarchy of reason over passion. Kant inverted the hierarchy of objects over concepts in his Copernican revolution. Finally, Heidegger inverted the hierarchy of Being over Nothingness. All these maneuvers belong to the deconstruction of rectification.

The deconstruction of rectification not only has to presuppose essentialism but also has to flout the Derridian principle of semantic indeterminacy and semiotic flux. By the time a categorial hierarchy is rectified, it becomes a semiotic fixture, which is inadmissible into the Derridian world of perpetual semiotic flux. For these reasons, the deconstruction of rectification is even a greater embarrassment for the Derridians than the deconstructions of effacement and contradiction. This is the Derridian predicament. The one positive mode of deconstruction is outright anti-Derridian, and the two negative modes are about to engulf all the Derridians in the universal vortex of self-contradiction. Is there any way out of this predicament?

In *Spurs*, Derrida makes a cautious attempt to find a way out. He expresses his resolve to launch "a new phase" of deconstruction, which is supposed to be an "affirmative" interpretation (*Spurs*, 37). Evidently dissatisfied with the negative modes of deconstruction, he appears to be in search of a positive mode. This new mode of deconstruction is designed to give affirmative rather than negative interpretations of Nietzsche's two sentences (1) "Truth is like a woman" and (2) "I have forgotten my umbrella." Derrida begins his affirmative interpretation of the first sentence by displaying the polysemy of the word *woman;* he parades all the different meanings this word can have, especially in Nietzsche's writings. He concludes that none of these meanings can give the essence of woman or establish her identity. Every one of them is only a simulacrum (*Spurs,* 49–51).

Derrida goes on to show that the meaning of Nietzsche's statement "Truth is like a woman" is equally undecidable. To demonstrate this point, he selects three principal interpretations of this statement (*Spurs,* 95–97). In the first, woman is taken as a figure or potentate of falsehood, who finds herself censured, debased, and despised. In the second, she is censured, debased, and despised as a figure or potentate of truth. In the third, she is recognized and affirmed as an affirmative power, a dissimulatress, an artist, and a Dionysiac. None of these interpretations can be taken as the true meaning of Nietzsche's statement; each is only a simulacrum.

Up to this point, Derrida's deconstruction is only semantic. How do these different interpretations interact with each other in defining Nietzsche's position? This is a pragmatic question. By the old method of negative deconstruction, Derrida should say that Nietzsche's text destroys itself, because it generates three mutually contradictory interpretations. This is the verdict he had meted out for Plato's text. But Derrida does not hand out this negative verdict for Nietzsche's sentence. Instead he says that all three interpretations are attributable to the author "simultaneously or successively" (*Spurs,* 101). But he does not say that such an attribution will destroy Nietzsche's text or his position by the force of its inner contradiction. Here lies the magic of positive deconstruction. It avoids the negative result.

* * Positive Deconstruction

How does this magic work? How can Derrida's new method achieve positive results in spite of the fact that his interpretation generates three incompatible readings? Although Derrida does not raise this question, the following appears to be his answer:

There is no such thing as a woman, as a truth in itself of woman in itself. That much, at least, Nietzsche has said. Not to mention the manifold typology of women in his works. . . . For just this reason then, there is no such thing either as the truth of Nietzsche, or of Nietzsche's text. In fact, in *Jenseits*, it is in a paragraph on women that one reads "these are only—*my* truths" (*meine* Wahrheiten sind). The very fact that "meine Wahrheiten" [*sic*] is so underlined, that they are multiple, variegated, contradictory even, can only imply that these are not *truths*. Indeed there is no such thing as a truth in itself. But only a surfeit of it. Even if it should be for me, about me, truth is plural. (*Spurs*, 101–3)

The idea that truth is plural or multiple is consistent with Nietzsche's perspectivism. The three contradictory readings of Nietzsche's statement "Truth is like a woman" do not have to contradict each other if they are parceled out as multiple truth claims via different perspectives. On the other hand, they cannot avoid a contradiction if they are taken as truth claims for a single truth or perspective. To avoid this contradiction, we need a theory of double truth analogical to Derrida's theory of double writing. Just as every signifier has more than one meaning, so every truth can be stated from more than one perspective. We can have no more access to the truth in itself than we can have to the essential meaning of a signifier. Only the partial or perspectival truths are accessible to us, and they are "irreducibly plural" (*Spurs*, 105).

The multiple and conflicting meanings of a text are employed for different purposes in positive and negative deconstructions. In a negative deconstruction they generate the self-contradiction of a text; in a positive deconstruction they yield competing interpretations. One result is negative; the other is positive. To make this point clearer, let us consider Derrida's deconstruction of Nietzsche's second sentence, "I have forgotten my umbrella," which is given as a further illustration of what an affirmative deconstruction is meant to be (*Spurs*, 123–39). This sentence was found in Nietzsche's unpublished manuscripts. As far as its textual meaning is concerned, Derrida says, "Everyone knows what 'I have forgotten my umbrella' means" (*Spurs*, 129). But there is no way of knowing the occasion for this writing or its purpose. Depending on the occasion and purpose for this writing, it can have so many different meanings that they cannot even be enumerated. Its indeterminacy is not textual but contextual, and yet it is equally impossible to determine what Nietzsche meant by it.

The problem of interpretation for "I have forgotten my umbrella" differs from the one for "Truth is like a woman." The one is the problem of contextual indeterminacy, and the other is the problem of textual indeterminacy. The textual problem arises from the multiple and conflicting meanings of the word *woman;* the contextual problem arises from the multiple and conflicting contexts. Derrida's doctrine of double writing applies differently to the two cases. It applies to "Truth is like a woman" on the textual or semantic level and to "I have forgotten my umbrella" on the contextual or pragmatic level. These two dimensions of double writing may be called the *textual double writing* and the *contextual double writing*. The textual double writing produces a self-contradiction. "Truth is like a woman" can produce a contradiction if *woman* is taken to mean the potentate of truth and falsehood at the same time. But the contextual double writing cannot produce a contradiction. "I have forgotten my umbrella" cannot contradict itself if its multiple meanings are parceled out to different pragmatic contexts.

In spite of these differences, Derrida seems to say that the problem encountered in the interpretation of the two sentences is basically the same. This is because he is converting the problem of textual double writing into that of contextual double writing. If he were to give a negative deconstruction to "Truth is like a woman," he would have to say that its multiple meanings cancel each other. Instead, he separate them out into different perspectives, which function as different contexts. By this contextual segregation, he forestalls the mutual destruction of the competing interpretations. This is why he calls the three principal interpretations of "Truth is like a woman" three "positions" (*Spurs,* 95). To be sure, the expression *contextual double writing* is ambiguous. Although it is meant to refer to the contextually multiple meanings of "I have forgotten my umbrella," it may be taken to mean either that those multiple meanings are placed in a single context or that they are segregated into multiple contexts.

The latter alone can forestall the mutual contradiction of those multiple meanings. That is what I mean by *contextual double writing;* it requires a series of different contexts.

Derrida himself recognizes the importance of the distinction between these two types of double writing, though he does not use the terminology I have introduced. He says, "What counts here is not the lexical richness, the semantic infiniteness of a word or a concept, its depth or breadth, the sedimentation that has produced inside it two contradictory layers of signification (continuity and discontinuity, inside and outside, identity and difference, etc.). What counts here is the formal or syntactical *praxis* that composes and decomposes it" (*Dissemination,* 220). In the last sentence of this passage, it is not easy to see what is meant by "the formal or syntactical *praxis.*" Let us try to translate it into some familiar language.

Derrida's idea of lexical richness or semantic infiniteness is already familiar to us. This feature of language, exemplified by the contradictory meanings of *pharmakon,* belongs to the semantic level, and I have called it textual double writing. On the other hand, what sort of sentences can be made from its semantic richness is a question of syntax, which deals with the problem of composing and decomposing sentences by using words and their meanings. But Derrida is not concerned with the simple syntactic operation when he talks about "the formal or syntactical *praxis.*" He is concerned with the problem of not only composing sentences by a syntactic operation but also placing them in pragmatic contexts. This operation belongs to what I have called contextual double writing. It belongs to the pragmatic level.

The secret of Derrida's positive deconstruction is to convert a textual double writing into a contextual double writing by replacing a single context with a series of single contexts. By this conversion, the deconstruction of "Truth is like a woman" becomes positive and undergoes the same basic procedure that "I have forgotten my umbrella" does. In both cases, the problem of competing interpretations leads not to the negative outcome of their mutual elimination but to the positive one of presenting a set of alternative readings. Hence Derrida talks about the undecidability of a text instead of its self-destruction. The notion of undecidability presupposes the notion of possible alternatives and choices.

In an affirmative deconstruction, the multiple meanings present themselves as possible candidates for a choice to be made. This is a question of choice that cannot arise in a negative deconstruction, because the self-destruction of a text leaves no possible candidates for such a choice. The idea of pragmatic choice distinguishes positive from negative deconstruction, and the choice is given to the deconstructor. Hence the deconstructor plays different roles in affirmative and negative deconstructions. Since a negative deconstruction presents no room for a pragmatic choice, the deconstructor has only to watch his or her text destroy itself. On the other hand, a positive deconstruction presents positive possibilities for a choice, and the deconstructor has to survey and compare those possibilities before making a choice.

Derrida refuses to make his final interpretive choice for either of Nietzsche's two sentences, because he has insufficient evidence on which to base such a choice. Instead of making such a final decision, he "oscillates" between the competing alternatives and pronounces them "undecidable" (*Spurs*, 99, 105, 121, 135–37). His positive deconstruction turns out to be the deconstruction of oscillation, whose hallmark is "undecidability." This is his conversion of negative to positive deconstruction, and he makes a similar conversion for the deconstruction of rectification. We have already noted that this mode of deconstruction is incompatible with his doctrine of semiotic flux because it produces a determinate result. He eliminates this problem by converting the deconstruction of rectification into another operation of oscillation. This is perhaps the most bizarre maneuver he has ever made for the sake of his theoretical integrity.

In an interview with Jean-Louis Houdebine, Derrida faces the question of how his concept of *differance* and deconstruction is related to the Hegelian synthesis.[24] He says that his notion of *differance* is meant for the destruction of the Hegelian *relève*, or *Aufhebung*

---

24. Derrida, *Positions*, trans. Alan Bass (Chicago, 1981), 39–41, hereafter cited in the text.

(*Positions*, 40–41). He rejects Hegel's optimistic view that all dialectical conflicts can be resolved via mediation and synthesis. He stresses the conflictual character of all binary oppositions and their categorial hierarchies and the impossibility of resolving their conflict. Hence the deconstruction of a categorial hierarchy only demonstrates the impossibility of finding a third term for a Hegelian synthesis (*Positions*, 42–43). Then he proceeds to demonstrate this point by using, for an example, his deconstruction of the speech/writing hierarchy.

This is a surprising development, because this deconstruction appears to be almost tailor-made for a Hegelian synthesis. As we noted earlier, Derrida demonstrated the essential identity of speech and writing against the phonocentric view, which stressed their essential difference. Moreover, he produced the new concept of arche-writing to capture their essential identity. In that case, this new concept can function as an ideal third term for the Hegelian synthesis, which can resolve the dialectical opposition between speech and writing. This is a Hegelian account of his deconstruction, and I cannot think of any better way of describing his performance. But Derrida tries desperately to disown this Hegelian account and gives a Derridian account, which is indeed compatible with the play of *differance*.

At the outset, Derrida notes, the deconstruction of a categorial hierarchy cannot be performed as a single or simple operation such as its inversion or reversal, because such an operation establishes another hierarchy and secures its stability. Such a stability is obviously incompatible with the Derridian play of *differance*, which dictates a perpetual flux for all signifiers. Hence, Derrida says, the deconstruction of a categorial hierarchy should be performed as an element in "a double gesture" or "a double writing, that is, a writing that is in and of itself multiple" (*Positions*, 41). This is an incredible extension of the doctrine of double writing to describe the nature of deconstruction itself. Prior to this point, Derrida had never described deconstruction as a process of double writing. He had only claimed that it was a process of exposing the nature of every text as a double writing. Now he makes the baffling claim that deconstruction itself should be performed as a double writing.

What does it mean to say that deconstruction should be performed as a double writing or a double gesture? Derrida says that it is to perform two different operations simultaneously, to overturn the categorial hierarchy on the one hand and to disorganize or neutralize it altogether on the other hand. For example, Derrida says, the deconstruction of the speech/writing hierarchy "*simultaneously* provokes the overturning of the hierarchy speech/writing, and the entire system attached to it, *and* releases the dissonance of a writing within speech, thereby disorganizing the entire inherited order and invading the entire field" (*Positions*, 42).

This is clearly an inaccurate description of Derrida's deconstruction of the speech/writing hierarchy. To be sure, it overturned and disorganized the phonocentric hierarchy, but it did not stop there. It established a new categorial relation under the general notion of arche-writing. This constructive part is missing from Derrida's description of his own performance. We should note that the constructive part is an embarrassment to Derrida, because it installs another stable categorial relation. So he is now trying to disown it. But this still does not explain how his deconstruction of the speech/writing hierarchy can be taken as a double writing. This is the most baffling feature of his account.

He starts out by saying that a categorial deconstruction should be performed as a double writing rather than as a simple operation. But he never explains what that really means. After giving an inaccurate account of his own performance in the deconstruction of the speech/writing hierarchy, he says that the deconstructive double writing should be understood as analogical to the "undecidables, that is, unities of simulacrum," as exemplified in the *pharmakon*, which "is neither remedy nor poison, neither good nor evil, neither the inside nor the outside, neither speech nor writing" (*Positions*, 43).

The logic of neither/nor is the logic of oscillation in the domain of undecidables; it can choose neither the one nor the other. But Derrida does not explain how this logic applies to the deconstruction of categorial hierarchies. Perhaps we should try to construct a model for hierarchical deconstruction that can embody the spirit of undecidability that underlies Derrida's positive deconstruction. Let us reconsider the deconstruction of phonocentrism, which asserts the superiority of speech over writing. We can deconstruct it by showing all the possible forms of ordering the relation of speech and writing: (1) the superiority of speech over writing (phonocentrism), (2) the superiority of writing over speech (graphocentrism), and (3) the essential identity and equality of writing and speech (Derridianism). We then pronounce all these forms as undecidable.

This undecidable result is clearly different from the one achieved by Derrida's own deconstruction of phonocentrism, which produced a decidable result. His deconstruction rejects (1) and (2) and endorses (3); consequently it allows no room for oscillation or undecidability. But our proposed deconstruction retains all three alternatives, which in turn jointly dictate the perpetual oscillation between the undecidables. This outcome makes a perfect fit with the play of *differance* because it secures a perpetual motion. This is the truly Derridian mode for deconstructing all binary oppositions and their categorial hierarchies. It is again the deconstruction of oscillation.

* * The Derridian Logic of Undecidables

In Derrida's lexicon, *oscillation* and *undecidability* are interchangeable, and he tries to express their central meaning by the logic of neither/nor. This is the logic of *pharmakon:* it is neither remedy nor poison. Strictly speaking, however, the logic of neither/nor cannot be the logic of undecidability, because it is a logic of decidability. To say that the *pharmakon* is neither remedy nor poison is to make a decision. What Derrida has in mind is something clearly different from the logic of neither/nor. What is really the Derridian logic of undecidables? This is one of the most baffling questions, and it has not even been noted by the Derridians.

Let us go back to the original source of *pharmakon*, "Plato's Pharmacy." The logic of neither/nor is absolutely improper for describing the polysemy of *pharmakon* in that essay. The *pharmakon*, which is needed for Derrida's deconstruction of Plato's phonocentrism, cannot be neither remedy nor poison, because its logic of neither/nor can produce no contradictions. The *pharmakon* has to be both remedy and poison to produce a contradiction. The polysemy of *pharmakon* is governed by the logic of both/and throughout Derrida's deconstruction of Plato's phonocentrism. To that extent, Derrida's logic is similar to Hegel's logic of both/and: both generate contradictions. But Hegel's logic resolves the contradiction by generating a third term, while Derrida rejects the possibility of a Hegelian resolution. Hence the *pharmakon,* or rather its logic of both/and, becomes the instrument for the deconstruction of contradiction, as we have already noted.

Let us now imagine that Derrida converts the negative deconstruction of *pharmakon* into a positive deconstruction. Instead of saying that it has two mutually incompatible meanings and that they destroy each other, he has to say that its different meanings can be parceled out into different contexts and that those contextual meanings are undecidable. To choose one of the two meanings requires the logic of either/or, which is a logic of decidability. To accept both of them and let them destroy each other belongs to the logic of both/and, which is also a logic of decidability. To avoid these two logics of decidability is Derrida's intent in resorting to the logic of neither/nor. He cannot adopt the logic of neither/nor in its normal sense, because it is just another logic of decidability. By the logic of neither/nor he means to say that he wants to avoid both the logic of both/and, and the logic of either/or.

Derrida's logic of neither/nor is meant to be neither the logic of both/and nor the logic of either/or. He can accept neither the *pharmakon* that means both remedy and poison nor the *pharmakon* that means either remedy or poison. Unfortunately, however, he cannot rest with this assertion either, because it is just another decidable position. To avoid all decidable positions, he has to go on and say that he can accept neither all the previous positions nor this one. Again, he cannot stop at this position either, because it is again just another decidable position. Hence he is driven into an infinite chain of denials; his logic is not the logic of simple neither/nor but an endless series of neither/nor's. For this reason, Derrida says that his logic of undecidables involves "an infinite calculus" (*Spurs,* 99). The

Derridian oscillation is an endless motion, as endless as the play of *differance*. It is an endless treadmill.

The perpetual motion of the Derridian treadmill involves an endless series of affirmations and denials. None of these can be a simple affirmation or a simple denial, because such a simple act is a decidable position. It has to evade both affirmations and denials; in fact, it suspends itself between affirmations and denials. It may be called the Derridian *epochē*, but it is different from the Husserlian *epochē* in one important respect: the latter can be stable and stationary, but the former cannot. It has to be a perpetually mobile suspension.

There can be two different grounds for this perpetual suspension or undecidability: epistemic and normative. The notion of epistemic undecidability is exemplified in Derrida's affirmative deconstruction of Nietzsche's two sentences. He finds no sufficient epistemic ground to choose any one or any combination of the competing interpretations as Nietzsche's intended meaning. Normative undecidability is a different matter; it concerns normative grounds for choice, which may involve our values, purposes, and normative standards. But normative undecidability cannot be totally disengaged from epistemic undecidability, because normative choice always require relevant information, which constitutes its epistemic ground.

In addition to the distinction between epistemic and normative undecidability, we should take note of one more distinction. These two modes of undecidability can take place for two entirely different reasons. Let us consider three different ways of ordering the relation between male and female: (1) the superiority of male over female (patriarchy), (2) the superiority of female over male (matriarchy), and (3) the equality of male and female (egaliarchy). We may pronounce all three undecidable because we have difficulty in comprehending the normative standards for ranking them or in applying those standards to the practical world. Our evaluations are so complicated that we may conclude that the problem is undecidable. We may also regard it as undecidable because there are no normative standards for our decision. One type of undecidability stems from the absence of normative standards, and the other obtains in spite of their presence.

To distinguish these two types of undecidability, let us call them the aporetic undecidability and the nonaporetic undecidability. Undecidability is aporetic if it stems from the absence of normative standards; it is nonaporetic if it takes place in spite of their presence. These two senses of undecidability are not distinguished by Derrida. Consequently his use of the term is highly ambiguous. For example, his interpretation of Nietzsche's sentence "I have forgotten my umbrella" is obviously undecidable on epistemic grounds, that is, the grounds of insufficient evidence. He is presumably operating on an unmentioned epistemic standard, and the undecidability is nonaporetic. But we can never be sure that he accepts such a standard. In a Nietzschean spirit, he may disavow all epistemic standards and even the notion of truth, in which case the undecidability of the same sentence is aporetic. These two senses of *undecidability* also obtain for the undecidability of Nietzsche's sentence "Truth is like a woman."

The aporetic undecidability is standard-independent; the nonaporetic undecidability is standard-dependent. The latter is generally reducible to epistemic undecidability. It is the uncertainty and indeterminacy of applying existing normative standards. By contrast, the aporetic undecidability has nothing to do with the epistemic problems, because it is rooted in the absence of standards. The ambiguity between these two notions of undecidability cannot be avoided in the Derridian world, because we can never be certain whether the Derridians ever accept epistemic and normative standards. But these two notions of undecidability present entirely different problems for the Derridians. If they have no normative standards, they face a serious normative aporia, which arises from the aporetic undecidability. On the other hand, if the Derridians have their own normative standards, they can avoid the normative aporia and have to cope only with the nonaporetic undecidability, which is much easier to handle than the aporetic one.

Which of these two types of undecidability does Derrida accept for his positive deconstruction? This is perhaps the most critical question for the Derridians. This question does not arise for his negative deconstruction, because it can be performed without appealing to any epistemic or normative standards. The principle of noncontradiction is all that is required for negative deconstruction. Because it destroys all competing alternatives by their mutual cancellation, it presents no undecidables and allows no room for choice. Hence there is no need for any criteria, epistemic or normative. The only choice involved in negative deconstruction is the choice of its targets. What kind of normative standard do the Derridians have for this choice? This and the other questions of standards are the most troublesome questions for the Derridian deconstruction as a practical enterprise. Let us now see how these practical questions are handled by the Derridians.

Subversion is one of Derrida's favorite aims in deconstruction. It can be performed by either positive or negative deconstruction. Negative deconstruction can annihilate any position by exposing its inner contradiction. This is the tactic of internal subversion. Positive deconstruction can destabilize any position by exposing its undecidability. This is the tactic of external subversion, as we will soon see. Here is an example. The internal subversion of patriarchy can be achieved by exposing its internal contradiction. Its external subversion can be achieved by showing that there are many other ways of ordering the male-female relation than patriarchy and that all of them are undecidable, that is, that there is no ground to choose patriarchy over the others.

What sort of undecidability is involved in positive deconstruction? Is it aporetic or nonaporetic? Does it presuppose normative standards or their total absence? If it presupposes normative standards, they cannot be the normative standards internal to the object of deconstruction, for example, patriarchy. Because those standards are in the process of being deconstructed, they cannot be used for pronouncing the deconstructive outcomes as undecidable. By its own internal standard, moreover, patriarchy is definitely better than its competitors, and there is nothing undecidable about it. Hence the normative standard required for recognizing the undecidables must be external to patriarchy. If the undecidability is aporetic, on the other hand, not only can it not depend on any normative standards internal to patriarchy but it must deny the existence of all external standards. This is the external dimension of positive deconstruction. Whether it presupposes external normative standards or not, it must take an external perspective before it can talk about the undecidability of its outcome.

Positive deconstruction cannot talk about its undecidability from the perspective of normative standards internal to the object of deconstruction. It has to take a vantage point outside that object, whether there are external standards or not. In the absence of such standards, the external perspective delivers the aporetic undecidables. In the presence of such standards, the same perspective delivers the nonaporetic undecidables. Either way, the external perspective takes the deconstructor to the outside of the text to be deconstructed. Consequently, positive deconstruction cannot satisfy the Derridian requirement that the deconstructor remain inside the text, as stipulated by Pierre Schlag. To that extent it is anti-Derridian. The Derridian requirement can be met by negative deconstruction, because it requires no external perspective. It is the only truly Derridian operation. The difference between the internal and the external perspectives thus turns out to be the central difference between positive and negative deconstruction.

These two perspectives require two different types of deconstructor: the immanent and the transcendent. The immanent deconstructor remains inside the text he is deconstructing; the transcendent deconstructor transcends it by taking a vantage point outside it. Let us now see how this difference shows up in the practical world of legal deconstruction. The tactics of internal and external subversion have been favorite ploys in Critical Legal Studies. Many have tried to subvert the legal establishment by exposing its internal contradictions or by demonstrating the radical undecidability or indeterminacy of legal concepts and principles. For example, Duncan Kennedy maintains that our legal system is systematically infected by the contradiction between two incompatible ethical positions, individualism and altruism.[25] A similar charge has been made against the

25. "Form and Substance in Private Law Adjudication," *Harvard Law Review* 89 (1976): 1685–1778.

liberal tradition by Roberto Unger and Allan Hutchinson.[26]

Individualism advocates the primacy of individuals over society; it stresses the importance of individuals as the agents of rights, initiatives, self-reliance, and well-being. Society is only an instrumental framework for promoting these individualist values. Altruism advocates exactly the opposite doctrine, the primacy of society over individuals. Society should not be regarded as a mere instrument, because it has its own ultimate end, which is much nobler than the individualist values. Its essential function is to be a community of mutual care and respect. Hence the duty of care for others is much more important than the individual rights. Although individualism and altruism are mutually incompatible, both have been accepted as the basic principles of liberalism. Consequently, Kennedy holds, their contradiction permeates the liberal legal tradition.

Kennedy has further expanded the scope of the contradiction between these two ethical views. He says that this contradiction is not unique to the modern liberal tradition but common to all societies.[27] It stems from the insoluble dilemma facing every individual and society. Since no human beings can live alone, they have to secure their well-being and even their self-affirmation in a social order. Hence they have to make themselves dependent on others, but this dependence is a perpetual threat to their well-being and integrity as free individuals. The principle of individualism protects the individuals against this threat. But it has the danger of rending the entire social fabric unless it is counterbalanced by the principle of altruism and its spirit of care for others. For this reason, Kennedy holds, the conflict between individualism and altruism is the fundamental contradiction of all societies, and the liberal tradition has only been the latest attempt to resolve this contradiction. But the resolution is obviously impossible.

In this expanded version, Kennedy's critique is not limited to the

26. Unger, *The Critical Legal Studies Movement* (Cambridge, 1983); Hutchinson, "Of Kings and Dirty Rascals: The Struggle for Democracy," *Queens Law Journal*, 1985, 273–92.

27. "The Structure of Blackstone's Commentaries," *Buffalo Law Review* 28 (1979): 211–21.

liberal tradition; it is a global condemnation of all societies. But his critique has been misconceived; his use of the term *contradiction* is as misleading as Karl Marx's. What he really means is not the contradiction of two ethical views but the conflict between two competing values. When two values compete against each other, their conflict is sometimes irresolvable. For example, if you are caught in the conflict between the freedom of being single and the happiness of marriage, you have to make a choice because they are incompatible values. But both choices may be unacceptable to you. In that case, it is a case of unreconcilable conflict; it is like the contradiction of two incompatible propositions. But there are cases where such a conflict is negotiable. Now suppose that you have to look after two things, your family and your career, that place competing demands on your resources of time and energy. You can negotiate their conflict by allocating your limited resources between them. This is a case of negotiable or adjustable conflict; it is not a case of contradiction.

As many critics have pointed out, Kennedy has never succeeded in making a case for his thesis of fundamental contradiction in our legal system. At most, he has shown that there are many different ways of balancing the two competing principles, individualism and altruism. This balancing act involves drawing a boundary line between the rights and the duties every individual should have in our legal system. The different ways of striking the balance between the two competing principles are the different ways of carving out rights and duties. The conflict between the two principles can generate these multiple possibilities but not their mutual destruction.

If Kennedy had successfully demonstrated the mutual destruction of the two principles, he would have given us his negative deconstruction of our legal system. Since his demonstration only shows the multiple possibilities for negotiating the conflict between individualism and altruism, it amounts to a positive deconstruction. This assessment is true of many other attempts for legal deconstruction insofar as they have conducted their critiques in terms of the contradiction between competing values or principles. As a mode of positive legal deconstruction, Kennedy's critique falls into the general argument for radical indeterminacy, that is, that legal concepts and principles are so indeterminate that their meanings can be fixed in any number of different ways.[28] This move is supposed to undermine and destabilize the established legal system. It may be called the deconstruction of destabilization.

The aim of destabilization cannot be achieved as long as the argument of radical indeterminacy is given in the mode of positive deconstruction. To be sure, this argument can show many different possibilities for the reorganization of our legal system, but those possibilities are only undecidables for the Derridians. There is no way to show that any of them is better or worse than the others. The authority of positive norms cannot be undermined by merely showing that they can be fixed in many other ways, because those alternative ways may produce a set of positive norms worse than the present ones. We can discredit the present norms only by showing that the alternative ways are better. To be sure, Kennedy and Unger have said that the principle of altruism will function better than the principle of individualism as the dominant legal principle. But this claim may be no more than an expression of their subjective preferences.

Can these deconstructors transcend their subjective preferences and present their claim on the objective ground? We have already noted that positive deconstruction requires an external perspective, external to the legal system under deconstruction. Sometimes Kennedy tries to transcend not only the positive norms but even the framework of his own preferences. In those rare moments he declares that there can be no justification for any normative choice.[29] This is the Sartrean position, which recognizes no normative standards on any objective ground. According to such a position, every normative problem is aporetically undecidable. The radical freedom of a Sartrean subject is rooted in this aporetic undecidability. Hence its decision is always absurd; it is impossible to give any reasons for its justification. But the Derridian subject is different from the Sartrean

---

28. See, e.g., Gary Peller, "The Metaphysics of American Law," *California Law Review* 73 (1985): 1151–1290; Clare Dalton, "An Essay in the Deconstruction of Contract Doctrine," *Yale Law Journal* 94 (1985): 97–1114; and Mark Tushnet, *Red, White, and Blue: A Critical Analysis of Constitutional Law* (Cambridge, 1988).

29. "Form and Substance," 1762.

subject in one respect: The Derridian subject does not have the will to make an arbitrary decision in the domain of the aporetic undecidables. Hence it is stuck on the endless treadmill of oscillation. The Sartrean subject is the knight of resolute absurdity; the Derridian, the master of infinite vacillation.

* * Platonic Transcendence

Some Derridians have vaunted their power of opening up new "possibilities of change that are incalculable."[30] If the incalculability of these possibilities is no more than their aporetic undecidability, they only constitute the endless series of aimless steps on the Derridian treadmill of oscillation. To bounce blindly between those undecidable possibilities is truly what Derrida calls "blind tactics" or "a strategy without finality" (*Margins*, 7). Derrida can get off this devilishly absurd machine and transform his deconstruction into a really positive program only by accepting some normative framework for his deconstructive decisions. Only such a normative framework can convert the undecidables into the decidables. Derrida has finally taken this positive step in "Force of Law: The 'Mystical Foundation of Authority.'"[31]

What sort of normative framework does Derrida accept in taking this huge step? All normative frameworks belong to one of the two perspectives for any system of positive norms, internal and external. The internal perspective is to accept the positive norms as the only framework for all normative judgments and choices. This is the Wittgensteinian perspective, which is articulated in Wittgenstein's *Philosophical Investigations*. It is sometimes known as conventionalism or institutional positivism. But the internal perspective is of no use for positive deconstruction; as we have already noted, it

---

30. Jonathan Culler, *On Deconstruction* (Ithaca, 1982), 158.

31. This was the keynote address for a special symposium titled "Deconstruction and the Possibility of Justice" at the Benjamin Cardozo School of Law on October 1 and 2, 1989. It appeared first in *Cardozo Law Review* 11 (1990): 919–1045 and then in *Deconstruction and the Possibility of Justice*, ed. Drucilla Cornell et al. (New York, 1992), 3–67. It is cited in the text as Force, the page references being to the latter.

requires an external perspective. What sort of external perspective does Derrida want? This is the only question left for him to answer.

There can be three types of external perspective: Sartrean, Nietzschean, and Platonic. The Sartrean normative perspective provides no normative standards, as we just noted. It is a perfect match for the deconstruction of undecidables. From this perspective, everything is aporetically undecidable; it gives no reason whatsoever to choose one alternative over another. The Derridian oscillation is the hermeneutic counterpart to Camus's Sisyphean movement. If Derrida wants to get out of this Sisyphean predicament, he has to disown the Sartrean perspective. So Derrida's choice narrows down to the Nietzschean and the Platonic perspectives. The Nietzschean perspective is to accept the subjective will and preferences as the only normative framework. The Platonic perspective is to appeal to the transcendental standards for all normative judgments and choices.

Between the Nietzschean and the Platonic normative perspectives, Derrida cannot be neutral. He has repeatedly told us of his irresistible fascination with Nietzsche, which he has shared with his revered mentor Martin Heidegger. At the same time, Derrida has also expressed his emphatic aversion to Platonism, which he has also shared with Heidegger. After all, for both Heidegger and Derrida, Plato is the great grandfather of logocentrism and the metaphysics of presence. So the Derridians have every reason to expect their master to go for the Nietzschean normative framework. In fact, many of them have flaunted the Derridian deconstruction as a Nietzschean play. But their natural expectation has been defeated; Derrida appears to have chosen the Platonic Forms for his normative framework.

Derrida begins with the necessity of acknowledging "the idea of justice" in the deconstruction of positive law. What is the idea of justice? He says that it is an infinite idea and that it is infinite because it is irreducible (Force, 25). He recognizes the basic difference between the idea of justice and the positive law. The law is subject to deconstruction, but the idea of justice, if such a thing exists, is not, because it is outside or beyond law (Force, 14). This is a startling statement from a man who has become famous for saying that there is nothing outside the text. Now he is talking about something evidently lying outside the text, namely, the idea of justice. It is not deconstructible, I presume, because it is not in the text, or rather because it has not been constructed. In Derridian language, the domain of text is coextensive with the domain of construction, that is, human culture. Positive law belongs to the domain of text, but the idea of justice lies beyond it.

How does the idea of justice affect deconstruction? Let us begin with the universe of discourse for justice. Derrida says that the question of justice and injustice arises only for a special group of subjects, from which animals and inanimate objects are generally excluded. But the demarcation of this special group has been unstable; it has excluded from the domain of justice different groups of people at different times (Force, 18). To demonstrate this instability has been one of the familiar moves in the Derridian deconstruction. This familiar move can be restated in terms of a binary distinction. The demarcation between the proper subjects and the nonsubjects of justice can be drawn in any number of ways, and all of them are undecidables. Thus it is impossible to say that any one of them is more just than the others. Nor is it possible to say that we can make progress in justice by expanding the coverage of justice for all human beings.

If the demarcations between the subjects and the nonsubjects of justice belong to the world of undecidables, we can only perpetually oscillate between all the possible demarcations and even efface those demarcations altogether. Derrida maintains that this familiar nihilistic consequence of deconstruction can be averted by his acceptance of justice as the normative ideal (Force, 19). And he gives two reasons in support of this claim. First, deconstruction is not a normatively neutral operation; it is an operation dictated by the infinite demand of justice. Consequently, it is "anything but a neutralization of interest in justice" (Force, 20). Second, there is a moment of suspense in deconstruction, evidently the oscillation in the domain of the undecidables. But he now claims that this moment is a moment of anxiety that can be motivated only by the demand of justice (Force, 20).

The idea of justice converts the deconstruction of undecidables to that of decidables. It is burdened with a sense of anxiety and responsibility. This sense of anxiety should not be mistaken for the Sartrean variety. It belongs to the domain of decidables, whereas the Sartrean anxiety belongs to the domain of undecidables. The new mode of deconstruction is truly positive in comparison with the old modes. This new mode, Derrida says, derives its force, its movement, and its motivation from nothing else than the idea of justice and its realizability (Force, 20–21). Hence deconstruction finds itself between the idea of justice and the positive law. So conceived, deconstruction is no longer an independent operation or an end in itself. It is a dutiful servant for the improvement and reconstruction of law in the name of justice. Instead of saying that all the possible demarcations between the proper subjects and the nonsubjects of justice are undecidable, Derrida can now say that they are decidable by virtue of the idea of justice.

What is the relation between justice and law in Derrida's new perspective? Apparently the best way to state their relation is in the Platonic relation of an Idea and its construction. Justice is an Idea that lies beyond deconstruction, but it can be realized only in a law, which can be constructed by the articulation of its eternal demand. Because the construction of a law is based on the Idea of Justice, its deconstruction or critique cannot be made without reference to the same Idea. The Idea of Justice is the common basis for the construction and deconstruction of law. Derrida endorses this point in the following statement: "But it turns out that *droit* [law] claims to exercise itself in the name of justice and that justice is required to establish itself in the name of a law that can be 'enforced'" (Force, 22).

To be sure, Derrida does not even mention Plato in his talk about the Idea of Justice, and he uses very guarded language in talking about the existence of this Idea. But his association of it with the Kantian regulative Idea is highly instructive and deserves to be quoted in full:

I would hesitate to assimilate too quickly this "idea of justice" to a regulative idea (in Kantian sense), to a messianic promise or to other horizons *of the same type*. I am only speaking of a *type*, of this *type* of horizon that would have numerous competing versions. By competing I mean similar enough in appearance and always pretending to absolute privilege and irreducible singularity. (Force, 25)

In his *Idea for a Universal History from a Cosmopolitan Point of View* and *Perpetual Peace*, Kant assigns a messianic eschatological role to the Idea of Justice. He says that this Idea is the ultimate end governing the development of the entire history and all the diverse forms of human culture. Derrida does not completely repudiate such a sweeping view of the Idea of Justice. He only says that he would "hesitate to assimilate" his Idea of Justice to the Kantian version. Moreover, the only reason for this hesitation is his pluralistic view of the Idea of Justice insofar as it affects the development of human history and culture. He would like to recognize "numerous competing versions" of the Idea of Justice rather than the single universal type. He admits that these competing versions are "similar enough in appearance and always pretending to absolute privilege and irreducible singularity."

The singularity, Derrida says, belong only to our historical place, but not to our vision of the Idea of Justice:

The singularity of the historical place—perhaps our own, which in any case is the one I'm obscurely referring to here—allows us a glimpse of the type itself, as the origin, condition, possibility or promise of all its exemplifications (messianism of the Jewish, Christian or Islamic type, idea in the Kantian sense, eschato-teleology of the neo-Hegelian, Marxist or post-Marxist type, etc.). (Force, 25)

Although our historical place is singular, Derrida believes, it still "allows us a glimpse of the type itself." The type is the origin for all different versions of justice, Christian and Islamic, Kantian and Marxist. They are different exemplifications of one and the same type. Derrida's pluralism accentuates the role of justice as the type and origin. The different versions of justice can compete against one another because they claim to exemplify the same Idea of Justice. The pluralistic view of justice can make sense only if we accept the transcendence of the Idea of Justice. This is Derrida's astute observation.

Derrida's idea of the different versions of justice can be restated in terms of constructivism. They are the different modes of construction, the different ways of articulating the Idea of Justice in this world. All the different versions have to share the same transcendental Idea because it is their common basis. Likewise, even construction and deconstruction have to share the same transcendental Idea for their common basis because they participate in the same enterprise of realizing that Idea. In this common enterprise, construction and deconstruction are two complementary operations that must work together like two hands for clapping. Our deconstruction can never be an end itself; it is always for the sake of improving our constructed normative ideals and standards. So every deconstruction presupposes reconstruction as its ultimate end. But construction also is in need of the service of deconstruction, because we can rarely begin our construction *ex nihilo*. Even such a revolutionary construction as the U.S. Constitution was largely an adaptation of previous constructions. The adaptation and reconstruction of old institutions require the service of deconstruction.

Our normative life is a series of constructions, deconstructions, and reconstructions; we keep on mending and fixing our positive normative standards by deconstructing and reconstructing them in reference to the transcendental normative standards. Only by this perpetual process of construction and deconstruction can we maintain the vitality of our positive normative standards. Without such an integral link to construction, any program of deconstruction can easily degenerate into a purely destructive enterprise. Without the benefit of deconstruction, any program of construction can easily fall into the danger of building only a house of cards. Hence their mutual dependence is essential for the integrity of both construction and deconstruction. But their mutual dependence cannot be established without recourse to the transcendental Idea, because it is the ultimate ground for their raison d'être. By accepting transcendental normative standards, Derrida has finally succeeded in converting the deconstruction of undecidables into that of decidables. Following Balkin's lead, I am tempted to call this new version the transcendental deconstruction.[32]

For this new version, Derrida sets forth three radical requirements. First, a free and responsible subject. It should have the freedom not simply to follow a positive law but to transcend it, that is, the freedom to destroy or suspend it for the sake of justice (Force, 22–23). This is to replace the Derridian subject, a mere appendage to writing, with a Platonic subject. The second requirement is to slay "the ghost of the undecidable": "The undecidable is not merely the oscillation or the tension between two decisions," says Derrida, but an essential phase in the ordeal of making a free and responsible decision (Force, 24). The undecidables are no longer aporetic; they have become epistemic undecidables. The third requirement is the urgency of justice. For any given case, we can never have the complete information to do justice because getting information is an infinite process. But justice cannot wait, Derrida says. So we have to make our decisions without the benefit of infinite information and unlimited knowledge. Every decision of justice has to be an act of urgency and precipitation (Force, 26). The third requirement turns out to be an extension of the second; both are concerned with the epistemic difficulty of making the decisions of justice.

All three requirements constitute one Platonic requirement. It begins with a Platonic subject and ends with the Platonic agony of realizing the Idea of Justice in this imperfect world. What initially appeared to be his Sartrean anxiety turns out to be his Platonic agony. By fulfilling the Platonic requirement, Derrida has now become a full-fledged Platonist, and his deconstruction has turned into a Platonic program of reconstruction. This Platonic turn clearly dissolves all the problems that have plagued Derrida's program from his negative to his positive deconstruction. This is Derrida's Platonic conversion.

This conversion is a long way from Derrida's fascination with the *pharmakon*. In "Plato's Pharmacy" he was captivated with the power

---

32. Balkin, "Transcendental Deconstruction and Transcendent Justice," forthcoming in *Michigan Law Review.*

of a text that can destroy itself by the single principle of contradiction. This fascination was a continuation of Kant's and Hegel's fascination with the same formal principle. Kant thought he found the magical power of constructing all normative standards from this single principle. By a dialectical transformation of Kant's formalist program, Hegel claimed to find even a greater power, not only the power of construction but also the power of destruction. Derrida refurbished the destructive part of Hegel's dialectical formalist program in his program of deconstruction. All three tried to achieve their goals by the formal principle of noncontradiction alone, although they characterized it in quite different terms.

As we have seen repeatedly in this volume, however, the vaunted power of formalism is a metaphysical illusion, because the principle of contradiction is totally vacuous. It can have no power of either construction or destruction. But to the two champions of pure rationality, Kant and Hegel, its purely formal character appeared to be the embodiment of pure reason, largely because they had lost faith in the notion of substantive rationality. They could not believe in the existence of substantive normative ideals and standards that transcend the world of positive norms. But Kant had the wisdom to recognize the vacuity of formal reason and the futility of his normative formalism and eventually returned to the Platonism of his earlier days. He came to see that only Platonic Forms can provide the normative ground for substantive rationality.

Derrida's fascination with the formal principle of noncontradiction was as obsessive as Kant's and Hegel's had been. But he could not share their optimism about the positive, or constructive, function of the formal principle, because he knew too well what had eventually come of their programs. So he tried to retain only the negative, or destructive, half of Hegel's dialectic. Derrida's negative deconstruction is the Hegelian dialectic without *tertium quid*, or *sans synthese* (*Dissemination*, 219). Derridianism is a truncated Hegelianism. But the formal principle is just too powerless to accomplish anything, whether it is dressed up as Kantian, Hegelian, or Derridian. It cannot achieve even the objective of negative deconstruction unless it is supported by a pragmatic decision. The self-contradiction of a text is achieved not by the formal principle of contradiction but by the deconstructor's pragmatic choice to read it as a chain of mutually contradictory signifiers. That choice cannot be made without appealing to some substantive goal or standard. So Derrida appears to have been forced to acknowledge the necessity of substantive standards and principles. This, I gather, is the background for his Platonic conversion.

In fact, this was what drove Kant to abandon his formalist program and to return to Platonic Forms. Hence Derrida's Platonic conversion is a miniature version of Kant's conversion. In his "Force of Law" Derrida is captivated not with the force of law but with the Idea of justice. If there is any force in law, it comes from this Idea. This new normative force cannot belong to the formal principle of contradiction. It is the power of substantive ideals and standards; it is the power of Platonic vision. Only this power of substantive ideals can release Derrida from the shackle of formal reason and the treadmill of endless oscillation. And this release can take him out of the dismal cave of "Plato's Pharmacy" and open his eyes to the Idea of justice in Platonic Heaven.

Index

* *